Issues an Cross-Cultural Management

An Asian Perspective

Margaret C. McLaren
Md. Zabid Abdul Rashid

Prentice
Hall

Published by
Prentice Hall
Pearson Education Malaysia Sdn. Bhd.
Lot 2, Jalan 215, Off Jalan Templer,
46050 Petaling Jaya,
Selangor, Malaysia
Tel: 03-77820466   Fax: 03-77853435

Pearson Education offices in Asia: *Bangkok, Beijing, Hong Kong, Jakarta, Manila, Kuala Lumpur, New Delhi, Seoul, Singapore, Taipei, Tokyo.*

Typeset in 11/16 Stone Serif

Printed in Malaysia, PA
ISBN: 983-2473-17-9

5 4 3 2 1
06 05 04 03 02

Perpustakaan Negara Malaysia   Cataloguing-in-Publication Data

McLaren, Margaret C.
  Issues and cases in cross-cultural management: an Asian perspective/
  Margaret C. McLaren, Md. Zabid Abdul Rashid.
  Bibliograhy
  Includes index
  ISBN 983-2473-17-9
  1. Management – Asia, Southeastern. 2. Management – Cross-cultural studies.
  3. Intercultural communication – Asia, Southeastern. I. Md. Zabid Abdul Rashid.
  II. title.
  658.00959

Table of Contents

Foreword

As the Asian countries are coming out of the economic crisis of the late 1990s, international companies from all over the world are once more focusing on Asia for investment and business opportunities. At the same time, Asian countries are expanding their international activities as well. The economic difficulties brought to the forefront a number of issues that are unique to that area of the world and may have contributed both to the deepening of the crisis as well as the overcoming of it. For example, on the one hand, Confucian values have been credited with the flourishing of Asian economies by emphasizing hard work, loyalty, and dedication, but on the other hand, these same values are said to have fostered shady business practices and corruption by emphasizing loyalty over sound business principles.

During the past decade researchers have focused increasingly on international business in Asia including government regulation, expatriate issues, and culture. We now have a body of research that goes beyond business practices in North America and Europe and focuses on countries that have their own unique business operations.

This book makes a major contribution to the teaching and understanding of the dynamics of international business. In the past, the majority of cases on international business tended to place Americans or Europeans at the center of the case and then explored the problems that these managers had to deal with when entering foreign countries. This approach almost exclusively placed westerners in the superior positions. McLaren and Md Zabid open the field and bring a fresh perspective to the study of international business.

The first three chapters provide the background of the cultural, business, and regulatory environment. While the theoretical model is based on the standard researchers, such as Hofstede, Hall, and Adler, the examples to illustrate the concepts are from Asia, thereby presenting a very different cultural orientation system.

Frequently, authors assume that students and instructors are familiar with using cases and, therefore, do not discuss methods for maximizing the case approach. This book is a welcome exception. Not only do the authors provide guidance for approaching cases, they also give specific questions and examples of how cases can make sense out of a complex reality where culture, regulations, religion, and financial considerations are intertwined.

The major contribution of this book, however, is the number and variety of the cases, many of them dealing with business issues between people from Asian countries. For example, "The Mess in the Technical Department" explores the cultural parameters for promotion of employees in a Malaysian subsidiary of a Japanese firm. In "Flooding the Indigenous Voices" Korean managers in Malaysia are confronted with the value system of indigenous traditional people. This case illustrates the cultural variations within Asia in general and within Malaysia in particular. After exploring this case, students will realize that there is not just one Asian culture, that to be effective in Malaysia, one needs to be aware of the rich cultural tapestry in Malaysia. The cases that involve western managers, such as "The Fijian Experience – The *Tau* Relationship" or "Romance at Entores" place the westerner in a business situation where he or she must deal with the cultural complexities of the host country. The western manager in these cases can no longer use his or her own culture as the sole reference point to deal with the problems.

This casebook illustrates globalization in its broadest sense and gives students experience in looking at international business issues from a truly multicultural viewpoint. It is an exciting addition to the international literature.

Iris Varner
Professor in International Business at Illinois State University at Normal, Illinois
2001 President of the Association for Business Communication

Preface

This book is intended for use in training sessions either in university courses or in organisations holding seminars to upgrade the skills and understanding of their staff. It contains management cases complicated and enlivened by cross-cultural dimensions.

Either doctoral or MBA students at the Universiti Putra Malaysia wrote the original cases. They are all real and at the time all seriously affected management in their different ways. Most have had names and other details changed for privacy reasons but for some cases, the organisations gave permission to retain some or all identifying information.

The opening chapters of this book serve as an introduction for both facilitators and participants. The first chapter suggests the approach users should take as they put themselves in the position of directors and managers confronted with challenging cross-cultural situations. The second outlines the nature of 21 cross-cultural dimensions seen differently in different cultures, drawing on the work of theorists like Edward Hall, Geert Hofstede and Fons Trompenaars. It also contains a discussion of stereotyping, ethnocentrism and negative attribution, three issues which decision makers must be constantly aware of. The third discusses the importance of the cross-cultural environment. Although many of the cases did not occur in Malaysia, and several were not contributed by students from other countries, all the cases were written in Malaysia. For this reason it was appropriate for the Malaysian environment, itself a microcosm of the multi-cultural world, to provide many of the examples used in chapter 3.

To make the cases easier to use, they have been divided into four groups: *Tug of the Heart, Trouble in the Workplace, Culture Clash* and *The Power of the Spirit*.

The Tug of the Heart shows six work scenarios, where personal relationships interplay with management in a way not dreamed of by those who became involved. In many western countries, nepotism rulings try to shut personal complications out of the workplace. In some Asian cultures, however, attempts to keep love and work apart are alien. Anywhere they may interfere unduly with personal rights, as the first case, *Romance at Entores*, illustrates. In contrast, mother-in-law worries at home can ignite in the office as happens in *Dilemma* when Mrs Tan explodes into her son's workplace to the embarrassment – and, in the laboratory, danger – of everyone there.

Similarly, there are long-term implications for where people should live in *Medicine, marriage and business*. In that case, two lovers, young doctors from different nationalities who trained together but who both have family ties of steel, have their professional roles put under enormous strain. The chance of overseas training is at stake in *Who should it be*? in which the most deserving candidate is likely to be passed over on the assumption that that she would not let work interfere with her family responsibilities. In *Time is running out*, problems arising from interracial romantic relationships seem certain to disrupt the smooth performance of work. And in *Coping with a new boss*, staff loyalty to the founder of a company makes his appointment extremely difficult for a new CEO given the post by the Board of Directors after the company has gone public.

The title of the next section, *Trouble in the workplace*, speaks for itself. It will be particularly useful in management courses and work place seminars. In the first case, *Why do we have to live together*? Malay and Indian women resent having to share accommodation and the company is torn between keeping to what seems a sound policy and the fear of losing staff. In *YTL Textiles Sdn Bhd*, a CEO in Taiwan who has developed a family business cannot bring himself to share responsibility when the business grows beyond one person's control. The third case in this section, *Why me*, involves a woman manager of a fast-food restaurant in Singapore who, without realising it, treats her Chinese and Indian staff differently and suddenly finds staff are walking out on her. The next case, *Hari Raya holidays in the year 2000*, arises from disparity between the Christian and the lunar calendars which caused problems in many companies in Malaysia until the government stepped in with a ruling that employers did not like.

Attitudes to gender and preferences about individual and teamwork vary across cultures. And these differences exist not in a vacuum but in the workplace where people know one another and work together. The result can be great unhappiness, especially when the issue of promotion looms, as in the next case in this section, *The mess in the technical department*. This time a local deputy manager and Japanese general manager have to choose between two candidates for promotion. The general manager's power seems to make his decision the final one but then an excellent worker may be lost.

The next two cases involve misunderstanding within multi-cultural Malaysia. In *Mr Tan's predicament* privileges accorded to one group upset another. Culture shock, not, as is usual, of a foreigner but of a Malaysian within Malaysia, is the crux of *On the plantation*, the last case in this section. A city man, devout and close to his family, feels anomie when promoted to a position in rural Sabah when the environment is totally different from the one he is used to.

The third section, *Culture clash*, is the core of the book. Those studying intercultural communication will probably choose cases here before any others. Several of them involve multinational companies where expatriate senior staff and employees have different windows on the world.

The first case in this section, *The Fijian experience – The Tau relationship*, has a young Fijian hotel manager, western-trained, in an impossible position with a junior member of his staff because of local customs. Then *Temper, temper!* focuses on two young (and age is an important factor in Asia) Swedish consultants unintentionally upsetting the Malaysian staff they are employed to help. Even when the real conflict occurs right outside the workplace, as in *Transmission lines*, in which feelings run high in off-site work because religious taboos have not been observed in providing the food at the campsite, the results can be disastrous. *Mr Braun in trouble* illustrates the difficulty different concepts of a written contract can cause. In *Pride and prejudice* expatriate managers are misfits in Malaysian companies and in *Expat blues* the same thing occurs with a Malaysian manager in Johannesburg.

In every section of this book, particularly in the last section, there are cases which can be traced to religious differences. But in *Insya Allah* communication barriers block financial dealings between two Islamic groups, one from Malaysia and the other in Saudi Arabia.

Resignations and *Va bene: A Japanese spy in Italy* both involve Japanese companies. In the former, the company faces severe staffing problems in competitive Kuala Lumpur. In the latter, a lone representative of the company, as it happens a Singaporean and not a Japanese person, is planted in Italy to see what is happening with supplies, and feels totally useless. In contrast, *Paying for cultural values* is a very different case, set in the hinterland of Malawi, in a joint venture with a Finnish manager, where locals expect the heavy expenses of funerals to be borne by the employer who has no such expectations. The section ends with a very short case, *Love letters*, on reaction in an office to food which may not be *halal*.

The final section of the book, *The Power of the Spirit*, illustrates the immense importance of the spiritual in much of the world. In *The pride of Mr Richard White* belief in a "superpower" disrupts work. In *Disappointment* it is religious commitment to prayers and the *haj* that worry management. And in *The gods must be angry* a Welsh manager gives orders to move a Hindu shrine at an inauspicious time, with disastrous results.

The next two disturbing cases, *Widetech Malaysia* and *The Thaipusam Tragedy* both develop out of misunderstanding of the importance of the Thaipusam festival. In *The month of the hungry ghost*, a Chinese manager blames her irrational behaviour on the influence of a "superpower" that possessed her. And in *Insensitive* the issue is overtime during the Muslim fasting month. The final case, *Flooding the indigenous voices*, occurs in Sarawak where the indigenous people threaten black magic if the land continues to be cleared for development.

The issues – resignations, work hours, personality clashes, promotion and so on, are universal and will occur in management anywhere. But in every case in this book they are complicated and heightened by cross-cultural influences that demand wise handling and genuine respect for all cultures.

Our thanks go to all the students who contributed cases, and to many members of the Universiti Putra Malaysia staff. Special thanks go to Ian McLaren and Tasneem Usmani for their thoughtful and constructive reading of the text, to Tee Keng Kok and Ho Jo Ann for their ever-willing help with corrections and printing, and to Netty Dzureena, Ima Yanti Ramly and Paridah Haji Hamid for their efficient secretarial work. The Pearson Acquisitions Editor for Malaysia, Hasri Hasan, gave full encouragement and support. And from Margaret, special thanks go to Naoki Kameda for his help with the Japanese words and phrases, and to Iris Varner, who inspired me many years ago to enter this stimulating and important field of cross-cultural management and has been warmly behind the idea of a cross-cultural management casebook.

Whatever errors remain in this text are, of course, ours. We would be grateful for follow-up or discussion of any points we make. Meanwhile our best wishes go to all who use these cases. We hope you find them as thought provoking as we did.

Margaret C. McLaren and Md. Zabid Abdul Rashid

SECTION 1
Introduction

Chapter 1
Using Cases

Cases are a wonderful help in the teaching of management, as in other professional fields. They enable everyone involved to bridge the gap between theory and practice. Those who use cases can learn from situations others have experienced to tease out the issues thoughtfully and independently, and to resolve problems without any risk to the organisations in which the cases occurred.

For any management case, there are several key steps that have to be taken to identify and resolve the real problems. The key areas that have to be addressed include identification of the problems and issues, analysis of the facts and situation, alternative solutions, and recommended actions. In a cross-cultural context, the problems can be resolved by adopting a cultural synergy approach. In this approach, the manager is expected to find potential solutions by recognising the presence of similarities and differences of cultures in a particular situation, and to seek, through the insights of diverse group members, creative solutions that minimise cultural misunderstanding.

What is sometimes called the cultural synergy approach involves three steps (Adler, 1986, p 91; Burke and Goodstein, 1980). The first step involves understanding the cultural context, that is, the existence of two or more separate cultures. Here, the case analysts need to recognise the source of the conflict from cultural perspectives. We assume cultural heterogeneity, that is we are all not the same. We believe that different cultural groups exist, and each group maintains its distinctiveness.

The second step is to understand the basic cultural conflicts. What are the cultural assumptions in one culture and in the other culture? How did the conflict arise? In this way, the case analysts can avoid being parochial or ethnocentric in understanding the issues or problems raised.

The third step is to seek a creative approach that fits in with the different cultural assumptions, and then to generate at least two or three potential solutions. From there on, the case analysts can choose the one they consider the best solution at the time for the particular problem. The solution must exemplify cultural synergy as it takes into account the sensitivities of each culture, and selects a reasonable and acceptable potential solution.

This book was written in Malaysia, a microcosm of the multi-cultural world, with three main races and many small groups of people from other races. Though many of the cases included here involve other countries and cultures, Malaysia itself supplies a wealth of challenging situations.

For example, in one cross-cultural case in Malaysia the employees consisting of Malays, Chinese, and Indians, believed that there was an evil spirit causing trouble in a manufacturing plant in Shah Alam. How should the expatriate (a westerner) handle this problem?

One possible method is to acknowledge the existence of three distinct cultural groups in the plant. Those in each of the cultural groups have their own beliefs and values. Some Chinese employees might recommend that the managers of the plant employ a Chinese priest or 'lamoloh' to recite special prayers in the office premises. The Indians might want the management to engage an Indian priest or 'shaman' to perform sacrifices and other rites. Some conservative Malays might insist that a 'bomoh' (traditional medicine man) be employed to transport the evil spirit elsewhere, while another Malay group might prefer to conduct special prayers (without engaging any 'bomoh') in the plant.

All the employees would also want the management of the plant to pay for the expenses of such rituals. As a manager of the plant, this could be a major issue as the expatriate would not know which solution to consider. Further, how could he justify paying for the 'bomoh', 'lamoloh' or 'shaman' to his superior in United Kingdom.

Members of all three cultural groups believe that an evil spirit is causing the problem to the employees in the plant.

However, engaging the services of any one of the three traditional medicine men could cause dissatisfaction and uneasiness to the other cultural groups. Therefore, a creative solution is needed to address this so that the expatriate would not be accused of being insensitive to the local problems. The best way to generate a solution would be to investigate the problem further to analyse the severity of the problems caused by the evil spirit.

For instance, if the event only happens during the period of the 'hungry ghost', then it may not affect the other cultural groups, as they do not have such taboos. Identifying the fundamental problem and generating creative cultural solutions would be a painstaking exercise yet may be acceptable to all three different cultural groups, and so well worth the effort.

Using cases of this and other kinds with a group has several special advantages. First, they can work well with concepts like leadership, negotiation, strategy and culture. Managers need to use holistic thinking when confronted with complex situations. Even decision analysis, sometimes taught from an entirely quantitative viewpoint, has strong personal and emotional elements that can be seen at work in some cross-cultural cases.

Second, cases have been used with convincing results by scholars researching issues like culture in manufacturing organisations (e.g. Filion, 1988; Shockley-Zalabak and Morley, 1989). Peters and Waterman' famous book, *In Search of Excellence (1982)*, is one example of research developed out of case studies, which has had a wide-reaching impact on management thinking.

Third, cases can, in a short time, provide something of the range and depth that might otherwise take years of experience to acquire. Knowing the facts and the implications of those facts in business is important, but hands-on experience is important too, and can be gained through practice with cases. It cannot, of course, be claimed that cases can replace experience. However, they can allow users the opportunity to work through challenging situations without any risk in time or money or anything else to the organisations in which the problems arose.

The Harvard Business School which first popularised the use of cases was making teaching and learning a participatory process, rather than an authoritarian one. Bryan Poulin (1990) suggests that the Harvard Socratic case method of encouraging questions provides users with a sound stand.

The first stage in handling a case is to let everyone read it, preferably in their own time, at home. After this, the case itself can be presented in three ways. The facilitator can go over it in the classroom, refreshing the memory of those who may have read it some days before. With a busy or pressured group, this may be the best approach. It is the only method to use if the facilitator is asking the group to read the case for the first time at the meeting.

The second method is for the facilitator to arrange ahead for one or more of the group to present the case, and to lead the session from then on. This gives those presenting a chance to present the case in an accurate and lively way, supporting the key points with either or both role plays or visual aids like transparencies or Powerpoint slides. It also gives good practice for times when they may have a similar responsibility in the work place. It is the recommended method when the group are able to read the case ahead. Almost every case has plenty of conversation to make role-playing easy.

The third, and the harshest method, only possible when the group have the case to read well before the meeting, is to warn the group ahead that any one of them will be called on to present the case and lead the session, so forcing everyone to be prepared. The last method ensures that those who come will have read and thought about the case, but it may result in some absenteeism and also a flimsy presentation and some resentment from the group.

Whichever method is used, members of the whole group need to consider these matters:

- What is happening here?
- How is it happening?
- Who is responsible?
- What should be done about it?

Answers to these questions can be discussed in small groups so that each member actually confronts the issues, rather than just listening to those who are more outspoken. That will give those involved chances they might not otherwise have. This discussion can take place either before the group meet, so that the leaders present the views once the case has been presented, or actually in the room, once the facilitator or some member (or members) of the group has presented the case.

Afterwards whoever presents the case can facilitate sharing of views, using the standard brainstorming technique of accepting and recording all points raised. The brainstorming session is extremely important.

Multiple solutions may be offered, for different reasons. And, as in the world outside, a degree of consensus must be reached so that the problem does not continue to bug the organisation. Through both the small group discussion and the later sharing, each participant can acquire something of the invaluable experience that distinguishes the wise person from others. Through the case they can receive several benefits:

- They can vicariously experience a world of work that may be very different from their own.
- They can reflect on what is happening in organisations they are not themselves in.
- They can decide what issues are involved from the theory they are either studying formally or privately reading about in current thought-provoking management books and journals.
- They can suggest solutions to the cases, both immediate and long-term.

Two approaches are involved simultaneously. One is the objective, analytical approach, derived from analysis and application of theory. The other is the practical approach, considering the background and the situation of the people involved in the caring and constructive way appropriate for a successful leader. Who is threatened by the situation? Who is advantaged? How can the underlying problem or problems be resolved so that both individuals and the organisation are hurt as little as possible? Can a more forward-looking strategy be worked out for the future?

As they read each case, participants will need to ask themselves:

- What is going on?
- What does this mean in the light of what I am learning in this course?
- How might the organisation proceed, both to evade the abyss that yawns before it and to avoid other similar chasms opening up in future.

Participants will find that making notes, either on the cases themselves or separately, can enable them to sort out the critical factors to share with others when it comes, first, to the small group discussion, and second, to the wider discussion with the larger group. Those presenting the case have to take over the role of others, and to do that they must fully understand the role.

The case approach has three stages. First, the participants read the case, sorting out the key facts and the issues involved. Causes, effects, constraints, threats and opportunities will all need to be considered. Making notes during the reading is very important since it is difficult to hold everything in mind at the same time. Alone at this stage, the participant has to visualise the trauma of deciding what to do. Evading this responsibility is tempting. It is so much easier to stay as a reader or observer than to decide what you would do under the particular circumstances. Mauffette-Leenders and others (1997, p.21) suggest the reader thinks: "If I got fired if I made the wrong decision and promoted if I made the right decision, how hard would I be working on this decision?" Thorough preparation by all participants will make the rest of the work on the case particularly worthwhile.

Second, the participants divide into small groups, in which they share what they found with the other members. These groups will discuss every case, before the larger group meets. In a small group every participant has the chance to explain to the rest of the group the insights he or she has gained. Because they have to voice their views, they will take the case seriously. Peer pressure is likely to ensure that every individual prepares the case and talks about it, sharing good ideas. All participants develop their communication skills, build their confidence, build relationships, and practise working as a team.

In the final stage, a representative of each group shares the group's understanding of the case with the others. The presenter will write each idea down on a flipchart or white board, as it is given, accepting everything in the brainstorming session. The process of recording each idea for the larger group to see gives it importance and allows it to be referred to later. After the recording is completed, some ideas may be discarded, if they are of little relevance. Members of the smaller groups may add details if it seems appropriate and if time allows. The aim is to enable everyone to understand the case and decide on the best way to solve it, both for the present and in the long term.

The problems that arise from cases are seldom simple. In the cases in this book various forces will play their part and will need to be considered carefully by the decision makers. But that is by no means the end. All the cases in this book are complicated by a mesh of the cross-cultural issues raised in Chapter 2 and set in a particular cross-cultural environment as portrayed in Chapter 3.

The conversations that take place in almost all the cases add the richness of human interest, bringing the people and incidents to life. They serve another purpose, too. If participants are busy people with many other matters on their minds, even though they have prepared the case meticulously, a brush-up in the meeting- room will be invaluable. Some members of the team presenting the case can take the main roles, reviving the case for everyone. In a boardroom, similarly, a chair might ask the main protagonists of a case, "Just go over it again for me, will you? I'd like to be brought up to scratch with all the details."

Often the cases will seem incomplete. So it is in the management workplace, though there you might be able to track down missing pieces of the puzzle. However, even in the workplace you rarely have all the information you would like to have. All you can do is make the best of the information you have.

Though a case may be remembered longer than any set of facts or figures, its main value is to stimulate the participants to bring all their analytical and personal training and skills to bear on the incident or set of incidents before them. The meeting room is no ivory tower but a laboratory where ideas are shared and tested so that their users later can help solve all the challenges their work brings. We ask that all participants prepare by reading and considering the case due for discussion thoroughly before the meeting, and come ready to contribute actively.

Once you are together, for each of the cases in this book, here is the recommended approach:

1. If the group has more than four or five people, break into small groups. Three or four is the maximum recommended number for each group. Select a spokesperson for the group. Sometimes you will choose a separate person to take notes of the group decisions; sometimes the spokesperson may prefer to do it.
2. Sort out the facts.
3. Decide what the underlying issues are. Chapters 2 and 3 of this book will help any participants who have not already studied cross-cultural issues.
4. Decide what causes the problems, and what might be done about those causes. Sometimes it may be useful to do a SWOT[1] analysis. In a cross-cultural case, a qualitative approach is

---

[1] An analysis of strengths, weaknesses, opportunities and threats facing the organisation.

more often called for than a quantitative approach, but if numbers play a significant part, as with sudden losses or conflicting information given to different decision makers, use them to formulate your conclusion.

5. Generate alternative solutions and weigh them all carefully. Try to take careful account of cross-cultural differences and include innovative solutions, not just the obvious ones. Arrange the possibilities in order of preference for the people affected most and for the organisation.

6. Decide what to do immediately.

7. Decide on a long-term solution.

8. Come together as a single large group and share ideas. The facilitator is likely to ask first for the facts, then for the issues, then for the possible alternatives and finally for the recommended solution. Remember, each small group should come to consensus but the larger group need not. Often there is not a single best answer to a complex case.

9. As a group, develop a plan of action as realistically as you can, with such details as time and cost carefully considered.

We hope users will both enjoy the cases and learn from them.

Chapter 2
Cross-Cultural Dimensions

The number of cross-cultural dimensions that may emerge from a case is legion. The list that follows gives some of the more recognised ones but is not intended to be exhaustive. Nor is it to be thought of only in terms of extremes. Every culture holds both sides of the various dimensions to some degree. And within every culture, individuals differ in themselves, some inclining far from the usual bent of those in the same culture. A particular German may be habitually late; a particular Malaysian may be habitually early.

All the same, if the tendency in a culture is to behave in a certain way, a sharp management team will know that and take it into account, recognising, at the same time, that some individuals will not fit into the pattern of dimensions. This chapter will enlarge on each of these dimensions, not in depth but enough for them to become recognisable to readers. They can then recall times when these and other dimensions were important in their work and share these with the others considering the cases. Here are the key dimensions that frequently affect cross-cultural situations in the workplace:

1. High versus low context
2. Collectivism versus individualism
3. Power distance
4. Ascription versus achievement
5. Uncertainty avoidance
6. Masculinity versus femininity
7. View of time
8. Long term versus short term orientation
9. Mode of activity
10. Worldview
11. Level of formality

12. Universalism versus particularism
13. Detachment versus emotion
14. Concepts of face
15. View of the environment
16. View of people
17. View of age
18. Problem solving
19. Attitude to the metaphysical
20. Importance of harmony
21. Use of silence

These dimensions will be discussed briefly in the following pages. So will three other tendencies that enter cross-cultural negotiations but are related to culture in a very different way: stereotyping, ethnocentrism and negative attribution. For a much richer understanding of all these and other cross-cultural matters, readers should explore the books and articles listed as Recommended Reading at the end of this book.

In the discussions, cultures will be seen to overlap and separate out in countless ways. The differences somehow need to be labelled, but no labels are really satisfactory. Some books divide the world into *east* and *west*, inaccurate terms at best. East and west of where? The term might work adequately for Europe, but even the continents like Africa and Australia do not really fit in. All the same, for concepts like **worldview** it is difficult to manage without them.

Developed and *developing* are even more objectionable except for economists who base the character of a country on gross national product. To call a country like China, with thousands of years of history *developing*, and a country like New Zealand with a short known history *developed*, seems truly ironic.

Some books divide the world into the *host country* and *strangers*, but those terms imply a distance, even opposition, that belongs to ethnocentrism, not to the kind of cross-cultural understanding which is the aim of this collection. And some cross-cultural problems occur within a single country, like Malaysia, Belgium or the United States, where several cultures co-exist.

Each case has the underlying dimensions interacting in different ways. Each reader will bring a different set of assumptions and a different store of knowledge to the cases, but it may help to provide some background to the dimensions that occur most frequently.

1. One frequent trigger of trouble is the dimension placed at the top of the list, **high and low context**, a concept developed by Edward T. Hall (1983). In a later book, Hall and Reed (1990) expressed the idea this way:

    > Too much information frequently leads people to feel they are being talked down to; too little information can mystify them or make them feel left out. Ordinarily, people make these adjustments automatically in their own country, but in other countries their messages frequently miss the target (p.11).

    In a high context culture, information resides in the person, not in the message. Communication will be general, assuming the listener or reader would know the context and be able to understand a message after little more than a prompt.

    In a high context society like China or Russia, an employee may not have a contract at all, or may have an oral one only. If a written contract exists, it is not likely to be detailed, and can easily be overridden by spoken agreement between employer and employee, or buyer and seller.

    In contrast, in a low context society like Germany or the United States, everything significant is expected to be recorded, and the details can be enforced in a court of law. One case in this book, *Mr Braun in trouble*, involves a joint venture between a German and a Chinese company whose members have very different understandings of the role of their written contracts.

    Victor (1990, p.144) gives five main differences between high and low context culture:

    1. Different emphasis on personal relationships
    2. Different attitude to explicit communication, the law, contracts
    3. Different reliance on verbal communication
    4. Uncertainty avoidance variations
    5. Different versions of face-saving.

    Any of these may have major repercussions in the workplace. Some of the differences will be discussed in more detail later in this chapter.

2. The second listed dimension, **collectivism and individualism**, can also affect management in serious ways.

    In a collectivist culture, employment is likely to be long term, even for life as used to be the case in Japan, and still is in many organisations there. The employer has an almost paternalist relationship with his or her staff. Hofstede puts it this way: "The level of individualism/collectivism in a society will affect the organization's members' reasons for complying with organizational requirements" (1984, p.153). Family problems and joys are the organisation's concern, as well as those of the person. Employment of family members of employees is common and liked, whereas in individualist cultures like the United States, it tends to be labelled *nepotism* and disliked, or even seen as illegal in many organisations.

    The family in a collectivist culture is likely to be extended, and a member is expected to attend functions and sometimes to support financially other members who have never lived in the same house. For instance, uncles, aunts and grandparents could be thought responsible for making regular donations to a nephew studying overseas.

    In cultures where either dimension predominates, the people form groups, but the groups tend to be different in kind. In some Chinese universities, students enter a class and take all subjects throughout their degree together. The bond among them, developed over several years, is retained for life. The other groups they belong to are similarly long term. In contrast, except in some professional schools, in most western universities students usually choose their own subjects and are in several different groups each semester and each year. They will form some friendships, and these friendships will change continually. The same happens with groups that members of a western community join. One year a person may attend a cycling club; the next he or she may drop the sport altogether and go to cooking instead.

3. The third dimension listed, **power distance**, is almost as important as the first two. It involves the extent to which a society accepts power differences, both in personal and in work relationships. People in high power distance cultures, like Mexico or Malaysia, tend to accept power and authority as facts of life. A vice-chancellor of a university can make a

decision the staff dislike, and, although they may express unease they will still accept it. *The Analects* of Confucius, which permeate the thinking of many Asians whatever their religion, require, before all else, submission to authority and submission to the mores of society.

In high context cultures, in most organisations power is centralised, and if it is challenged the challenger is swiftly dealt with. Unions may not be allowed; if they are, what they can and cannot do is strictly controlled.

In contrast, low power-distance countries like the Scandinavian countries or New Zealand have firm laws to see that those with power do not take advantage of those without. The office of Ombudsman, a person to whom anyone who feels ill-treated can appeal, is seen as important, and the courts will listen to any employee at least as closely as to an employer.

4. **Ascription and achievement** are useful concepts, not only in understanding power distance but for other issues as well, like view of age, view of people and attitudes to problem solving. Ascribed status is given to a person simply for being whatever he or she is. Judgement of where a person rates in a society depends on an amalgam of birth, age, gender, social connections, education and profession (McLaren, 1998, p. 92).

However slight the distance, in some cultures it will be openly recognised where ascription is the norm. In Mandarin, as in the language of various other collectivist cultures, there is no word for "brother" but there are words for "older brother" and "younger brother". In some cultures an acquaintance, even a customer in a shop who has never met the person serving before, may be called "uncle" or "grandma", the status depending on the perceived age.

The most extreme example of ascription is perhaps the now illegal caste system once regularly practised in India, in which status was built into a person's name and could not be changed. In Malaysia, simply by being male, a man has privileges not accorded to women. For instance, a male visiting professor has his wife's fare to and from the home country paid, whereas a woman professor does not have her husband's fare paid. Who you know is important everywhere, but is especially important in a culture where merit is accorded by ascription.

Education is slightly different since it is the result of effort. All the same, interviewing candidates with the highest academic qualifications for a position may result in the best person not being considered at all. Profession, too, is slightly different since it is the result of effort on an individual's part. However, to assume a medical doctor is someone extremely important in New Zealand but unimportant in China (and correspondingly remunerated in each country) seems to make little sense in either society.

In an ascription-oriented culture, titles are used invariably. In Malaysia the authors of this book are "Professor Doctor" to their graduate students, whereas in New Zealand they would simply be addressed by their given names, just as the students are. Respect for your superiors in an organisation, whatever their ability, is required in an ascription-oriented culture and seen as a measure of your commitment to the organisation, whereas in an achievement-oriented organisation it would depend on the quality of the superior's performance.

5. **Uncertainty avoidance** can be variously defined as "the extent to which the members of a culture feel threatened by uncertain or unknown conditions" or "the degree to which the members of a society feel uncomfortable with uncertainty and ambiguity" (McLaren, 1998, p. 70).

The concept was originally developed by C.R. Berger and R.J. Calabrese in 1975. Of all the dimensions, it may be undergoing the most change in Asian cultures at the time of writing this book. Insurance, once rare in Asian and African cultures, is becoming increasingly popular as people fear that continuity of jobs can no longer be assumed, and that in their old age the family may no longer be able to welcome them into their homes.

In 1983 Gudykunst carried out research that showed a positive correlation between high uncertainty avoidance and high context cultures. Certainly leaders in organisations in high context cultures do tend to prefer to work with those they have known a long time and learnt to trust, whereas those in organisations in low context cultures may be very willing to enter into negotiations with newcomers. However, this needs much closer examination. People in some high context cultures, such as those of Thailand and China, are much less likely to have taken out insurance than those in low context cultures like the United States or Australia, yet taking out insurance is surely a sign of *high* uncertainty avoidance.

Although some people consider *feng shui*, or belief in the supernatural powers of wind and water, to be based on scientific evidence, others see it as a way of avoiding the unforeseen dangers of life. Even in parts of the United States, the United Kingdom and Australia, all low uncertainty avoidance cultures, *feng shui* experts are called in by some members of the community, not necessarily Asian, to give advice about such matters as placing the furniture when a building is officially opened. *Feng shui* will be raised again in the section on metaphysics in this chapter.

6. **Masculinity versus femininity** is a difficult concept to explain, because it does not equate with male and female roles in all societies. In Hofstede's work (1980, 1984, 1991, 1997), a masculine society is seen to be one in which strength, performance, achievement, competition and ambition are admired. A high proportion of a country's income is likely to be spent on the military. In contrast, a feminine society is a caring society with a generous welfare system, where the very young, the old, the disabled and the unemployed are supported by the state. Hofstede sees his own culture, the Dutch culture, as extremely feminine, and the Scandinavian cultures also. Japan is seen as the most masculine society, far more masculine than the next in his data, Austria (Hofstede, 1991). Hofstede's findings have been challenged (eg. Md Zabid and others, 1997) but the underlying notion still remains an interesting one.

   In a masculine-oriented culture, most senior managers will be male. To send a woman, however qualified, to travel abroad to head a multinational company in a masculine society, might be taking a risk, even though she would be seen first as a member of her own society and only secondly as a woman. The case entitled *Insya Allah* shows the kind of unspoken but crucial way different attitudes to the roles of men and women can influence decisions.

7. Every manager working in a multicultural environment will be aware of the differences in the **view of time** and the ways these influence the behaviour of employers and employees.

Some see time as cyclical, independent of people, a base into which people fit activities as they choose. Relationships are seen to control time, not the other way round. The present matters more than the past and more than the future. Such societies are sometimes labelled **polychronic**, meaning that people within them are comfortable doing several things at the same time. In the words of Edward Hall: "Matters in a polychronic culture seem in a constant state of flux. Nothing is solid or firm, particularly plans for the future" (1976, p.47). A clerk at a counter may stop serving a customer to answer a question from somebody else. A manager will answer the telephone during a meeting, keeping the person who had an appointment waiting. Nobody seems to mind. A guest invited to dinner may accept and then not arrive because something else more interesting has come up. In some societies this would be seen as the height of rudeness; in others it would be simply accepted and considered not at all important.

In a **monochronic** culture the tendency, especially in business, is to do one thing at a time. The diary controls the day. A manager who has an appointment with an individual will, if possible, route all telephone calls through a secretary and only take one during a meeting in an emergency. If the manager does not have a personal secretary, he or she will either ignore the telephone or answer it briefly, arranging a call at a later time. The relative importance of the visitor is not an issue. The fact that a previous appointment has been made dictates the action.

Time is seen as the only non-renewable commodity. People say time is money. They talk about "spending time", "saving time", "giving time", "allocating time" and "wasting time". Compare this with the polychronic view in which each activity will be done in its own good time. A university can change the dates of its teaching term with two weeks' notice, whereas in a monochronic society such a decision would need to be made years in advance and widely notified in writing.

This dimension is one that individuals are likely to hold strong views on. The manager in an organisation may give habitual lateness as the main reason for terminating an employee's contract, not recognising that flexibility with time has many advantages. The manager in a polychronic society may make it difficult for an employee to see him or her privately, while thinking his or her open-door policy is truly kind.

A westerner who has travelled a distance or has turned down attractive offers in order to keep an appointment only to find that the person who made the appointment has taken leave that day will mind greatly. Similarly, when the westerner is in the room for an appointment and the officer answers the telephone for a long conversation – or even a series of conversations – the waste of the visitor's time will seem galling and will certainly disrupt good business relationships.

A manager who does not understand the different attitudes may become the victim of them. Hall (1976) suggests that Japanese negotiators in Japan delay making final offers until they know their American visitors have a confirmed flight home, realising that Americans, with other commitments awaiting them at home, are likely to agree to anything rather than change their schedule.

8. **Long and short term orientation** is usually a natural corollary, polychronic societies tending to have a long term orientation and monochronic societies a short-term orientation. Both personal and business relationships are likely to be for life.

Kluckhohn and Strodtbeck (1961, p.12) identified three cultural approaches to time: past, present and future orientation. These overlap with the **being**, **becoming** and **doing** attitudes identified in the **activity orientation** dimension, number 9 in this list.

People in a past-oriented society see history as the key to understanding the present and the future. Applicants for an academic position would include a detailed listing of all their publications, emphasising the most significant even if they were produced many years before.

In a short-term oriented culture, immediate goals are more likely to be set and observed than long term goals, and to have a precise time limit set on them. Planning is considered extremely important. People assume that what they do will make an immediate difference and will be correspondingly appreciated. Profit figures will be given for short periods, perhaps quarterly, and key personnel will be kept informed. An applicant for an academic position would emphasise recent publications and achievements, not those of years before.

The organisation choosing the applicant, too, may have expectations that are not met. A survey of 2,500 young applicants in the United States found that 78% planned to work for their first employer for three years or fewer (Locker and Kaczmarek, 2001, p.508). Compare that with the Japanese system, now changing but still widely held, of life-long employment, or with the Malaysian and Thai system of paying for staff to undertake advanced training and then bonding them for several years for each year of training.

A company planning to do business with a company in, say, China, Japan or Mexico, would need to show how long the relationship between the two companies has lasted already, how it can be trusted long-term, and how reliable it has been in the past. Visits on both sides and close personal contact between senior individuals will help considerably. In contrast, in the United States, Canada or Australia, the strategy would be to show how efficient and how busy the company is, and how it is using the latest technology.

9. **Activity orientation** is sometimes referred to as the preference for **being**, **becoming** or **doing**. The concept derives from a framework developed by Kluckhohn and Strodtbeck (1961, p.3) and mentioned already.

    The **being** orientation to them is usually practised by people in a past-oriented culture. Leaders will talk about the lessons of history. But they will throw themselves into happy occasions with abandon. The Mexican attitude of *manãna* (Let it wait till tomorrow) is characteristic. It may be that the **being** orientation is linked to climate, as in the Pacific Islands where the people tend to work and play in the same communities or in Thailand where the word *ngan* means both work and play. In such a culture, managers who insist on a stern differentiation between work-related and outside activities might meet heavy but unspoken resistance.

    The **becoming** orientation is a natural result of a belief in incarnation, in the cyclical pattern of life. Everything is in a constant state of flux, of rhythmic movement, including business and life itself. Life and death are alternating stages, like sleeping and being awake." Just as sleep prepares us for the next activity, death can be seen as a state in which we rest and replenish ourselves for the next life." (Ikeda, 1996, p.153). What can a lost hour matter to those who think that way?

Fate and fortune play their part, and must be accepted as part of life. People are concerned with who they are, not with what they are doing. This orientation is likely to be held by Buddhists and Hindus. People will be present-orientated, but forward-looking, in a calm manner.

The **doing** orientation is the norm in the west. People are future-oriented and competitive. Companies will keep a close watch on their own market share and that of their rivals. In a doing-oriented culture, managers will feel they are responsible for the outcome of their work, will plan meticulously and do all they can to control their own results.

Beamer and Varner (2001 p. 83), though, point out that even in the west this attitude is changing:

> Even some Westerners think Western rationalism, which is our heritage from Aristotle through Voltaire to modern technocrats, has travelled too far from human experience. The discounting of fate and the belief in human planning and engineering seem foolish to some Western thinkers.

10. **Worldview** is a particularly difficult concept to grasp. In the words of Samovar and Porter (1995): "The issues associated with worldview are timeless and represent the most fundamental basis of a culture" (p.68). How do people view religion, each other, the universe they live in, their place in the world and the role of their culture in the world? Are explanations usually mystical or logical or practical? Young Young Kim gives an Asian perspective, which Westerners are not likely to accept:

> The Western view of the universe is characteristically dualistic, material, lifeless. Assuming a relatively barren universe, it seems only rational that humans exploit the lifeless material universe. . . On the other hand, the Eastern view is profoundly holistic, dynamic and spiritual . . . (McLaren, 1998, p.56).

This worldview may seem abstract and unrelated to management situations but it is not. If people in a culture see the world in a particular way, that vision can translate into what they do. Germans are obsessed with technical quality and so they produce exceptionally good quality cars. The Japanese are fascinated with spatial arrangements and so they produce meals exquisite in appearance, with each item tiny and perfectly set out.

Worldview involves both how people in a culture see the world, and how they see their own position in the world. What is their role? How do they think they are seen? Do they see themselves as leaders or victims or poor relations of the rest of the world?

11. **The level of formality** in a culture is extremely important in the early stages of any management negotiation. Casual dress and the assumption that others can be addressed by their personal names may be taken for granted by many in the United States, Canada, Australia and New Zealand. In countries like Japan, Malaysia, Germany and Belgium, they may seem to indicate a lack of respect and seriousness.

Meetings in some cultures will tend to be much more formal than in others. New Zealand Maori will expect to begin meetings with prayers, formal greetings and acknowledgements of ancestors, family, and all those present. In other cultures such as in South China meetings may often be casual, even without agenda or minutes.

When agenda and minutes are prepared, the level of formality will dictate the language used. At a formal meeting, close friends will address one another by official titles and this will be reflected in the minutes. The minutes themselves will have no contractions of pairs of words (like "don't" for "do not") and will contain no unexplained slang. Numbers under ten occurring in the text may be written in words rather than in digits.

Age, gender and social status can all affect the level of formality expected. In some cultures, such as the Japanese and Korean cultures, this goes as far as controlling the choice of words used, especially the choice of personal pronouns.

12. **Particularism and universalism** are dimensions which might be expected to coincide with individualism and collectivism, but do not. **Particularism** sounds close to **individualism** but is the opposite. A person from a

particularist culture is likely to behave according to the particular circumstances, not according to the rules and regulations laid down by the society. In a court of law a person from a **particularist** society may give unreliable evidence, because it is his or her duty to support a friend in trouble.

Trompenaars (1993, pp.33-35) cites an experiment in which two close friends are envisaged as being in a car which hits and injures a pedestrian. There are no witnesses. The court orders generous compensation for the pedestrian. The driver's lawyer tells the passenger that if he testifies under oath that his friend was driving at only 20 miles an hour it might save him from a jail sentence. The friend has to decide whether to testify or not.

Notice that the result will make no difference to the pedestrian, only to the driver. In the experiment almost everyone from the universalist cultures said they would refuse to testify on the friend's behalf, considering it would be corrupt to do so. But of those from particularist cultures, nearly a third were willing to testify.

In contrast, a person from a **universalist** society will take laws as sacrosanct and tend to obey rules and regulations even when it might seem unnecessary. There are stories about motorists coming to a complete halt at stop signs in the Arizona desert when visibility is completely clear and no vehicles can be seen anywhere. The rationale would be that there must have been a reason for the law, (perhaps a hidden side road might bring unexpected traffic) and flouting it would be wrong.

In a **universalist** culture, legal contracts are normally drawn up for any business, and a reliable organisation is one which honours whatever has been agreed to. In a **particularist** culture, agreements are likely to be oral. If they are written they can be easily changed by oral agreement. A good organisation is thought to be one that adapts promptly to changing circumstances.

13. Business behaviour can be dictated by the relative attitude within a culture to **detachment versus emotion**. In some societies, people show their emotions visibly. In others, they keep them utterly under control, showing nothing. This does

not mean they feel strongly about issues; simply that they do not show their feelings to the world.

Princess Diana, when she was alive, was criticised by senior British officials for publicly kissing AIDS victims, and, when she was supporting a Red Cross campaign against land mines, for speaking graphically about children who had lost limbs. Masses of the British people adored her for that very behaviour. The official "stiff upper lip" attitude, the disapproval of "wearing your heart on your sleeve" of those in authority may not represent the attitude of the majority within a culture.

Sometimes, of course, it does. In Japan it is unlikely that any public shows of emotion will be made, whether the emotion is joy or sorrow or anything else. *Tatenae,* or the Japanese facade suitable for the world to see, is carefully cultivated. The stereotype of the "inscrutable Oriental" has developed because of the difficulty Westerners have had in assessing just how some of their Asian associates felt about matters.

In a business context, it is necessary to remember that overt shows of emotion may reflect cultural views about the display of emotion, not the real depth of feeling. People in Mediterranean cultures who show emotion openly in their gestures and their voices do not necessarily feel more strongly than people in more restrained cultures like those of Sweden or Japan. The Japanese have a saying "Only a dead fish has an open mouth" and are much more guarded than Italians or French might be. In such cultures understatement or irony may be used and may cause serious trouble. To thank someone for a "generous concession" when you think very little has been offered may be either misunderstood or understood and considered extremely rude by people from a more open culture.

People in a culture where banging on the table or forceful gestures in speech may be thought to indicate immaturity and lack of control may not respond favourably to those who assume that showing their feelings reflects their strong concern. And those in cultures where people expect feelings to be exhibited may assume those who show only restrained emotion are lukewarm and may not be the best to do business with.

Two kinds of ability are useful in this aspect of cross-cultural management, both depending on recognition of different attitudes to showing feelings. One is to ensure that our own expression of emotion is acceptable to the other party. The other is to put the other party's expression of emotion into its cultural context and try to take it as it was intended.

14. **Concepts of face** differ greatly according to the culture. They always matter greatly, but David Victor (1992) points out that the more high context a particular culture is, the more important people in it will consider face-saving to be.

Face is the self-image presented to the world. In individualist societies, each person must protect his or her own face. The aim is always to separate the person from the actions, so a superior can find fault with what is done without the person taking it to heart as a personal insult. If reprimanded, the person may explain the background to the behaviour, as a form of justification, so protecting his or her face.

In collectivist societies, however, the emphasis is on protecting the face of others. A student may know that a lecturer is wrong but not say so in class, because doing so might hurt the "face" of the instructor. A technician may know that reinforcing to the structure of a building or safety procedures are inadequate, but will not bring the danger to the attention of superiors. In China, *mianzi* (face) and *ren qing* (human feelings) are of extreme importance (McLaren, 1998, p. 180) so to challenge the worth of the superior's actions is to challenge the personal worth of the superior, which would be unthinkable.

In a management situation, the different views of face must be respected or the repercussions may be serious. Public reprimands – or even public praise – can upset people in societies where managers need to respect the face of others. The message itself is not the important factor but the way of delivering it. In a culture where a person's own face is important, the absence of public praise may discourage a worker from exertion another time.

15. **The view of the environment** involves both nature and what are called "built" areas. Until relatively recently, collectivist cultures were thought to treat nature as something to be guarded carefully for future generations, whereas individualist cultures were seen to treat it as a series of forces to be harnessed to improve life for the people.

In many countries, roads, flyovers, bridges and dams can alter the land significantly but were constructed, sometimes ruthlessly, to supply transport and electricity. But the continuum is changing, almost reversing. With technology reaching more widely, collectivist cultures are controlling nature when they can, as with the huge Yangtse River project in China. Yet on 31 July 2001 a government-owned railway in Hong Kong, now part of China, was forced to stop its plans to build a train track through wetlands where a rare species of birds nest (Pottinger, 1 August 2001, p.4, col.1). An earlier ruling by the Hong Kong Environmental Protection Department had been challenged but was upheld in court. And individualist cultures like those of the United States and Australia, are listening to environmental groups and working out their civil engineering projects with extreme caution.

To some extent the built environment reflects the population density of a people. In the rural areas everywhere, people tend to have their own separate dwellings, however primitive. In cities like Taipei with far more people to the hectare, than in, say, the back blocks of New Zealand, apartments will be the norm. Consequently concepts of privacy will be very different. An American businessperson brought to Japan may be extremely uncomfortable sharing a large office with many others; a Japanese businessperson may feel isolated in an office by him or herself.

A culture in which full employment is seen as of extreme importance may have employment conditions that would be unacceptable in a culture where safety of employees is more important. Young girls will do close work for hours in a Chinese doll factory, and staff will work without earmuffs in a noisy Chinese factory, yet there is no doubt that the workers in both situations are happy to have the work.

16. **The view of people** rouses controversy wherever it is addressed. Whether individuals are religious or not, within a culture it goes back to the underlying religion. For part of the world, especially those parts with a Christian or Jewish tradition, it is rooted in the Old Testament view of original sin. A baby is born totally self-centred, crying for food and attention. Over the years the child is trained to consider others more and more.

For much of the rest of the world, however, the Buddhist view of innate purity is held. A baby is understood to be born utterly pure and good, until worldly influences develop evil in him or her.

These assumptions, usually subconscious, will have an effect on how people behave towards others. But they interact with other assumptions, particularly those like individualism versus collectivism and universalism versus particularism, touched on above. Should a manager reward individuals or the group they work in when a task is well done? Is society, the employer or the family responsible for caring for an injured person? What if the person is not employed but is injured through the actions of an employee? Should company activities be arranged out of work time? Is gift giving in business acceptable or not? Should there be a compulsory retirement age or not? Answers to all such questions will depend to a considerable extent on the view of people held by those making the decision.

In any culture, a respect for others can help managers solve problems. The Buddhist leader of the Peace Movement known as Soka Gakkai, Daisuka Ikeda (2000), lecturing at Moscow University in 1975, reminded his audience: "When one person recognises the humanity of another, walls that may have separated them crumble."

17. Issues such as retirement, mentioned in the previous dimension, lead naturally on to the **view of age**, which in turn ties in with other dimensions such as power distance and ascription.

In some cultures, age confers status. In the words of Beamer and Varner: "In cultures that value age, the older a businessperson is the more credibility he or she has" (2001, p. 107). To send what the Americans call a " whiz-kid", a very young person with some outstanding technical skill but little or no experience, would seem unacceptable.

In other cultures, age is seen as irrelevant. The expertise is all that is considered, and a young person is no more and no less acceptable than an older one.

In still other cultures, age is seen as evidence of uselessness, as words like "has-been" show. People over fifty may find it impossible to get a new job of any importance, whatever their skill. Beamer and Varner cite the terms used to get rid of older people in some American organisations: they are "kicked upstairs" or "put out to pasture" (2001, p.108).

When joint ventures involve cultures with different attitudes to age, promotion and senior positions will need to be thought about carefully, with people of each culture being informed about and sensitive to the differences. Even the language used or the depth of the bow is likely to be age-related.

18. **Problem-solving** differs in both obvious and subtle ways in different cultures. When a problem or set of problems arises, the solutions will depend on the decision makers' attitudes to several of the dimensions in the list given in this chapter. But whatever the particular dimensions, they may be taken together, holistically, or separately, one by one and balanced one against another for relative importance. Students applying for jobs, for example, are sometimes urged to make a "forced choice" weighing against each other factors like salary, promotion, location of the organisation and many others.

Western texts on such subjects as management, business strategy and business communication all stress the direct manner of approaching a problem and thinking it through, using step-by step Aristotelian logic. William Deming called it "Management by Objectives" and though this philosophy is now considered dated, it still underlies much of the decision making in western business. There is one solution and one only. Western courts, in which a person is either guilty or not guilty, show how westerners tend to see solutions in terms of opposites. However, a quarter of a century ago, Edward Hall was reminding readers that linearity can get in the way of mutual understanding (1976).

Daisaku Ikeda, the Soka Gakkai Buddhist thinker quoted twice already, is one who challenges the western concept of causation as mechanistic and divorced from subjective human experience:

> When an accident or disaster takes place, for example, a mechanistic theory of causation can be used to pursue and identify how the accident occurred. It is silent, however, on other points, including the question of why certain individuals and not others should find themselves caught

up in the tragic event. Indeed, the mechanistic view of nature requires the deliberate dismissal of existential questions (1966, p.160).

In Asian and Middle Eastern cultures, therefore, a more cyclical or gyrating pattern of thought might be more acceptable. In business documents diffuse language patterns, with liberal use of poetic devices like alliteration and metaphor can be greatly admired (McLaren, 1998). Relationships rather than causes are sought. Gudykunst and Kim explain how much can be gained by going beyond logic:

> What seems to be of central importance in Asian thinking is a certain repose of the personality in which it feels it is grasping the inner significance... The intuitive style of thinking provides a powerful cognitive mechanism for developing a harmonious rapport with the other person and the environment. (1992a: p.149).

In all cultures both linear thinking and divergent thinking will be used to solve problems, but in some the emphasis is on the former, while in others it is on the latter.

19. **The attitude to the metaphysical** is wider than the attitude to religion discussed more fully in the chapter on the cross-cultural environment. The metaphysical is far from sectarianism. It includes all matters that go beyond the physical and cannot be explained otherwise. Ancestor worship does not necessarily have a religious base. Spiritualism, mysticism, grace, a sense of the sacred, superstition, belief in good or bad luck, belief in ghosts and devils, and animism (or the belief that all living things are in themselves divine) may be part of a particular religion but need not be. Sometimes they are explained as having geophysical implications. *Feng shui* beliefs, for instance, such as the value of hanging a picture of a mountain behind your chair in times of adversity, are taken extremely seriously by many in the business world, and not only the Asian business world.

Francis Schaefer (1968) divided the world into secular cultures, or those that presuppose a natural cause for everything, and sacred cultures, or those that presuppose a spiritual dimension. But the division is not as clear cut as it might seem. In both secular and sacred cultures metaphysical views do have a link with the physical world, whether they are held as part of a religion or not. Jewish and Islamic dietary laws, Hindu beliefs about valuing and not ever killing cows, early Polynesian views about cannibalism, and even western notions of the evil that will strike those who walk under a ladder, have developed out of physical behaviour believed necessary at certain times and places for safety.

20. **The importance of harmony** is stressed in some cultures but not in others. In the west, smoothing over difficulties without getting at the root cause is not considered acceptable. When William Clinton, the President of the United States, had an extramarital affair with a young woman, the courts came down heavily on the fact that he had untruthfully denied it, not that he had had the affair. His defence, saving anguish to his family, was considered irrelevant.

    Confrontation and intense argument are considered desirable in cultures like those of Italy, France, India and Israel. A Yiddish proverb says, "Where there are two Jews, there are three arguments." But in a collective culture strong and open argument is viewed seriously as threatening the face and so the dignity of others. When a person loses his or her temper in a meeting everyone is hushed and those not there learn about it afterwards. Relationships are precious and must not be treated roughly if they are to persist. The person and the incident are one and the same. Arguments are not enjoyed as they might well be in, say, France. The implications of this for doing business with those who do not understand the difference are considerable.

21. The final dimension in this list, though by no means the only remaining dimension, is the **use of silence**. Imagine a meeting between people of one culture where silence is valued and another in which they are uncomfortable with silence! The notion that if Americans are kept waiting long enough they will agree to anything has been called a popular "in-joke" among the Japanese (Smith and Luce, 1979).

    In Japan, silences can last more than half an hour and mean that something is being seriously considered (Smith and Luce, 1979). But even short silences may be misunderstood.

Japanese people consider it courteous not to speak for a few seconds after the other person has spoken. Since in some cultures turn-taking is quick, with the second person even speaking sometimes before the first has finished and certainly the very second the first finishes, Japanese people may never get a word into a conversation with others.

Even within a single country, people of different cultures may have very different attitudes to silence. In New Zealand, Maori use silence as a control strategy. Sometimes it means "No"; sometimes it means: "We will consider your proposal." If Pakeha (or non-Maori New Zealanders) assume it means "We accept" after a question like "Has anyone any objections?" serious miscommunication can occur. Similarly, Basso found that in the United States people of the Apache culture have a totally different attitude to silence from that held by most Americans (1970).

* * * * * *

The twenty-one dimensions discussed so far, and others like them, are reflected in the behavioural patterns in different cultures. Like all aspects of culture, they tend to be learnt, transmitted from one generation to another, shared, partly physical, partly emotional and partly mental, and slowly changing. Unless we are conscious of them, they may blur our understanding so that we behave in ways that can interfere with successful cross-cultural relationships.

Three other dimensions can damage our understanding seriously, but, if they are aligned at all, it is with personal level of education, not with culture. They are **stereotyping, ethnocentrism** and **negative attribution**.

Stereotyping is a natural and necessary process, our way of making sense of the world we live and work in. We observe differences in others and generalise from them. When we stereotype we make judgments from what we hear or read or notice about members of groups, and apply those judgments to others in the same groups.

The process has at least two serious dangers. One is that the observations may be complete or inaccurate. For example, the stereotype that Belgians make group decisions might be safe for doing business with people from the Flemish part of Belgium but unsafe for Wallonia where the business culture tends to be more hierarchical and only the highest person in authority makes the final decision. (Aini Suzana Haji Ariffin, 2001, p.24). Even more unfounded, we might form a stereotype about a whole region. European cultures differ greatly from one another. So do Asian cultures. So do African cultures. The list could go on and on. Druckerman reports that Argentines "often deride Chilians as unsophisticated and money-grubbing, while Chileans see their neighbours as arrogant and self-indulgent" (2001, p. 1). However, the more we know about individual cultures, the less likely we are to stereotype rashly.

The other danger is that those we apply the judgments to may differ significantly from others in the group. Many people hold the stereotypes that Scots are frugal and Japanese use an indirect style of communication, but a Scot may be extremely free spending; a Japanese person may be direct in thought and word.

Stereotyping, then, may be useful for cross-cultural understanding. It is better, at least in the beginning, to know that the Dutch expect people to keep to deadlines than not to know, if we are to do successful business with them. At the same time, we must recognise that stereotyping is only the beginning of understanding and can lead us badly astray unless we are open to additional information about particular people or groups of people.

Ethnocentrism is a concept introduced almost a century ago by the psychologist, William Sumner (1906). He defined it as "the technical name for the view of things in which one's own group is the center of everything, and all others are scaled and rated with reference to it"(p.13).

All of us are ethnocentric to a degree. The culture that we have learnt to see as the norm and to like forms the basis of our attitude to all other cultures. Unfortunately, the corollary of seeing other cultures from our own standpoint is the conviction that our culture is not only different from but also better than any other culture. It can both result from and cause stereotyping.

To make it worse, most of us do not recognise that we see our own culture as superior and allow the sense of superiority to cloud our judgment of the behaviour of others. Managers who think they are making objective and fair decisions may be extremely biased. Power distance may compound the problem, making it unlikely that others will suggest what is happening.

A further complication can enter into decision making when **negative attribution** occurs. Stereotyping from an ethnocentric viewpoint, managers may make what psychologists call the "fundamental attribution error". This means that they attribute behaviour to the culture and character of individuals rather than to the situation, so blaming people when the particular circumstances are the cause of the trouble.

That is, they make their own judgment of workers from another culture, and measure it against what they think is right. To start with, the original judgment may not apply to the individuals concerned. And then the judgment on what has happened in a particular set of circumstances may be wrong.

If those making decisions are aware of the dangers of stereotyping, ethnocentrism and negative attribution, they can then use the cultural dimensions listed in this chapter to help understand difficult situations. Cross-cultural problems arise not just because people of different cultures have different sets of values and beliefs but because they either do not realise that differences exist or recognise but fail to respect the differences.

Chapter 3
The Cross-Cultural Environment

In the business environment, several factors – political, economic, technological and social – affect the operations of the firm. The political environment encompasses issues relating to forms of government, political stability, legal systems, and foreign policy. These factors can affect directly or indirectly the operations of the firm in the local and international context. Economic forces like the level of economic growth, fiscal and monetary policies, foreign investment, Gross National Product (GNP), and stage of economic development also affect the operations of the firm. The level and availability of technical skills, infrastructure, technological capability, research and development, and technological support policies, also have a direct and indirect bearing on the operations of a business firm. The political, technological and economic forces indicate the level of sophistication of the society, and consequently are reflected in the social forces in a society or community.

The social forces include religion, language, race, social systems, ideology, and education. These forces largely determine the *culture* of a particular social environment. Culture has been defined as the 'norms, values and beliefs' of a particular group or community in a particular area or geographic location, and shared by its members (Hofstede, 1980). This means that the influence of the beliefs and value systems will lead to the members of a community behaving and acting in a predictable manner, and will become part of their perceptions of the world. For example, it is the culture of the Malays not to speak with a high tone to an elderly person or superior, as it is perceived to be 'uncultured'. It is also considered improper not to address close relatives with titles like *Mak Cik* or *Mak Long*.

These are but some examples of values adhered to even in the twenty-first century, and expected to be upheld and practised in the future. Values are community ideas about what is good or bad, right or wrong, like the belief that stealing is immoral and unfair. Values will also determine how individuals will respond to a given situation or circumstances.

In the globalisation era, businesses will face communities from different parts of the world. Interactions among the different cultural groups form an integral part of the present and future life styles. The United States of America (USA), United Kingdom, and Canada are among those countries with communities from different parts of the world converging towards one set of basic values: the language and communication mode.

Like Singapore, Malaysia is a multicultural country in which the major communities – the Malays, Chinese and Indians – interact harmoniously in their everyday living. While this may be considered to be a colourful cultural community, it cannot avoid tensions and crisis among the communities due to cultural misunderstandings or the lack of cultural awareness or comprehension of different cultural values, beliefs and norms.

In a western community, cultural variations may not be seen as major as the community has mainly been grounded in one religious faith – Christianity. In the Malaysian context, the cultural diversity is further intensified by the divergent religious faiths and practices. For example, the Malays have adopted the Islamic religion; indeed the Malaysian Constitution lays down that a Malay in Malaysia cannot remain a Malay if he or she rejects Islam. Members of the Chinese community may be Taoist, Confucian, Buddhist or Christian. Indians in Malaysia may be Hindu or Muslims, and a minority are Christians. This adds complexity to understanding the cultural diversity among the Malaysian ethnic groups, and consequently, enhances possible tensions and misgivings.

However, since independence was gained in 1957, Malaysia has experienced only one major crisis, in May 1969, that can be related to cultural differences. Some Malaysians argue that even that crisis was more due to political differences and social inequalities than to cultural differences. The usual harmony can be attributed to the high level of socio-political tolerance among the ethnic communities, and generally accepted norms in the Malaysian society.

Cultural variables like values, norms and beliefs can also determine the basic attitudes, towards life, work, time and change. Such attitudes can affect an individual's expectations and so his or her behaviour.

Therefore, in trying to understand better the cross-cultural environment, it is imperative to comprehend the basic elements of a particular environment. This will provide the fundamental framework for analysing the cases presented in this book. The cross-cultural environment is shown in Figure 1.

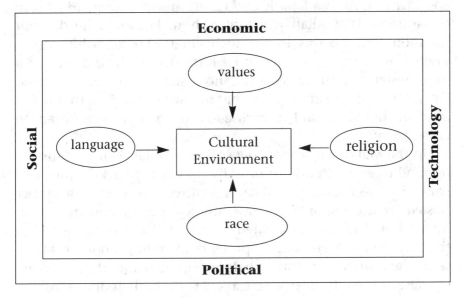

Figure 1 Cross – Cultural Environment

The basic elements of the cross-cultural environment include religion, race, language, and social systems (including values, beliefs, and norms).

Religion

Religion is a person's faith in the existence of a creator, God. Different religious faiths have different views of the world and its *raison d'être*. In certain societies, religious faiths have a limited impact on everyday life and are considered personal. In other communities, religious faith is as inseparable as life is to an individual.

The cross-cultural environment has a major impact on the global community in circumstances where one community adopts religion as a way of life and another sees it as a personal belief. This is particularly true in the case of a Muslim living in a Christian community in the West. For example, Ali is a Muslim and he believed that it is important for him to consume food that is considered *halal* (food prepared according to Islamic rites). Because of this, Ali would have to be cautious and check the availability of *halal* food when he is travelling in Western countries. A person who sees religion as personal faith would consider that Ali is a fanatic and taking an extreme stand instead of assuming that Allah will forgive him, knowing the difficult situation that he was in. In such circumstances, when Ali is invited by George, a Christian by birth, to lunch or dinner at a meat restaurant in Texas, USA, how should Ali react? Would George accept his explanation that he cannot eat food that is not *halal*, or should Ali find an excuse to avoid any embarrassment to either party?

In the Malaysian scene, how should a Malay, being a Muslim, respond to an invitation or offer by his client to drink brandy or wine? In one incident, a Malay executive was attending dinner hosted by the major client (a Chinese-owned company) in an international restaurant located in one of the five-star hotels in the city. There were others present, including another Malay senior executive. As usual, before commencing the elaborate Chinese dinner, the guests were asked to order their drinks. All the guests (including the Malay senior manager) ordered the alcoholic drinks (beer, whisky, brandy or rum) except for the Malay executive. At the beginning there were no problems but toward the end of the dinner one of the hosts, the general manager of the major client, asked the Malay executive why he did not drink like the others. By that time, the senior Malay manager had left the dinner to attend another function. The general manager asked: "Zainal (not his real name) is a Malay, and you are a Malay. You both are the same. Why can't you drink this brandy?" The Malay executive was overcome with embarrassment and could not explain to the general manager why he chose not to drink brandy. The incident ended up in a sour relationship between the Malay executive and the Chinese general manager who took the situation to mean that the Malay executive did not want to cooperate with him and so did not drink the brandy. But how could the Malay executive drink the brandy when he knew that it is forbidden to do so?

These are some of the possible situations in cross-cultural

settings that could be related to religion yet have nothing to do with extremism or fanaticism. It should be noted that the accepting someone's offer (to eat non *halal* meat or drink alcohol) does not imply that the individual is open minded but rather indicates his or her lack of commitment towards his or her religious faith. Malays have been brought up to observe full commitment strictly and it is very difficult to change this attitude even after staying abroad for a number of years.

The dietary constraint of the Indians is also similar to that of the Muslims. The Indians are predominantly Hindus, and beef is strictly prohibited to them. Many Hindus are expected to eat only vegetarian meals on all occasions, and no Hindu eats beef. Because of this, serving beef to Hindus is provocative and insulting behaviour. However, there are also Indians who observe other Hindu rites, and consume other meat (like fish, lamb or chicken) though never beef.

Like the Hindus, the Jews also observe certain dietary requirements like the consumption of *kocher* meat. One Moroccan Muslim was travelling from Canada to Asia and the airline ordered *kocher* food for her, thinking that the traveller could consume it in lieu of a *halal* or Muslim meal which was unknown to the airline. In such an incident, one Muslim may consider it acceptable but another Muslim would not accept it at all.

On one occasion in a European city, one Arab was commenting to a Turkish guest that the salami (considered *nonhalal*) contained pork meat. The Turkish guest replied: "So what?" The Arab was stunned and kept quiet. One or the other community can misinterpret this response to mean a high or low level of tolerance.

The extent to which business practices are affected by religion depends on the degree of religious fervour and the support of either the government or the community or both for it. The case of the *Thaipusam Tragedy* clearly illustrates the extent of religious faith and the potential seriousness of intercultural misunderstandings. Similarly, the case of the *The Month of the Hungry Ghost* shows that religion plays a more critical role in some communities than in others.

Race

In countries like Japan, China and India, where the community is predominantly homogenous, the need for cross-cultural understanding may be lacking or taken for granted. In most developed countries, the issue of race is not identified. It is feared that the concept of race could create communal conflicts; it is thought that the principles of 'human rights' dictate that any consideration of race should be avoided.

In certain countries, the registration and identification of race have been conceived of as racist. This has been inappropriately misinterpreted, as there are few communities that wish to discriminate adversely on the grounds of race. In Malaysia, one reason for race being considered important in the national registration database is to determine the individual's faith and heritage. A Malaysian may have Chinese or Indian features but actually be Malay and hold the Muslim faith. In case of an accident, the unfortunate person would easily be buried according to Muslim rites.

In countries with multicultural communities like Malaysia and Singapore, the identification of race also has socio-political and economic implications. In both countries Malays have been given some privileges so that they can continue to compete with the other racial groups in the society. For example, in Singapore, Malay students have to pay lower tuition fees while studying in a university than do Chinese or Indian students. In Malaysia, some Malay businessmen are given priority or first offer of selected business projects so as to allow them to compete with the other communities in the country. These moves are protectionist approaches to conserve Malaysia's national heritage and national identity in the years ahead.

The case of *Time is running out* illustrates the importance of race in the cross-cultural setting. It should be realised that the issue of race may not have anything to do with religion but can result from a cultural perspective. While the Malays and Arabs are Muslims, they do have difficulty working together in business because of racial differences. Similarly, racial differences can also have impact on the issue of gender. For example, in certain cultures, such as the Chinese and Indian cultures, women are considered the 'fairer sex' but not equal in some ways. It is considered unacceptable for a Chinese man to marry a Chinese woman who is better educated and has more income than the potential husband. In the Indian community, it is also difficult to accept such a situation. However, this is not the case for Malays.

Malay women, even if they are highly educated, can accept husbands who have a lower income or education. This is due to the fact that Malay men and women accept the different roles of men and women in the community (Sarachek and others, 1984).

The issue of race has also been related to discriminatory practices in the Malaysian society. For example, in an application form for an entry visa to Malaysia, one applicant wrote 'white' on his application form instead of writing his nationality. Another applicant wrote 'Caucasian' on the application form. These incidents suggest that the meaning of race has more than one interpretation. In the Malaysian context, for a local, the term 'race' refers to the ethnic group or identity. In the western context, 'race' might refer to the colour of the skin or the anthropological definition of the human race: Aryan, Caucasian, Mongoloid and others. It should be noted that in terms of racial groupings, the Malays include those ethnic groups in Malaysia, Indonesia, Thailand, the Philippines, and perhaps some parts of Cambodia. For this reason, this geographical location is known as the 'Malay Archipelago'.

Language

Language is the means of communication among communities in a particular society. The simplicity or complexity of a community will determine the extent and level of communication among the members of the community. In Malaysia, it is believed that the Malay language originated from various major languages, including Sanskrit, Hindi, Arabic and regional ethnic languages (such as the Javanese, Minangkabau, Riau-Johor, Bugis, Bawean and many others). In earlier times, the Malay language was dominated, first by the influence of Arabic, and subsequently by English. The Arabic language had influenced the Malay language structure and vocabulary up to the 1970s. Then, with economic development and progress, coupled with the English language education system, the English language style and approach became influential.

In relation to the cross-cultural setting, language appears to have an influence on the style and approach of communication. Due to the sensitivities of the Malays, the language used in communication has an impact on the listener and speaker. For example, a Malay would not bluntly tell a person if he or she did not like an action or behaviour. The idea is not only to show that one is polite but also to show some respect for another person's feelings. More importantly, it is also the concern of the speaker to show that he or she has an *adab* (good manners) when interacting with others.

For example, when a westerner asks a Malay visitor what drink he or she would like to have, the typical response of a Malay is: "Anything will do."

What does this mean to a westerner? Does it mean offering a beer is acceptable or not? If a westerner does not know that a typical Malay does not drink beer, then a beer might be offered which would be a disaster. In reality, the response of the Malay to the westerner is meant to suggest that the Malay visitor does not wish to cause the person making the offer much difficulty and so allows serving of any beverage consumable by the typical Malays – tea or coffee. Because of this, the westerner would have to ask the Malay twice, once more than in the west, whether coffee or tea is acceptable.

In other words, Malays have been known to be very indirect in communicating their ideas so as to avoid hurting the other person's feelings. Communicating bluntly among Malay community members is considered ill mannered (*biadab or tidak sopan*), impolite (*tidak berbahasa*), and crude (*kasar or tidak halus*). It should also be noted that misunderstanding could occur when speaking to Malays in different regions or parts of the country, as different regional Malay words have different meanings and connotations. Certain words have offensive meanings in the typical or standard Malay language but not in all regional dialects. For these reasons, the language used in communication in a multi-cultural community can cause considerable unintended stress.

In a multi-cultural community like Malaysia, a word can have negative connotations within a certain community, yet positive connotations in another community. For example, the word 'Proton' has no negative meanings to the westerner or Malays. Yet to the Chinese community, it can have a negative meaning if it is not pronounced properly. Pronounced as 'ploton' it means 'silly or stupid'.

Although it is known that the *lingua franca* of the people in the Malay archipelago is the Malay language, in Malaysia it is known as *Bahasa Melayu* and in Indonesia as *Bahasa Indonesia*. Both languages have similar origins but they have been differently influenced. Javanese and Dutch influenced the latter more while Arabic English influenced the former. Because of this, certain words used in communicating in Indonesia are considered acceptable there but not in Malaysia.

Even within the Malaysia peninsular, the dialects have different meanings in different regions. For example, the word *beradu* as spoken by royalists can mean 'to sleep', yet could also mean 'to compete' in the state of Kelantan (on the east coast in peninsular). Communication among the Malays also needs to be addressed with caution as some words are only used by the members of the royal family and not by the common people. Consider the following:

Royal language	Common Language	Meanings
gering	*sakit*	sick
beta	*saya*	I or we
santap	*makan*	eating/dining
murka	*marah*	angry
mangkat	*meninggal dunia or mati*	died

The rulers or members of the royal family when communicating with the general public should only use the royal language. This is to indicate the finesse of the speaker and the humility of the recipient.

The use of a poem and 'pantun' has been considered a 'finesse' way of communicating with people in a cultured way. For example, Malays would say a 'pantun' as follows: (Asma, 1996, p. 21)

> *Pisang emas di bawa belayar,*
> *Masak sebiji di atas peti,*
> *Hutang emas boleh dibayar,*
> *Hutang budi dibawa mati.*
> *(With golden plaintain sail away,*
> *Whilst on a chest lies one that's ripe,*
> *The debts of gold we can repay,*
> *But debts of kindness last throughout life.)*

Such a 'pantun' means that the stability of a home lies in its support, the strength of man lies in his deeds. Proverbs are commonly used in communicating among Malays to avoid disappointment.

For example, a Malay proverb suggests the importance of discipline and of manners in life:

Hidup didunia biar beradat,
Budi bahasa bukan dijual beli
(Let us live in this world according to discipline
for manners are not bought or sold)

Malays also use their own sayings when communicating with other people. For example, 'Pinching one's left thigh the right thigh feels the pain' (*'Cubit peha kiri paha kanan merasa sakit'*). This saying means that if one is offending the brother, the sister will also feel offended. Similar sayings exist, like 'Because of a cow, all the cattle are affected' (*'Kerana seekor lembu semuanya terpalit'*). In other words because of one person, all the others have to be blamed or affected by the incident or problem. This means that the language in a culture has implications for the type of relationships among, and the behaviour of, the people.

The influence of language in cross-cultural settings should not be overlooked as it also has implications for the potential relationship between the speaker and the listener. While inappropriate use of the language can be tolerated by the listener in the host country, the mind set of the non-native speaker of the host country can often produce misleading interpretations of the communication. The indirectness in communication among the Malays, for example, can make business negotiations difficult. In one business negotiation between a Malay businessman and a Chinese businessman, it seemed that the Malays were fickle and also unable to state their demands. Instead, the difficulty was that the Malay businessman had indicated his demands in an indirect way that was not visible or understood by the Chinese businessman. This had resulted in several deadlocks and renegotiations of business deals. One possible way to resolve this issue is for the Chinese to demonstrate willingness to have a 'give and take' attitude and maintain a balance between a 'humbling and belittling' position so as to preserve the dignity of the Malay, and know when to exit graciously (Asma, 1996, p. 79).

In the Malay culture, due to the practice of indirectness, metaphors and analogies are often used to express intention or desire. In this way, the speaker can help to minimise discomfort to the listener in the most subtle way or with the least offensive approach. It would not be desirable to be directly critical as this may cause the recipient to lose face.

It should be noted that Malays tend to be forgiving but will remember the person who had caused them to lose face. As a consequence, the use of a *pantun* or *sindir* to convey hidden messages can soften the impact of direct spoken messages. One common expression would be *'biar mati anak, jangan mati adat'* (you may let your child die, but never let your culture degenerate). This expression has deep meanings about the extent to which one should realise the importance of one's values and culture. Some may even say *'kerana seekor nyamuk, kelambu di bakar'* (because of a mosquito, you would burn the mosquito net). In other words, even if you are angry with someone, do not over react about it.

Other expressions abound like *'biar pecah di perut, jangan pecah di mulut'* (you can let your stomach be open but don't let your mouth break). This means that one must keep a secret at any cost. As a consequence, the indirectness in communication often leads to misinterpretations or misperceptions of certain information, events or incidents. In an effort to avoid saying 'no' to someone, Malays are often misunderstood by others and this can lead recipients to act inappropriately.

Values

The values of a community are derived from the assumptions and beliefs of the members of the community. The assumptions of a community refer to the basic (unconscious or unseen) views of the relationship between man with God, nature and other people. In certain cultures, it is important to take control of the environment, while in other cultures it is important to have a harmonious relationship with the environment.

For example, if a Malay is to pass through an unfamiliar place, say on a jungle path, then the Malay would say loudly, 'O guardian, please let me pass through'. This is to safeguard the adventurer so that he will not be lost in the jungle when trekking. Similarly, the Chinese and Indian communities also have their own views and beliefs of the natural environment. These beliefs were instilled because of the unknown phenomena in the natural environmental setting. They may appear to be outdated but they are still widely practised in the twenty-first century.

Further, the Malays believed that man must live in harmony with nature. For this reason Malays have to adapt and take whatever comes that induces an attitude of humility, non-confrontation or even submission in the interest of the community (Asma, 1996). In some cultures, the underlying assumption in the relationship with people is less important than the task, while in other cultures, the relationship is more important than the task. The relationship with God is personal in one culture, but in another culture it can be considered a public domain that is of primary concern to everyone or rather that there exists a holistic view combining material and spiritual aspects of life. That is why the problem of an 'apostate' can be considered a serious issue in certain cultures yet is viewed as non-controversial in another community.

The Malays, for example, believe strongly in the concept of a Supreme Being – Allah the Almighty. Malays generally perform their daily prayers five times a day, and consider it offensive if they are not allowed to perform such rituals, especially in a work place. That is why it is not uncommon to find places for prayers in shopping malls or hotels or office complexes. It is even considered unacceptable if the employer does not allow the male employee to perform the weekly Friday afternoon prayers.

Considering the differences in the underlying assumptions and beliefs of the members of a community, the values upheld by the members also vary and differ. Asma (1996) considered values as those elements or aspects that are referred to as 'shoulds', 'oughts', and 'musts', which were instilled and imbued in life without realising their influence. Cultural values have determined what is worthwhile holding to, what is worthy to be protected, and what allows people to do what they are doing.

In Malaysia, it is generally believed that one of the most important sources of values is the family. Parents, aunts, uncles, cousins, and other elderly people (relative or non-relatives) they had contact with in the early years taught them the 'dos' and 'don'ts'. In fact, there were more 'don'ts' than 'dos' in the Malaysian community. For example, it is more common to hear Malaysian parents to say "Don't climb the tree, . . . then you will fall" than "Be careful, you may fall". This attitude may be due to the protective nature or 'uncertainty avoidance' style of the Malaysian parents so as to reduce the risks of unforeseen circumstances. Problems are not considered a challenge or positive stance; instead they are viewed as hindering advancement. The concept of 'learning' and 'trying to know' is not encouraged.

Some of the selected ethnic values of the Malays, Chinese and Indians are shown in table 3.1 (adapted from Asma, 1992, p.30)

Table 3.1 *Selected Values of Malays, Chinese and Indians*

Malay values	Chinese values	Indian values
Respect for elders	Food	Fear of God
Spirituality/ Faith in God	Hard work/diligence	Sense of belonging
Humility	Pragmatism	Brotherhood
Face/self-respect	Perseverance	Family
Tact/Indirectness	Education	Hard work
Generosity	Wealth/ Prosperity/ Money	Filial piety
Sensitivity to feelings	Family oriented	Karma
Politeness	Face	Champion of causes
Relationships	Harmony	Loyalty
Apologetic	Gambling/risk taking	Face

These values are in contrast with American values. Asma (1992, p.30) found that Americans were more individualistic, valued success, punctuality, equality, achievement, hard work, privacy, freedom of speech, independence, informality, innovation and competition. Such values clearly show the marked differences in the emphasis of each cultural context.

Further, it was found that Malaysians have different expectations of the Americans and Americans also have different expectations of Malaysians in the workplace. For example, Malaysians expect Americans to show respect for hierarchy and senior elders; give face by not putting a person in a tight spot; avoid face-to-face conflict, listen more; be more patient; speak from the heart; and seek a win-win solution. On the other hand, the Americans want the Malaysians to be more open with their feelings; be direct; get to the point; be more specific; give data, facts; build credibility; be more persistent; admit problems or mistakes; avoid taking criticism personally; be more informal; ask questions to clarify; and not be too shy to confront. This suggests that the Americans and Malaysians have different perspectives and assumptions of their expectations in the workplace.

In comparing the interpretation of values between the western and eastern (Asian) values, Asma (1996, p.130) found differences in at least eleven dimensions: group/individual preference, honour, objects, respect, managing differences, time, success, risk taking, reverence, style of interaction, and communication. In the western culture, freedom and independence are valued while in the eastern culture, belonging, harmony, family, security and guidance are valued. The western community values privacy, while the eastern community values networking and family connections. Nepotism, cronyism and favouritism are despised in the west, whereas in the Asian culture, they are important and not considered unethical. Indeed, the danger of personal relationships causing industrial espionage seems very real in some western cultures, whereas close relationships in competitive organisations are totally acceptable in Asia. Is the issue in *Romance at Entores* ethical or cross-cultural or both?

In the Asian culture, respect is given due to age, seniority and authority, while in the west it is competence or equality that earns respect. The Asian community values cooperation and compromising attitudes in managing differences, while the western society values competition. The eastern culture adheres to hierarchy and formal admiration when interacting with people; the western culture values informality. Finally, the western culture values directness, clarity and speaking to the point, while the eastern culture admires subtlety, indirectness and third party intervention. Comparison and contrast clearly show the differences in the approach needed in handling cross-cultural settings.

While much has been said implying that western values appear to be similar, it cannot be denied that there are also differences among western communities. For example, the Russians appear to value family security, freedom, self-reliance, openness and material possessions. The Swedish society values freedom, relationship, cooperation, family security, and openness. The French community values self-reliance, freedom, openness, relationships and time. The Americans value freedom, independence, self-reliance, equality and individualism (Elashmawi and Harris, 1994, p.63). In contrast, eastern communities, for example the Japanese, value belonging, group harmony, collectiveness, age and seniority, and group consensus. Arabs value family security, family harmony, parental guidance, age, and authority. The Malaysians, in general, value family security, group harmony, cooperation, relationship and spirituality (Elashmawi and Harris, 1994, p.58). Table 3.2 shows the selected values of the Japanese, Russians, French, Swedish and the Arabs.

In the Thai culture, Smuckarn (1979, pp. 91–94) found that there are differences between the urban Thai and the rural Thais with respect to the terminal values and instrumental values. Terminal values refer to values held by individuals as goals in life, while instrumental values are those held by individuals as means of attaining their goals.

Table 3.2 Ranking of Selected Values of Japanese, Russians, French, Swedish and Arabs

Russian values	Swedish values	French values	Japanese values	Arab values	Ranking values
Family security	Freedom	Self-reliance	Belonging	Family security	1
Freedom	Relationship	Freedom	Group harmony	Family harmony	2
Self-reliance	Cooperation	Openness	Collective-ness	Parental guidance	3
Openness	Family security	Relation-ships	Age/seniority	Age	4
Material possessions	Openness	Time	Group consensus	Authority	5
Co-operation	Competition	Spirituality	Co-operation	Compro-mise	6
Spirituality	Self-reliance	Material possessions	Quality	Devotion	7
Equality	Privacy	Equality	Patience	Very patient	8
Time	Equality	Competi-tion	Indirectness	Indirect-ness	9
Relation-ship	Reputation	Group consensus	Go-between	Hospi-tality	10

Source: adapted from Elashmawi and Harris, 1994, pp. 58 and 63

With respect to terminal values, in the urban Thai culture, personal values such as family happiness, a sense of accomplishment, self-esteem, education and a world of beauty were highly valued. In contrast, the rural Thais placed high importance on social values like national security, a world of peace, brotherhood spirit, social recognition, spiritual life, status and wealth. For instrumental values, the urban Thais placed high importance on self-reliance, competency, courage, broad-mindedness, creativity, ambition, and hard work. The rural Thais emphasised interpersonal moral values like being grateful, caring, forgiving, obedient, mutually dependent, clean and neat. Runglertkrengkrai and Engkaninan (1987, pp. 10–11) noted that as a result of changes in economic and social development in the country, urban Thais do not follow traditional values but have instead adopted the more pragmatic and atypical western types of values. They also examined the managerial behaviour of the Thai managers and found that 69% of the managers were relationship-oriented and 31% were task-oriented. It is also believed that the leadership style of the Thai managers is consistent with the Buddhist belief in the Middle Path.

Using England's Personal Value Questionnaire (PVQ), Danandjaja (1987, pp. 2–3) found that 71% of Indonesian managers had a high score on pragmatic value orientation, 14% had moralistic value orientation, and 3% had affective value orientation. These results appeared to be similar to the value scores of the Japanese and Korean managers. The managers in India seemed to have higher scores on moralistic value orientation, followed by pragmatic orientation, and mixed orientation.

In the Philippines, the Filipino value system is based on social acceptance. When people are taken by their fellows for what they are, they will be treated in accordance with their status and will not be criticised improperly (Lynch, 1970, p 9). This social acceptance is effected through smooth interpersonal relations, which entails the facility and effectiveness in getting along with others as well as sensitivity to and consideration for the feelings of people (de Leon, 1987, p 29).

The four major values, which sustain the smooth interpersonal relations, are personal worth (*amor propio*) sense of shame (*hiya*), concession (*pakikisama*), and reciprocity (*utang-na-loob*). The sense of personal worth arises from the expectation that one should be treated as a person and not as an object so as to preserve the dignity of the person (Guthrie, 1968). *Hiya* is sensitivity to avoiding personal affronts; it prevents the violation of social propriety (de Leon, 1987, p.29). To describe someone as 'without a sense of shame' is an insult to a Filipino as it implies the lack of awareness of appropriate behaviour. *Utang-na-loob* refers to the voluntary or informal form of reciprocity, which develops a strong sense of personal obligation to those who have done one a service, especially to relatives or friends. *Pakikisama* shows the Filipino's propriety for camaraderie, trust, confidence and loyalty towards others.

According to Dong Ki Kim (1981, p 24), the Korean values are based on the five codes of Confucian ethics. The attitudes that exist between people are as follows:

1. Between friend, trust
2. Between elder and younger, respect
3. Between husband and wife, distinction in position and function
4. Between father and son, intimacy
5. Between king and servant, loyalty

Koreans also have great respect for learning and scholastic achievement, and place scholars high in society. Merchants or businessmen are placed at the lower echelon of the society. As in the Japanese society, the Koreans value seniority and age. It is difficult to promote someone who has performed well without giving due respect to the elders. Thus, younger superiors often have difficulty in managing older subordinates in Korean firms.

In making decisions, Korean managers often make decisions because they value certain ways of action even though it may be costly to do so. Consequently, Korean firms value judgment and give it priority over factual data in making important decisions. Compared to the Japanese, the Koreans appear to be less collectivist. The Japanese also have higher uncertainty avoidance and are more concerned with efficiency than the Koreans (Kelley and others, 1986). In spiritual matters, the Koreans have higher values than the Japanese. These examples suggest the existence of great differences in the Asian context.

In Africa, according to Jones (1986, p.208), the Malawians tend to view organisations as having a wider mission than is generally understood in the west. Organisations are expected to provide socially desirable benefits such as employment, housing, transport, and assistance with important social rituals and ceremonies. Profit maximisation and efficiency may be viewed as secondary or incidental. Malawian workers generally have an instrumental orientation towards work and have high expectations of the benefits to be extended to them and their extended family. Malawian society also seems to emphasise prestige and status differences, and the creating of relationships of dependency, particularly between managers and workers. Culturally, Malawians have collectivist culture, and the managers have a high regard for their subordinates as people. They view workers as a network of people rather than as human resources. For this reason they are reluctant either to accept individual blame for mistakes or to criticise individual subordinates in a direct manner. The case entitled The *Cost of Cultural Values* illustrates the importance of such values and practices.

It cannot be denied that the values held have an impact on the nature of management practices in an organisation. For instance, in terms of managerial planning, the Malaysian culture values flexibility rather than timeliness or deadlines as in the western culture. It has also been found that the Chinese agree more to act on wisdom in planning, evaluating and innovating management practices. The Malays prefer energy; they consider that younger people should be relied upon because of their knowledge of current problems and modern techniques in dealing with organisational issues (Md. Zabid and Choong, 1994, pp.574–582). When it comes to organising, the western system advocates democracy, a participative approach and a mechanistic or incremental style, while in the Malaysian context, benevolence, autocracy, organic and holistic approach are more valued.

In Malaysia, the leadership role is perceived as belonging to someone who is personally powerful while in western society, power is attached to the office. Leadership characteristics like total character, humility, deference, respect for elders, observance of relationships, trust, maturity, consensus, respect for role models and paternalistic views are appreciated in the Malaysian context. In the western society, skills, competence, assertiveness, being ahead of others, measuring outcomes, being achievement-oriented, separating roles, self-actualisation, and a combative spirit are valued.

In motivating the Malaysian workforce, values like affiliation, close relationships, group fulfilment, and spiritual meaning are important. In contrast, western values emphasise self-actualisation, task orientation, individual achievement and are worldly based. In recruiting staff, values like nepotism, support network, favouritism, group loyalty, long-term commitment, and social obligations are important as opposed to competence, fairness, equal opportunity, objectivity and an individualist approach in the western culture. As for the controlling function, it is centred on the authority of the person and externally driven and expressed by the person controlled in the form of shame. In the western culture, controlling is done through self-control, internally driven and expressed as guilt (Asma, 1996, pp. 240–241).

In decision-making, culture has an influence on the styles of making decisions. Europeans tend to base decisions on experience, while the U.S managers are more future-oriented and favour a group and participative approach (Ronen, 1986, p 220). In Argentina, Chile, and Uruguay, decision-making is equated with authority and therefore based on speed rather than on information seeking or rationality (Heller and Yuki, 1969). In Malaysia, decision-making is based on a myriad of factors: age (respect for elders), status (authority), harmony (knowing the values of each ethnic group), on developing connections with high status allies, and communicating decisions that affect people discreetly so as to maintain face, harmony and relationships. (Shephard, 2001, p. 71–80). The Chinese agree more on the "being" approach in decision-making while the Malays agree more on the doing approach (Md Zabid and Choong, 1994).

In the Malay culture, hierarchical relationships are important and uneven distribution of power is perceived to be natural and appropriate. Authoritarian relationships between young and old, superior and subordinate are adhered to and revered. The values of filial piety and respect for elders and authority are emphasised among the Malays (Asma, 1996). In the Chinese and Indian communities, similar patterns and trends may also be observed.

On the other hand, Malays, Chinese and Indians have different values on the status and role of women. In the Malay community, a Malay female executive may easily be found married to a Malay non-executive employee (perceived to be lower status in the job). The Malay community accepts that women have different roles, and the female Malay still plays a secondary role in the family as compared to the husband. In the Chinese community, it would be difficult to find a highly educated Chinese female manager married to a lesser-educated Chinese male executive or employee. Similarly, it is unthinkable to find such a situation among the Indians. One explanation from the Malay viewpoint is that the level of tolerance and differentiated roles of the female are recognised, while in the Chinese and Indian communities, the status and roles of women are considered inferior.

Superstition is another value-related aspect peculiar to the cross-cultural context. This value is adhered to due to the basic assumption of the culture in viewing the relationship between Man and Nature or God or, more precisely, in viewing the 'unknown'. It has also been viewed as a habit or belief of someone based on irrational fear of the unknown or mysterious events or incidents. For example in the Malay culture, it is considered taboo to whistle at night, for fear that the whistle may attract unwelcome company. Young unmarried girls should not sit at the front doorsteps of the house as it may cause them to remain unmarried.

In a Chinese community, the number eight is considered to be a lucky number. This is because the number eight, when pronounced in the Cantonese dialect, sounds like the word 'prosperity', which is liked by the Chinese community. Similarly, the number four sounds like the word for death in South China and should be avoided. The Chinese may pay a high price for the car registration number with eight and avoid the number four. For example, the number 'one hundred and sixty eight' is considered good, as it sounds like 'continuously prosperous', while the registration number 'one hundred and sixty four' would imply that the person would continuously die. Beliefs in such phenomena are still prevalent today. In most high rise buildings, the management or owners will avoid using the 'level four' and instead use 'level 3A' or jump to 'level 5'. The Chinese Hospital in Kuala Lumpur does not have a fourth floor; instead it moves from the third floor to the fifth floor. Office spaces on the eighth floor are generally sold out even before a building is launched publicly, or booked in advance.

The Chinese also believe that during the month of the 'hungry ghost', generally in the seventh month of the Chinese lunar calendar, special prayers and presentations must be made to entertain the roaming souls (ghosts). During that month, it is common to find special candles being lit near the roadsides or corners. At special altars located near the roadsides, offerings are made; oranges, apples and other types of food are left at the altars located near the roadsides or corners. On a more elaborate scale, there would be a Chinese opera shown in open grounds, the purpose being to entertain the hungry ghosts. During that month, it is also not recommended to leave homes at night. If such rituals are not observed, then a bad omen or accidents like unforeseen consequences may occur. On Chinese New Year day, it is forbidden to use a broom to sweep the floor as it is believed that all the good luck will be swept away.

Like the Chinese, the Malays are also superstitious. A Malay girl must not sing in the kitchen while preparing a meal. If she does, she will be doomed to marry an old man. If a man has a mole near his eye, that means the man has a roving eye. The Malays also believe that if the left palm is itchy, it means that a person is going to spend some money, while if the right palm is itchy, it means that the person is going to get some money.

The Indians also have their own superstitions. For example, Indian women do not welcome flattery where newborn babies are concerned. It is believed that a comment like: 'Oh, what a cute and lovely baby' will attract the attention of evil spirits and the spirits would bug the baby. If a stranger did pass such a comment, the mother would paint a large '*poto*' (black spot) on the forehead of the baby or blacken his or her eyes to ward off the evil spirits.

To relieve the beliefs of superstitions in a culture, the Chinese may use *feng shui* or engage a *lamoloh* to handle the problem in a particular situation. Some Malays may engage the services of a *bomoh* (traditional medicine man) to handle this or make special prayer services to overcome the situation. The Indians may engage a '*shaman*' to perform similar rituals to handle difficult situations. The extreme importance of recognising the superstitions is important in the Asia Pacific region as it is perceived as maintaining harmony with the environment or 'unfamiliar terrain'. While efforts have been made to reduce the beliefs in such incidents among the Malays through religious advice, such beliefs are still prevalent today.

Another important value to the traditional Malaysian is gratitude (*syukur*). The feeling of great gratitude is predominant among the Malays, and also the Chinese to a certain extent. The Malays have special *kenduris* (special prayer and meal sessions) and invite friends and relatives to attend the gathering. Special religious citations and verses and chants are made to express the feeling of gratitude to the Almighty for success or safety. It is not unusual to find a Malay organising a *kenduri* or *doa selamat* (special prayer session for safety) session after receiving an award or appointment or promotion in a job. In a western society, such joy may be celebrated in a less elaborate style than in the Malay or Chinese societies.

These sessions are held at home or in the office or at the local mosque. The Chinese may also have such sessions in their temples. Malays outside Malaysia have similar practices. For example, in Singapore it is not an uncommon feature to receive invitations to attend a *kenduri* or *doa selamat* session for someone who is going to perform a pilgrimage to Mecca or *haj*. In Malaysia such invitations are generally made through the 'word of mouth' invitation while in Singapore, the invitation is made through specially printed greeting cards.

SECTION 2
The Tug Of The Heart

This section contains cases in which personal relationships and feelings need to be considered thoughtfully by managers. As though they were members of a board of directors, the audience needs to sift out the key issues in each case and decide on short and long term strategies to overcome the cross-cultural differences.

Chapter 4
Romance At Entores*

Romance at Entores illustrates how important it is that foreign organisations understand the local culture and the way businesses are conducted locally. The case highlights an individual's dilemma when an American company that she works for claims a conflict of interest between her personal life and the company's business.

Mei Li was angry and humiliated. Andrew Cunningham's words were still echoing in her mind: "Stop dating Matt Sullivan or face possible demotion."

"They have no right to interfere with my personal life!" thought Mei Li angrily to herself. All that she had worked for all these years was for nothing. She had never expected an employee's personal life to come under so much fire.

Entores Ltd.

Entores Ltd. was an American company with annual sales of RM100 million. The company's core business was providing software solutions and marketing computer hardware and office equipment. Entores had offices all around the world and its Malaysian branch had approximately 650 employees. Being an American company, it valued results highly. Staff with excellent performances were quickly promoted while those who slacked were given the ultimatum of either "shape up or ship out". There were no two ways about it. Usually such staff would voluntarily resign from the company to avoid the humiliation of being asked to leave. Bonuses and salary increments were based on the employee's performance ratings.

---

* This case was written by Ho Jo Ann and Ling Ching Nee, while graduate students in the Malaysian Graduate School of Management at Universiti Putra Malaysia.

There were manuals and handbooks that outlined every procedure in each department and these guidelines were regarded as sacred by the staff. Many of the rules and regulations, however, were not adapted to the local requirements. Disciplinary action leading to dismissal would be taken against any staff who dared to disregard these rules and regulations. Each new employee was also given a Performance and Recognition (PAR) Manual. The manual contained Entores' policy concerning the conflict of interest. Relevant passages from the manual include the following:

> A conflict of interest can arise when an employee is included in activity for personal gain, which for any reason is in conflict with Entores' business interest. "Moonlighting" is defined as working at some activity for personal gain outside your Entores' job. If you do perform outside work, you have a special responsibility to avoid any conflict with Entores' business interests.

> Obviously, you cannot solicit or perform in competition with Entores' products or services offerings. Employees must be free of any significant investment or association of their own or their immediate family's, in competitors or suppliers, which might interfere or be thought to interfere with the independent exercise of their judgement in the best interests of Entores.

The number of staff in each department was kept to the minimum. For example, the Human Resource Department had only three staff, including the Human Resource manager. As a result, everyone in the organisation was overwhelmed with work and employees had hardly any time for friendly office chats. Everyone in the organisation kept to themselves, each trying to impress their managers, and relationships were very superficial. When Mei Li first joined the organisation, she was not used to the working environment at all. She was so miserable that at times she just felt like leaving the organisation. However, determination and the good pay kept her working for Entores.

Mei Li

Before joining Entores, Mei Li had worked as a general clerk in a small local company which had only 20 employees. Everyone knew each other. There were company trips during which all staff would participate and this fostered a family atmosphere in the company. Due to the close relationships between the employees, it was not surprising that some of the staff had close personal relationships. One of the employees was even married to the company's supplier. There were no rigid guidelines to be adhered to and all staff basically did what they were supposed to do. While working, Mei Li attended part-time classes and earned a marketing degree. She was later transferred to the company's sales department as a sales representative.

Two years later, Mei Li was offered a very lucrative position at Entores. She was assigned a sales territory, to sell office equipment. Mei Li was soon promoted to the position of senior sales executive and received numerous awards for her excellent performance. Entores' management judged her as one of the most successful sales people in the division and placed her in the "Growth, Opportunity and Leadership (GOLD) Program". Soon after, Mei Li was promoted to a management position and she continued her successful career. She was awarded a RM4000 merit raise the following year and was told by her Managing Director, Andrew Cunningham, that she was doing an excellent job.

The Ultimatum

Before this time, Mei Li had met Matt Sullivan, an accounts manager for Entores, and they started dating. Sullivan later left Entores to join IBM, a competitor to Entores in the computer products field. Sullivan was transferred to Singapore but then he returned to Malaysia and they began dating again. Entores' management knew of this relationship well before promoting Mei Li to the management position. Neither Jason Tan, Mei Li's supervisor, nor Andrew Cunningham, the Managing Director, raised any questions about this at the time of her promotion. A week after she received the raise, Andrew Cunningham left a message that he wanted to see her.

Cunningham: Are you dating Sullivan?

Mei Li: What difference does it make if I am dating Sullivan?

Cunningham: I'm sure you're fully aware of how the company feels about our employees getting involved with employees from competitor companies. I think . . .

Mei Li: Mr. Cunningham, I can see the point that you are driving at. Please be assured that I will not do anything which will violate the company's regulations or jeopardise the company's sales.

Cunningham: I think we have a conflict of interest, or at least the appearance of a conflict of interest.

Mei Li: Mr. Cunningham, Entores' management knew of my relationship with Matt even before my promotion. I just don't understand why that would have pertinence to my job now. I just got my job and you said that I'm doing really well. Besides, I don't even have access to any sensitive information that could be useful to the competitors.

Cunningham: Well, as I've said before I'm afraid we have a conflict of interest. I'll tell you what, I'll give you a couple of days to a week. Think this whole thing over.

Mei Li: Think what over?

Cunningham: You either stop dating Matt Sullivan or I'm going to take you out of your management job.

The Decision

The next day Cunningham called Mei Li in again and announced that he was removing her from management effective immediately. When Mei Li responded that she thought she had a couple of days to think it over, Cunningham answered, "I am making the decision for you." Mei Li repeated her earlier claim that she had been previously assured that no business was being lost to IBM and that she had been doing a good job. Cunningham once again mentioned the conflict of interest and stated that she was to be removed from management. When Mei Li pointed out that this demotion appeared to be more of a dismissal, Cunningham said, "If you feel that way, then give me your I.D. card and your keys to the office."

Mei Li was very angry and upset. She asked one of her colleagues, Thomas, about the matter. Thomas has been working in the company for six years. According to him, she should base her claim of wrongful discharge upon Entores' policies regarding employee privacy and conflict of interest. Much of Entores' policy regarding privacy was outlined in a memo circulated to all management by the former chairman of Entores, Tom Watson. In this memo, Watson pointed out that the line between an employee's business life and private life is not always clear. To draw that line, Watson directed management to use "clearly set standards" that follow from "our primary objective as Entores' managers which is to further the business of this company". He went on to describe this standard as performance:

Watson: This is performance – and performance is, in the final analysis, the one thing that the company can insist on from everyone. We have concerns with the employees' off-the-job behavior only when it reduces his or her ability to perform regular job assignments, interferes with the job performance of other employees, or if his or her outside behavior affects the reputation of the company in a major way, I can think of few situations in which outside activities could result in disciplinary action or dismissal.

Mei Li was even more confused. She interpreted her romantic relationship as her private life that had nothing to do with the conflict as interpreted by Entores. It was true that she and Matt were more than friends, but they had never discussed any issues regarding Entores or IBM. Besides, Matt and she were not even married! Mei Li remembered attending the wedding of one of her friends. Both husband and wife were from the same industry. Her friend, a banker, had married someone from a foreign-owned bank. In fact, many people have friends in the same industry. Furthermore, there was no policy in Entores requiring employees to terminate friendships with co-workers who left Entores to work for competitors. In fact, Matt himself continued to play on the Entores softball team after he went to work for IBM.

What should she do now? Does Entores have the right to dismiss an employee for a conflict of interest? What are the values that Cunningham has to look into before making such a decision in Malaysia? Does Entores have the right to even demote her when she is not even married to Matt?

Chapter 5
Dilemma*

Dynamic Batteries (M) Sdn Bhd is a wholly owned subsidiary of Dynamic Batteries Ltd. in England. The principal activity of the company is the manufacture of plastic lithium ion batteries. The Malaysian factory was set up a year before the situation in this case developed, to capitalise on the cheaper labour and overheads so that production cost could be reduced. The research and development section is headed by Tan Ah Beng, a 32-year-old chemical engineer who was transferred from the head office in England and has problems to cope with within his family.

Tan Ah Beng, a Malaysian, had been working in the head office of Dynamic Batteries (M) Sdn Bhd in England for the previous five years. As he was a hardworking and dedicated researcher, and showed considerable promise, he was the obvious choice to head the research and development section in the new Malaysian factory.

Two weeks ago, there was an explosion in the laboratory and 3 laboratory assistants were seriously injured. Investigations indicated that it was due to Ah Beng's negligence.

Ah Beng had to face a panel of inquiry where he had to answer the charges made against him. After a gruelling three-hour session of interrogation, Ah Beng was asked to wait outside the boardroom while the panel of inquiry deliberated on the case.

As Ah Beng waited outside the boardroom, he regretted accepting the Executive Chairman's offer to relocate back to Malaysia. He reflected on the events which culminated in today's inquiry.

About two and a half weeks ago, Ah Beng's mother paid him a visit in the office.

---

* This case was written by Chan Wai Yee and Tan Ai Bee, while graduate students in the Malaysian Graduate School of Management at Universiti Putra Malaysia.

Ah Beng: Mother! Why are you here?

Mrs Tan: I need to talk to you without your *gwei por** wife being present.

Ah Beng: Why? What has she done this time? Lately, you seem to be complaining endlessly about her.

Mrs Tan: Beng, I have had enough. I have tried my best to be tolerant towards her knowing that she is from a different culture and would need time to adjust to life in Malaysia. That is why I have been keeping silent about our clashes. But she has been here for almost a year. Instead of adapting, she has become more critical of our ways. Today is the last straw. We had a serious argument this morning and she accused me of sponging on you. She even had the audacity to ask me to move out of the house and go back to Penang.

Ah Beng: What sparked off the quarrel?

Mrs Tan: I mentioned to her that today is the twentieth anniversary of your father's death. To commemorate it, we will be having a small feast at home tonight. She ignored me and went out.

Ah Beng: Maybe she didn't understand you.

Mrs Tan: You are always making excuses for her. If she didn't understand she should clarify. Anyway I prepared the food and left it on the kitchen table and I went to take a shower. When I went back to the kitchen, I found that woman eating the food for her lunch.

Mrs Tan: I was so angry and scolded her. I told her that she had no respect for the dead and she should not eat the food until it has been offered to our ancestors at the altar. She laughed at me and called me a stupid, superstitious old woman. (*She starts to raise her voice and cries.*)

Ah Beng: Mother, please lower your voice. Everyone in the office is staring at us.

---

* *gwei por* is a derogatory term for a foreigner.

Mrs Tan:	Beng, you must talk to your wife. If she is married to a Chinese she has to accept our way of life. Our ancestors are very important to us. Without them we won't even exist!
Ah Beng:	Mother, you must understand. This is the first time that she is living in a foreign environment. You must give her more time to adapt.
Mrs Tan:	Time? She has been here for almost a year. Isn't that long enough? You are just making excuses for her. (*She cries even louder.*) Beng, how can you side with your wife all the time. You don't seem to care for me any more. I have sacrificed so much for you.
Ah Beng:	Mother, you are disturbing everyone in the office and you are embarrassing me. Why don't we talk about this at home tonight?

As Ah Beng accompanied his mother to the door, he could feel that everyone was staring at them.

After his mother's visit, Ah Beng could not concentrate on his work. He kept wondering why his mother was becoming so unreasonable. When he first came home with his wife, Angela, he expected that there would be some clashes of opinion between his mother and Angela but he did not expect this sort of conflict between them.

He decided to go for lunch. At the canteen, he met the Human Resources Manager, Mei Leng, with whom he was on very good terms.

Mei Leng:	Hi! Ah Beng, you look preoccupied. What's bothering you?
Ah Beng:	Big problems. My mother is not getting along with my English wife.
Mei Leng:	Oh, it's the typical case of mother-in-law problem, eh?
Ah Beng:	It's not only that. My case is very complicated.
Mei Leng:	It's very simple. Just separate the two of them.
Ah Beng:	How?
Mei Leng:	Don't live together with your mother.

Ah Beng: Mei Leng, I can't do it. I owe my mother a lot. What I have become today is due to her. You know, my father died when I was 12 years old. My mother worked hard and sacrificed a lot to ensure that I had a good education. Now it is my turn to look after her in her old age.

Mei Leng: But Beng, you must be realistic. We are now in the new millennium and should not cling to old traditions. I know that we must respect our elders but we should not let them dictate our lives.

Ah Beng: You don't understand, Mei Leng. You come from a very untraditional Chinese background and you are not bound by customs and rituals.

Mei Leng: Well, Beng you should be more liberal considering the fact that you have lived overseas for so many years.

When Ah Beng arrived home that evening, he was confronted by Angela. Her suitcases were placed in the hall.

Ah Beng: Angela, what is all this about?

Angela: I am leaving this hellhole. One day, your mother will burn down the house. My life is in danger.

Ah Beng: Don't be dramatic Angela. Mother would never do such a thing.

Angela: You did not see it. She was burning bits of coloured paper and fake money. There was smoke everywhere. I am surprised that the neighbours did not complain.

Ah Beng: Angela, you have to be a bit more tolerant and understanding. Most Chinese believe that the coloured paper represents cloth for the dead and the paper money is for the dead to spend in the other world.

Angela: Baloney! That's not the only thing she does. Every morning and evening she burns those smelly joss sticks and it is giving me migraines. Either she moves out or I move out.

Ah Beng: Angela, don't be so rash. I want the best for both of you. Please give me some time to sort this out.

After a sleepless night, Ah Beng went to the office in a poor frame of mind. He managed to convince Angela to stay but he knew that another minor incident would ignite the tense situation at home.

He felt that the only solution to this problem would be to request a transfer back to England. At least then, if he was residing in another country, he would not be duty bound to stay with his mother. If questioned by his relatives, he could blame the transfer on his company. So he decided to speak to Mr Martin, the Managing Director of the company.

Ah Beng: Good morning, Mr Martin, may I speak to you on a very urgent matter?

Mr Martin: Sure, Beng. Have a seat. What's the problem?

Ah Beng: I am thinking of requesting a transfer back to the head office in England.

Mr Martin: Why? You are doing so well here. When we offered you the posting here, you accepted it with enthusiasm.

Ah Beng: Yes, Mr Martin. When I heard of this offer, I was very happy because it gave me an opportunity to come back to Malaysia to be with my mother. She is getting old and I am her only child. So, it is my duty to take care of her.

Mr Martin: If this is the case, why do you want to go back to England?

Ah Beng: Well, the reason is because my English wife cannot get along with my mother. I am caught in between and I don't know what to do.

Mr Martin: Have you tried talking to them?

Ah Beng: Yes, but it is no use. My wife wants my mother to move out. But I can't agree to that even though my mother has her own house in Penang. In our society, the son is expected to take care of his parents and stay with them. If my mother has to go back to Penang, the relatives in Penang would think that I am a bad son and it would cause my mother to lose face.

Mr Martin:	I don't understand. In England, the children are not expected to live with the parents once they are adults.
Ah Beng:	I suppose that this is the difference between the east and west.
Mr Martin:	If you are transferred back to England, won't your mother feel that you are deserting her?
Ah Beng:	No. She will be very proud of me and this will give her a higher status in the eyes of our relatives because she has a son who is very successful.
Mr Martin:	Beng, what you are asking has to be thought out carefully. I'm not sure whether we can agree to your request. You were specially chosen for this job because of your experience and knowledge. Give me a week to think about it and I'll get back to you.
Ah Beng:	Mr Martin, I hope you will give me a positive answer.

Ah Beng went back to the laboratory in a better frame of mind. As he was working on his experiment, the telephone rang. He left what he was doing and went to answer the telephone.

Ah Beng:	Hello, R & D.
Mrs Tan:	Beng, that *gwei por* threw all the joss sticks into the dustbin. She has no respect for our religion. You must come home immediately, or else . . .

(*At this point, Angela grabbed the phone*)

Angela:	Beng, don't listen to her. She is so unreasonable. When I got up this morning, the first thing I smelt was the incense. Then, when I came downstairs, she thrust two joss sticks into my hands and insisted that I pay my respect to your ancestors. What nonsense! Of course I refused and threw the joss sticks away.
Ah Beng:	Angela, calm down. Let me speak to my mother.

(*Bang! There is an explosion in the laboratory.*)

Ah Beng saw Mr Martin approaching. Mr Martin smiled at him and went in to the board room. They must have made a decision, Ah Beng said to himself.

Mei Leng: Mr Martin, the panel has just concluded deliberating on Ah Beng's involvement in the explosion two weeks ago. The panel members have found him guilty of negligence. Now it is up to the management to decide what is the next course of action to be taken.

Mr Martin: What is your opinion?

Mei Leng : I agree that Ah Beng was negligent. But we must also consider the circumstances leading to this incident. In addition, we must also look at Ah Beng's past performance which has been exemplary up to now. In addition, he is the most qualified engineer we have.

Chapter 6
Medicine, Marriage and Business*

A young Chinese man who successfully qualified as a doctor at a Japanese University fell in love with a Japanese woman during their years at medical school. Parents on both sides – with some reluctance - accept the idea of their marrying, but the Chinese parents want their only son to settle at home in Guangzhou, while the Japanese father is adamant that the young couple settle in Tokyo for business as well as personal reasons. What can be done?

After years of studying and living in Japan, Tan Ah Kow has successfully passed his Japanese government medical examination and obtained a practice licence as a General Practice Medical doctor.

Tan Ah Kow comes from a family very much oriented to Chinese customs. He is the only son in his family, with three older sisters. The family lives in Guangdong, China. Dr Tan's father depends much on the only son of his family to be the Tan successor in China, especially since the only son has obtained the 'Dr' title in front of his name and everybody in the family is proud of him.

After graduating from a leading Japanese University, Dr Tan found a job in one of the famous hospitals in Tokyo. He planned to work in the hospital for about five years, get his experience, and return to China.

It took Dr Tan six years in university and two years working as a trainee in the university hospital before he passed the government medical examination and so earned the title 'Dr'. During this period of time, Dr Tan fell in love with a colleague,

---

* This case was written by Chee Chee Meng while a graduate student in the Malaysian Graduate School of Management at Universiti Putra Malaysia.

Ms Suzuki Yoko. The relationship began when Dr Tan was a second year student at the university; from being good friends they became lovers as time went on.

It started with Ms Suzuki being very kind to Dr Tan during his studies in university, helping him with language problems and with his studies, too. Ms Suzuki comes from a family of doctors. Both her parents are doctors and Ms Suzuki learned so much from them. This really helped her in her studies in the medical school.

In time, both Dr Tan and Dr Suzuki graduated from the university, worked together in the university hospital and finally passed the government medical examination. Dr Suzuki's father invited both of them to work in his private hospital because he planned to retire in two years' time and to pass his hospital business to Dr Suzuki.

Because Dr Suzuki is the only child in the family and a woman, the assumption was that eventually she would marry, and the hospital would belong to her husband. Dr Suzuki's father was, therefore, very much concerned with her choice of a life partner. The future husband of Dr Suzuki must be a medical doctor and must be able to take over the family business.

Initially, when Dr Suzuki met Dr Tan in university as a friend, Dr Suzuki had brought Dr Tan to meet her parents and introduced him to the family. The parents were not very happy because he was not Japanese but a foreigner. They advised their daughter not to become seriously involved with any foreigner because, eventually, the foreigner would most probably return to his country and whoever he married would follow him there.

However, Dr Suzuki didn't intend that Dr Tan would be her future husband at the beginning of their studies. It just happened that, after a year of studies together, the relationship developed to the stage where they became lovers and could not leave each other.

After the fourth year of working in Dr Suzuki's father's hospital, Dr Tan planned to return to China and asked Dr Suzuki whether she would return with him to China and get married there.

Dr Tan: *Suzuki-san, kekkon shite kuremasenka?*
              (Suzuki, will you be my wife?)

Dr Suzuki: *(happy yet worried) Kekkon . . . ? Ii desuga, demo . . .*
              (Your wife? I want to be but . . .)

Dr Tan: *(holding Dr Suzuki's hands) Isshoni Chugoku ni kaette kuremasenka?*
(Let's go back together to China)

Dr Suzuki: *(with her eyes fixed on Dr Tan's) Watashi wa ii no desuga, Otosama ga nanto iuka . . .*
(I would be happy to come, but I am not so sure what my father would say.)

Dr Tan: *Soredewa Suzuki sensei ni sodan shimasho!*
(Well . . . Let's talk to him and see.)

Dr Suzuki: *(pulling away Dr Tan's hands and preparing to take her handbag) Ima sugu ikimasen?*
(Why not see him now?)

Dr Tan: *(looking at his watch) Yoshi . . . Ima sugu ikimasho! Imanara mada okite irassharudesho kara.*
(Yes . . . let's go now while he is still awake!)

By 9.30 p.m. both of them reached Dr Suzuki's parents' home. Dr Tan started to ask whether Dr Suzuki could return with him to China and marry him.

Dr Suzuki's father: *Tan sensei, watakushi mo anata no kotoga sukidesu. Demo moshi Tan san ga Yoko wo tsurete Chugoku ni kaette shimattara, watakushi no byouin wa dou narrimasuka.*
(Dr Tan, I like you, but if you take Yoko back to China, what happens to my hospital?)

Dr Tan: *Suzuki sensei, watakushi wa hitorikko nano desu. Watakushi wa kuni ni kaeranakereba narimasen. Yoko san wa watakushi ni tori totema taisetsuna hito desu. Doka kekkon sasete kudasi. Yoroshiku onegai itashimasu! (looking at Dr Suzuki Yoko at the same time)*
(Dr Suzuki, I am the only son in my family, I have to return to my home country and Yoko is very important to me. Please let us marry! Please!)

Dr Suzuki's father: *Uun . . . iitowa omoimasuga . . . watakushi . . . no musuko ni naru to iu no wa dodesuka. Watashi ga intai shitara futaritomo nihon ni modori byoin wo hikitsugi,*

*jigyou wo keiei shite iku, Moshi soreni sansei naraba,
futarino kekkon ni goui shiyou.* (Mmmm . . . perhaps
. . . what if you become my son? When I retire, you
both must return to Japan and take over the
hospital and continue to run the business. If you
agree to that, I will agree to your marriage in the
meantime.)

But it seems that Dr Tan cannot meet this requirement to
become the son of Dr Suzuki senior, and to have to return to
Japan to take care of the hospital business.

The problem is that to be the son of a Japanese family, he
would have to change his family name from Tan to Suzuki and
register with the registrar. And he would have to return to Japan
upon Dr Suzuki senior's retirement.

After about half an hour, Dr Tan returned to his apartment
and said goodbye to Yoko and her parents. Dr Suzuki (Yoko's
mother) had not said much during Dr Tan's visit. She just sat
beside Yoko and listened to the conversation.

Usually, in Japan, after a woman marries, she has to change
her family name to the husband's family name.

While taking the sub-way back to his apartment, Dr Tan
thought about Dr Suzuki's requirement, "You must be my son and
must take over the hospital business after my retirement." How
can he accept the condition from Suzuki's family without
consulting his own parents? What other alternatives exist? If only
family and work did not overlap to such an extent!

Chapter 7
Who Should It Be?*

NITTAYA GROUP has acquired new technology to improve its rice milling processes. A senior manager from the Beijing branch asks that one of the best agricultural officers be sent from Thailand for training so that his staff can handle the new equipment. He promises generous remuneration. To what extent should status, age, gender and technical expertise affect the choice of who to send?

Company Background

After its privatisation in 1998, the rice business remains the core activity in NITTAYA GROUP. As a continuation of its long-term strategy, NITTAYA has taken crucial steps towards vertical integration by venturing into both upstream and downstream activities in order to strengthen its position as the leader in the paddy and rice industry. Steps taken include strategic alliances with relevant business partners in areas such as seed production, large-scale farming, and rice wholesaling and retailing. By so doing, NITTAYA hopes to establish a strong presence at each level of the rice value chain, starting from farming to retailing. This will eventually reduce the costs in maintaining both price and supply stability in the industry as well as enhancing the Group's future earnings.

In addition, NITTAYA has created its own mission statement and vision to portray its corporate image to its clients. The mission is this:

* This case was written by Juliana Johari and Yvonne Seow, while graduate students in the Malaysian Graduate School of Management at Universiti Putra Malaysia.

> To implement our social responsibilities effectively, whilst ensuring an optimum return to our shareholders and to pursue the highest standards in product quality, delivery and service to our customers and business partners.

And here is the vision:

> To be the leading force in the Thailand rice industry and to establish a significant presence in the rice business of the ASEAN region and to transform NITTAYA into a well diversified company with a wide spectrum of business activities spanning the ASEAN region and beyond its shores.

Although NITTAYA has been so ambitious towards its privatisation there is a major problem that needs to be attended to immediately. The transfer from a government-owned company to an independent, corporate firm creates a gap between the current work culture and the vision NITTAYA hopes to achieve.

The Operation

Currently, the major changes stem from the effects of the prolonged Asian financial crisis, which caused the economic slowdown and the sharp realignments of exchange rates on Nittaya's pricing policy. Nittaya also lacks the ability to source and lock in sufficient supplies of the desired quality, grade and timeliness.

At the international level, Nittaya has joint venture operations in Malaysia, Pakistan, Beijing, Hong Kong, West Africa and the Republic of Guinea.

The People

The average length of service for most employees ranges from 6 to 15 years. The employees have extensive capabilities from managing an integrated rice business while working with NITTAYA. However, they have not been exposed to a multi-skilling environment. They are also still unclear of the vision, mission and the implementation and evaluation of their job performance.

Process

The company is still applying the process methods for their production that were developed when NITTAYA was established in 1960. Because of this, waste of paddy and lack of integration in the process continues.

Technology

NITTAYA has acquired new technology in the rice milling industry to improve the manufacturing processes. However, most employees still adopt the old techniques. In regional mills, training hardly exists due to budget constraints and the time the training could take.

In order to achieve its vision, NITTAYA has identified the requirement of the desired future state in four areas:

(a) Operation

NITTAYA wants its future operations to be more efficient and competitive. The management wants more integration between business units in NITTAYA. The future state for NITTAYA's operations can be summarised as follows:

- To promote and implement vertical and horizontal integration of the business units in NITTAYA.
- To develop a high level of synergy among the different businesses.
- To develop competitive capabilities in order to sustain the business challenges of the globalisation era.

(b) People

Even though the current employees in NITTAYA have the capabilities to manage the operations, NITTAYA still needs to equip its employees with the new ways of managing the business. Some of the skills and capabilities that NITTAYA wants its employees to have in the future are:

- Capabilities to manage business integration.
- Skills in managing customer service.
- Possession of the capabilities to manage the globalisation of NITTAYA.

(c) Process

NITTAYA expects to have high efficiency and a more flexible business process in order to be more responsive to the needs of customers. Characteristics of NITTAYA future process are that it will be customer-driven, technology-driven, with empowerment and process efficiency.

(d) Technology

NITTAYA plans to make available the technology that it has acquired in all regional mills. They also expect to have an on-line information service that is available in all the regional mills so that all the mills can update each other on important information such as inventory, delivery schedule and others. In addition, it also wishes to improve all the technology that it currently has.

Gap Analysis

As a conclusion from the gap analysis, in the area of operation, it is obvious that a gap exists because NITTAYA lacks synergy between business units. As far as the employees are concerned, their skills and attitude are not adequate to meet the new business challenges. Meanwhile, the process is seen as inefficient and less flexible. Finally, the company certainly needs wider implementation of modern technology to support its operations and manufacturing facilities.

With the gap that exists, NITTAYA will have difficulty in achieving its vision. The difficulty of making organisational changes from the so-called 'being' to 'doing' culture of most NITTAYA employees can best be seen in the case between Mrs Aisyah Kamal and their manager, Mr Sarayarntanawut.

Aisyah has been with NITTAYA for about 11 years. With a high school background, she first started as an administrative clerk. Later in 1995, she pursued her first degree from the University of Calcutta in Business Administration. Despite having to take care of her 6 sons, she successfully finished off her part-time studies in 1998, when she was appointed as the Human Resource Executive. For the new position, she had to report directly to the Human Resource Director of NITTAYA GROUP, Selveraj. Although she has been exposed to organisational changes through her studies, somehow she sees changes in her own organisation as unnecessary.

Manager:	Mrs Aisyah, I am sure that you are aware of the changes in the company.
Mrs Aisyah:	Yes, but don't you think that the changes are a bit drastic? In the 11 years of experience I have worked here, I have never been more uncomfortable.
Manager:	Why? Aren't the changes likely to bring about positive changes to the company? The shareholders are very much satisfied with the new objective of the company.
Mrs Aisyah:	I couldn't agree more. But the staff are unhappy. Nothing is clear-cut any more. And there is no agreed standard of performance.
Manager:	Don't worry about that. A new system will be implemented to help ease the workload, which is why I called you up for a meeting today. I think I need to explain briefly what the new system is all about.
Mrs Aisyah:	What? A new system? What's wrong with the old one?
Manager:	Well, the process methods used now are old and wasteful. Before long, all staff will be required to undergo training in IT.
Mrs Aisyah:	Why? Why the sudden training? There is nothing about the new objectives or mission or whatever that requires this! You have to know we have other commitments like our families. There is no way people like me will agree on undergoing any training.
Manager:	Well, to be able to pursue the highest standard in product and service quality to the customers and business partners, IT is of great assistance. I bet you know that before the privatisation some of our staff were computer illiterate, and continuously refused to take courses. If we make it compulsory, everybody will go.
Mrs Aisyah:	God! Why so troublesome!

After the meeting, Sarayarntanawut is certain that his job of convincing other workers will be tough. Just a week after that incident, the Beijing partner calls.

Sarayarntanawut: Hello.

Beijing: Hello. Can I speak to Mr Sarayarntanawut, the Human Resource Director?

Sarayarntanawut: Speaking. Yes, what can I do for you, Sir?

Beijing: I am calling from Beijing. We would like to know whether you could send one of your best agriculture officers here. He or she will need to undergo this new technique training for 6 months.

Sarayarntanawut: Over there in Beijing?

Beijing: I am afraid so, Sir.

Sarayarntanawut: Well, I'll fax the detail of your future trainee as soon as possible.

Beijing: Great, that's the kind of co-operation we are looking for in our partner. And I'll fax the details to you by this afternoon. See you then. Bye.

Sarayarntanawut: Bye.

The phone call again makes Sarayarntanawut confused. He doesn't know how his workers will react. If they can refuse a small, simple and short training, 6 months' training in China will certainly be a no-no. After going through the list of officers' profiles, he calls upon Mr Kamal, the head of agriculture. Mr Kamal is one of the oldest employees in NITTAYA. He has been there for 28 years. He does not have any degree, but he had been promoted because of his seniority.

Kamal: You want to see me?

Sarayarntanawut: Oh it's you, Kamal. Come in, have a seat. So how's your department?

Kamal:	Doing fine. What could go wrong if I'm still there? Ha . . . ha . . . haaa . . .
Sarayarntanawut:	You're the best, I know that.
Kamal:	So what's the rush? Anything new?
Sarayarntanawut:	Actually, this morning, our Beijing partner called in. They want one of our best agriculture officers to undergo six months' training, over there in Beijing.
Kamal:	It sounds like a good opportunity. But who is to be sent? Normah?
Sarayarntanawut:	I'm thinking of sending Shahrul. He is new. But with his good academic background and excellent work quality, he will be our guy.
Kamal:	Him? But he's only been here for 6 months. Normah has been here for 6 years.
Sarayarntanawut:	You have to remember. Normah has 3 children to take care of. She has other commitments (thinking about what Aisyah told him earlier). Shahrul is single. He's just perfect. I also know that you and Normah are good friends. But refusing to send her to Beijing won't do any harm to her. She won't take it personally.
Kamal:	It's not about that. Sarayarntanawut, I know my department better. Like it or not, I'm sending Normah! I guess there is too much of the profit-oriented mission statement and vision in your head right now.

Again, Sarayarntanawut was left with confusion, depression, aggravation and all other kinds of negative feelings. He just could not find the root of the problem. Also he was wondering whether training itself was sufficient to adjust from the 'being' to 'doing' culture? In terms of long-term solutions, what should be done to implement the 'doing' culture? And why is Kamal commenting on the mission statement and vision of the company? "Should I call up other department managers for a meeting to find the solution?" he pondered.

Chapter 8
Time Is Running Out*

A firm providing expertise in medical facilities has Chinese and Indian staff. When interracial romantic relationships developed, the families began to interfere and work is severely disrupted. Is there anything management can do?

Euro-Asia Consultants Sendirian Berhad is a company providing expertise in medical facilities. They work hand in hand with turnkey projects and provide all the required advice before and after the healthcare facility is ready and handed over to the owners who are usually the Ministry of Health. The healthcare facilities that they have worked with and for are the Selayang Hospital and the newly completed Slim River Hospital. At present the government, together with Universiti Putra Malaysia, has embarked on a new medical referral centre for cardiac patients in Serdang.

This Healthcare centre and facility would support the residence of Serdang, Kajang, Bangi and surrounding areas. This facility would also supplement the Kuala Lumpur Hospital, a 3500–bedded hospital, and provide a cheaper alternative and than the National Heart Institute.

The proposals for the new facilities are about to be presented.

Mr Jayaraman is one of the directors of the company and he oversees the running of the company and its operations. He is a Malaysian Indian and has been involved in hospital facilities management since 1993. Mr Jayaraman had worked very hard to establish the company to be one of the prominent medical facilities consultants. His wide range of networks and contacts

* This case was written by John Rajamani & Krishnan Atiaappan, while graduate students in the Malaysian Graduate School of Management at Universiti Putra Malaysia.

around the world has enabled him to provide the best products at a reasonable price.

He is answerable to his board of directors who are mainly prominent medical practitioners and also well-known businessmen. The firm operates from the fifth floor of Megan Phelio.

The firm has three main executives and many other support staff.

Ms Mei Lin, Malaysian Chinese, graduate in medical sciences, has been with the firm since 1996. She has had experience working in hospital environment in England. She is in her late 20s and single. She comes from a small family of 4 and now stays with her mother.

Mr Ram, a biomedical engineer, has been with the firm for five years. He is a strong believer and follower of numerology and astrology. A bachelor in his mid 30s, he comes from Kulim, Kedah and he lives on his own in Kuala Lumpur.

Mr Thambi is a business graduate, young and energetic. He is 27 years old. He is the oldest in his family and he has a brother and two sisters. His father is a retired army officer and handles family matters like an army general. He has a girlfriend who works in the next block. They plan to be married in the coming year.

Ram and Mei Lin have been working together since the Selayang Hospital project and they have a very good working relationship. It has been observed that they make a good team and their coordination and cooperation have brought credit to the firm.

One Monday, Mr Jayaraman called for a meeting with Mei Lin, Ram and Thambi. The meeting was to assess and evaluate the progress and development of the Serdang proposal.

Mr Jayaraman has observed that the situation in the firm is rather quiet and tense. He is of the opinion that his project team have been working very hard to meet the deadline until he overheard the clerks talking about the affair.

The Affair

Mr Jayaraman overheard the clerks talking about the affair between Ram and Mei Lin.

Clerk 1:   You know what is happening to Mei Lin?

Clerk 2:   What?

Clerk 1:   Lin's mother has been calling the office and asking about who she is going out with and what kind of work she does?

Clerk 2:   Why is the mother such a busy body?

Clerk 1:   Its appears that the mother heard that Lin is being close with an Indian guy and she does not like it.

Clerk 2:   Do you think that's why she looks so distressed now and often looks like she has been crying all night?

Clerk 1:   I think something is going on with Lin and Ram. You can see them together all the time and they work together, stay back late finishing work. You can catch them smiling to each other often and you can know one that something is happening between them.

Clerk 2:   I do hope it works out for them. But Ram is Indian and Lin is Chinese, I think her mother won't like it.

Mr Jayaraman smiled to himself after hearing the conversation. He is happy for the two of them. They are perfect for each other and he wished that their union would be beneficial to the firm.

At The Meeting

Thambi wondered whether it is possible for him to take a week off. He has to settle some personal matter.

Thambi: Boss, I need a week off.

Mr Jayaraman: What? You want a week off! Do you remember that we have a proposal to submit regarding the Serdang project and we only have about two weeks.

Thambi: I know, Boss, but if I can't settle this matter my head will explode. The sooner I clear this mess, the better. I would be able to concentrate on the Serdang project.

Mr Jayaraman: What is your problem?

Thambi: You know that I have a girlfriend and we want to marry early next year.

Mr Jayaraman: Still a long way to go. What's about it any way?

Thambi: My parents, in the beginning adored her and made her part of our family. A few days ago, in the preparation my dad called an astrologer to check on the "*porrutum*".

Mr Jayaraman: Still believe in that . . . and then.

Thambi: The stupid astrologer said that Asha's fortune is not good and I cannot be married to her. My dad is totally against her and does not agree to her any more. I can't leave her. I love her very much. I rebelled against him and he being the commanding officer of the house said that as long as I am under his roof and still have his name as my father, I have to listen to him. I disagreed and he disowned me and said that I'm not his son any more. My old man has chased me out of his house for going against him.

Mr Jayaraman: What you have done so far?

Thambi: I met Asha's parents and told them what happened. They are of the same opinion as my old man and being believers of astrology and numerology, they believe that for a good future, the fortune teller is right and to follow it. But being parents of Asha, they are worried about Asha's future and how its going to affect her other sister.

Mr Jayaraman: I think your old man has considered the future of your sisters too. He wants the best for you and you being the eldest son. But you just can't elope!

Thambi: I have found a house and we have decided to marry with or without their consent.

Mr Jayaraman: But Thambi, I understand your situation but for me our firm's reputation and credibility are at stake. You have proven yourself in the Selayang project and I know you can do a good job for this project too.

Thambi: Boss, please show some mercy on me. Asha threatens to commit suicide if I were to delay or leave her. I really need time off. I promise I will work all night and day later to make the proposal a success.

(Thambi rushed out of the meeting room)

Mr Jayaraman: Now Ram, how is your proposal coming up?

Ram: Boss, I'm sorry, I don't think I can work on the proposal.

Mr Jayaraman: What ??? (Stands up . . . Surprised)

Ram: Even if I did it would be a failure. My astrologer said that I'm going through a bad period. Whatever I undertake would be a failure or lead to disaster. I need to observe a time of fasting and to consume vegetarian food only for 40 days so that this bad luck would pass.

(Shouts are heard outside the meeting room)

Madam Khoo: Who is Ram? Where is Ram? How dare he mess around with my daughter?

(Clerk 1 peeks in the meeting room and signals Mei Lin out)

Mei Lin: Mama, why are you here. You cannot do this to me . . . Come, we go out.

(Mei Lin drags her mother out)

Ram: You see boss, my bad luck has started. It's affecting the firm. Thambi is having problems and now another has erupted.

Mr Jayaraman: What has the commotion to do with you? Why was your name shouted outside and why did I see Mei Lin running out?

Ram:	Boss, we have become close in the last couple of months. Her family has recently found out about our relationship and her mother is against it. They are not in favour of us being together and Lin is being pressured by her mom everyday to leave me. She is given the choice whether it's her family she wants or me. I feel sad and distressed to see her in tears and also am unable to put my mind to work. Just as my astrologer warned me, my bad luck is true and happening. I do not want my bad luck to ruin the firm. Sorry boss, I would like to be excused now to check on the situation outside.

In the Late Afternoon

Mei Lin goes to see Mr Jayaraman, apologizing for the commotion earlier by her mother. She regrets the actions of her mother and she feels ashamed by the developments. She also told him that she enjoys working with the firm but the recent developments have taken her concentration. She would do her best to ensure the Serdang proposal gets through.

However she would like a few days to clear the air before she gets back to work.

Dilemma

Mr Jayaraman leans back on his chair and his thoughts begin to wander . . .

Chapter 9
Coping With A New Boss*

The owner of a successful information technology company, who works well with his staff, lists the company on the stock exchange, keeping a 30% interest. To his and the staff's shock, the new Board decided to replace him as CEO. Should the staff walk out, complain to the board or give the new person a chance? What price loyalty?

Introduction

A company listed on the Kuala Lumpur Stock Exchange Second Board, e-Way.com Berhad, has a staff force of 250. It was founded by Mr Nick Wong five years ago. The company's principal activity is in the sale and distribution of information technology (IT) products, mainly modems and servers. The company has a nationwide network of dealers totalling more than 150.

Nick, together with three friends, started this company and, through hard work and dedication built up the business to be a profitable one. The company now has six active subsidiaries, all trading in IT-related products. His dream, his vision for the company, is to be the leader in providing total e-business solutions in the near future. In order to achieve his dream, he embarked on the following :

- Listing the Company on the Kuala Lumpur Stock Exchange Second Board; and
- Recruiting young, enthusiastic, energetic, dynamic and high potential staff.

---

* This case was written by Chan Jing Min and Regina Fang Mei Leng, while graduate students in the Malaysian Graduate School of Management at Universiti Putra Malaysia.

Over the years, Nick built very good rapport with his staff. He valued his staff's opinions and gave them a lot of freedom in managing his company. He has gained their respect by practising what he preached and one of his principles that they most admire is his fairness in rewarding the staff according to their capabilities and merit. The company has a very flat organisation structure, with 10 managers (5 male and 5 female) heading the various divisions. The managers know that his door is always open to them especially when they have any problems, be they work or otherwise.

The company was successfully listed on 9th September 1999. The organisation was structured in such a way that Nick has only 30% interest in the company. When he was elected the Chief Executive Officer (CEO), he thought that he was on his way to realising his dream. Unfortunately, one month after the listing, some shareholders, who were unhappy with the way Nick managed the company, called for an Extraordinary General Meeting and voted him out of office.

The news of the removal of Nick from the company shocked the staff and caused great distress among them. They waited with anxiety for the arrival of the new CEO, Mr CK Phua.

Friday evening, 6.30 p.m., one month later

Rosie, the Human Resource Manager, Newton, the Finance Manager, and Sue, the Operations Manager, gathered for happy hour at Finnegan's.

Rosie :   Ahhhh (*Sigh*) . . . I don't understand this Mr Phua at all. He has been giving me a hard time since the day he stepped into the office. Do you know that I have to conduct counselling sessions very often nowadays? Just today, four staff came to see me.

Sue :   Yes, I know what you mean. I have been warned by one of my assistants to expect mass resignations within the next few days.

Rosie :   What? Actually, I do understand the reasons behind their decision to resign. The thought of leaving has crossed my mind as well. Do you know how difficult it is to counsel the staff when I myself do not believe in what I am saying?

Here are their most common complaints about the new CEO:

- He picks on petty things and makes a big fuss out of them.
- He is so suspicious of the staff that instead of asking the division heads about operational matters, he interrogates junior staff, sometimes keeping them for two hours.
- He ignores the staff when they greet him, as if they do not exist.

I, myself, have had such experiences. He finds faults with company policies that we have been practising all along. Even little things like the design of our staff claim forms and leave forms irritate him. When I try to explain the rationale behind such policies or why the claim forms were designed that way, he cuts me off and says, 'I don't want to listen to history! I want it changed this way. How soon can it be implemented?' He probably thinks that I should just drop everything that I am currently doing and do as he says. What about my other operational tasks?

Sue :   I get that from him, too. I guess you just have to see which task is more important. Do you think he has something against female managers? There was one day when he asked me, 'How come there are so many female managers in the company' and then he gave me this funny grin. What does he mean by that?

Newton : You guys haven't heard my story yet.

(The story swings back to three weeks before, when the following discussion was held between Newton and Mr Phua)

Newton : Good morning, Mr Phua. I would like to speak with you about the problem with the upgrading of the accounting system.

Mr Phua : Newton, where is my secretary? I don't believe you have an appointment with me this morning.

Newton : Oh, I am sorry. I did not know that I had to make an appointment to see you. Previously, we could just pop in to see Nick any time.

Mr Phua :   Well, I am not Nick. I am a busy man, Newton. So, please check with my secretary when I am available next and make an appointment.

(Back in the present with Rosie and Sue)

Newton :   I have never been so embarrassed in my life . . . though being embarrassed seems to be the order of the day nowadays. Do you know what he was doing when I walked in? He had just got off the line with his stockbroker and was just going back to reading the newspapers!

Sue :   The stock market was probably not being kind to him (*giggle, giggle*).

Newton :   Anyway, just because I had to make an appointment to see him, the problem about the upgrade of the computer system was not solved till a week later. As a result, I could not meet the deadline for presenting the accounts of the Group. Mr Phua flew into a rage and gave me a piece of his mind right in front of my staff! He went on and on about how important it is to meet deadlines and how I was not doing my job properly. Get this and I quote, "You are a manager and you can't even handle a bunch of females? I expect you to be more assertive and firm with your staff. You are basically weak!"

Sue :   That is not so bad. At least it happened within the four walls of the company. There was a meeting with our business partners two days ago and Mr Phua scolded one of my staff in front of them, for not being sure of her facts ... just because she said, 'I think ...' Can you imagine what went through the minds of the visitors and the shame my staff felt? I nearly had a heart attack. I just didn't know where to put my face.

Rosie :   I really miss Nick. He would never do this to us. He would never insult us or play us down like that. By the way, Sue, did you notice that there were two strange-looking old men in the room previously occupied by Nick?

Sue :   No. What about them?

Rosie :   Mr Phua had these visitors in the room. That was the first time I saw him stepping into Nick's office. After a few minutes, he walked out with both the men and mentioned to me that he preferred to stay in his present office.

Sue :   Why? I thought Nick's room was so much bigger and better furnished. Strange.

Newton :   You mean you don't know? You call yourselves Chinese? It has all got to do with *feng shui*.

Rosie :   *Feng shui*? There is no such thing as *feng shui*. What's wrong with the room?

Newton :   Well, the person seated in the room would have his back against the windows of the room. As a businessman, he would want to have a concrete wall behind him as a wall signifies support for his position. Why do you think he is spending unnecessarily to renovate his present office? We don't even have a budget for it.

Sue :   What is wrong with his room now? He already has a wall behind him. Don't tell me he wants to have another wall to replace those windows?

Newton :   Of course not. He says that his room door faces the entrance to the office which leads to the staircase.

Rosie :   Wait, don't tell me. He is so insecure that he needs an extra wall to support him and he is afraid that some unknown force would push him down the stairs!

Newton :   Rosie, Rosie . . . You've got a vivid imagination. You know you've got to respect other people's beliefs.

Sue :   Coming back to the problems we have with Mr Phua. I seriously think that we should do something about them before the threat of mass resignations comes true. We have got some really good and dedicated staff working for us and I am sure that we do not want to lose them to our competitors.

Newton :   I agree . . . but what should we do? What say we approach someone to voice our grievances. It will need to be someone who is in the position to do something about it?

Mr Phua is the CEO and he reports to no one except the Board of Directors . . . I've got it! We can go to the directors and let them know what is going on.

Sue :   I am not sure if that is a good idea. What happens if all the directors agree with the way Mr Phua is managing the company? Moreover, it would not look too good for Mr Phua if we went to them without talking to him first. Therefore, I feel that we should approach Mr Phua first to tell him how we feel about the issues and see what he says. He may not realise the consequences of his actions.

Rosie :   Another alternative would be to go on strike or maybe stage a management walkout . . . I think that we should get the rest of the managers together and discuss the next course of action as soon as possible. As you know, two heads are better than one. In our case, it's more heads are better than three (*laughter*).

Sue :   This coming Monday would be perfect since Mr Phua will not be in the office. His secretary mentioned that he would be attending a meeting in Penang. Rosie, maybe you could arrange for the meeting on Monday morning. I know all my sales managers will be in the office since I have earlier arranged for a sales meeting with them.

Rosie :   Okay. Let's not talk about office matters any more. I am feeling very depressed and I've got cravings for icecream now. Why don't we drown our sorrows in icecream and go next door to Haagen Dazs?

The three colleagues left for the next activity of the evening.

SECTION 3
TROUBLE IN THE
WORKPLACE

Every workplace has its problems. Many of these involve personal relationships and can occur with people of the same and similar education and background. When the cultures are diverse, the likelihood of problems soars. They arise from lack of knowledge and especially with people of other cultures and may become explosive if not handled correctly. This section presents eight situations that need careful thought in handling.

Chapter 10
Why Do We Have To Live Together*

Workers in Micro Dynamic Industries are given free accommodation, but the Malay and Indian women do not want to live the same way, and there is constant friction between them. Those in charge have different views about handling the situation. Can it be sorted out?

Micro Dynamic Industries Sdn. Bhd. (MDI) is a company which is 80% owned by Japanese and 20% by Malaysians. MDI provides free accommodation for its workers. The accommodation is on a sharing basis with 10 production operators sharing a flat. As for the technicians who are higher in rank, 7 are accommodated in a flat. Most of the technicians and operators are Malay and Indian. Each flat is furnished with the basic amenities such as double-decker beds, pillows and mattresses, tables and chairs, kitchen utensils, gas stove and gas cylinder, electrical items such as ceiling and table fans, electric kettle, rice cooker, television and so on.

As the Human Resource Manager, Ms Grace was often faced with difficult employees. One such person was Ms Ganga, a technician. She constantly approached Ms Grace as she wanted a room all to herself. One day she arrived in Ms Grace's office.

Ms Ganga: Excuse me, Ms Grace. Could I speak to you?

Ms Grace: (*cordially*) Certainly, please have a seat.

Ms Ganga: This is about the hostel accommodation. I cannot stay with anyone in my room. I want a room all to myself.

* This case was written by Lee Lee Yong & Shirley Joseph while graduate students in the Malaysian Graduate School of Management at Universiti Putra Malaysia.

Ms Grace: I'm sorry, but as I've already explained to all of you, we cannot allocate a whole room to anyone. For the technicians, it has to be on a sharing basis.

Ms Ganga: But my head of department has already agreed to this.

Ms Grace: It is not up to your head of department to decide for you, Ms. Ganga. Hostel matters come under me and it is the policy of our company that all rooms must be shared.

Ms Ganga leaves Grace's office angrily.

Ms Ganga's head of department was a Japanese who spoke and understood very little English. He began to pass remarks about Ms Grace's department to show others that her department was inefficient.

A few days later, a group of Malay technicians approached Ms Grace.

Cik Zalina: But Ms Grace, these Indian girls cut limes and put them at the front door and burn incense in their rooms. We don't like the smell of the incense. Furthermore, it is dangerous to burn incense inside as this can cause fire and our safety is at stake. Why don't you just shift them into house No. B5 which is currently occupied by three Indian technicians?

Ms Grace: I'm so sorry but all of you will just have to learn to live with each other. The company has been good enough to provide all of you with shelter so I think that this is not our problem and you all have to find a way to get along.

When they left, Ms Grace read the letter of complaint they had submitted to her. A copy of the following letter was given to the person in charge of hostel matters, Ms Janet, for filing.

Letter translated from Bahasa Malaysia

House B103 Ocupants
Kasawari Block
Jalan Damar 2
43000 Balakong
Selangor

Ms Grace
Human Resource Manager
ISC Micro Precision Sdn Bhd
Taman Taming Jaya
Selangor   14 February 2000

Dear Ms Grace

Complaints Regarding Accommodation and Housemates

We, the Malay technicians, are making known our grievances we hold against our Indian housemates for the following reasons:

1. **Religious matters**
   The Hindus are burning incense in their rooms during their prayers.

2. **Damages that have occurred**
   a) Food is thrown in the sink causing it to become clogged from time to time.
   b) The toilet also becomes clogged from time to time due to them throwing rubbish and food.
   c) They do not use the utensils and facilities in a proper manner. Even the bathroom door is giving way due to their negligence and improper usage. The kettle provided by the company has been spoilt by them and now that the kettle has been replaced, we sometimes cannot find it when we need to use it. We feel that they purposely hide it so that we will not use it.

3. **Complaints regarding cleanliness**
   We cannot use the toilet to take our prayer water because they don't keep the toilets clean. As all the Indians have long hair, the hair that is left behind in the bathroom is never cleaned up.

> ### 4. Other
>
> Initially we all decided to share the gas tank when it came to cooking. But we realized that the Indians were doing more cooking than us. We felt that it was not fair to divide the cost of the gas tank equally. We decided to buy our own gas tank and now we are using separate gas tanks.
>
> We are also requesting the following Malay technicians to be housed together with us. They are Aminah Yanti and Anita Ismail. With this we end this letter by saying that we can no longer tolerate the attitude of the Indian technicians in our house. We hope that the management will see the need to either relocate us or the Indian technicians as soon as possible.
>
> We are looking forward to receiving a favourable answer from you in order to prevent further unpleasantness and misunderstanding between the Malays and Indian technicians.
>
> Yours truly
>
>
> Zalina, Siti, Azizah, Zurita
> (Malay technicians of B103)

Two days later, the supervisor in charge of two of the Malay technicians, Mr Mokhtar, who himself is a Malay, confronted Ms Janet about the hostel issue. He went up to Ms Janet and asked her if she would spare some time to talk to him.

Mr Mokhtar: Ms Janet, I want to tell you that the QC assistant manager and I are very worried that you have not taken any action to resolve this hostel problem. We are worried that if the technicians are not happy, they will resign and we will be left in a dilemma.

Ms Janet: I'm sorry but this matter has already been decided. The policy of our company is that everybody will have to learn to get along with each other.

Mr Mokhtar: You cannot say that. You must try to understand how these girls feel. This is quite a sensitive issue. As Malaysians, we have to be sensitive to all races. Will you help me find replacements for them and train these new people if my present staff leave?

Two weeks later, the Quality Control (QC) Manager, Mr K. Tanida, brought up the same issue with the Director, who was also the Factory Manager, Mr T. Suzuki. "Suzuki-san, we have a problem here. Two of my Malay staff are resigning because they cannot get along well with their Indian housemates." Mr Suzuki asked, "What is the problem?" Mr Tanida explained the whole incident to him and how Ms Grace had decided that the girls would just have to live together.

Immediately, Mr Suzuki walked to Ms Grace's room to discuss her decision on this issue.

Mr Suzuki: Ms Grace, do you know that two staff in the QC department have tendered their resignation due to some hostel problems? Mr Tanida is quite upset because they are from his department.

Ms Grace: Mr Suzuki, these girls are making a big fuss. I've already resolved this matter with them. Why is Mr Tanida interfering in hostel matters? If the girls are not happy, then they can find another company which is willing to give hostel accommodation to technicians for free.

If you ask around, there are hardly any companies that provide accommodation for their technicians. Hostel facilities are only given to production operators. Can you imagine how many more units of flats we would have to rent just to suit each person's living requirements? What happens if a new Indian operator arrives but there is no vacancy in the flat where the Indians are housed? Do you think that we should go and rent another flat just for the new person when there are vacancies in flats that have other races in them? It will cost us a bomb.

Mr Suzuki: I think that we all should have a meeting to see how best this problem can be resolved.

At the meeting, Ms Grace, who was furious, blasted, "Who do you all think you are? If you are not happy staying together, by all means find a place you like. The company never forced you all to stay in the hostel." Ms Grace continued, "Don't give me all sorts of excuses to get the Indian technicians out of the house. I am aware that some of you are bringing in guys to the house and you actually want to shut the Indian girls' mouths because you already know that they have reported this to Ms Janet." Not giving the slightest chance for anyone to speak, Ms Grace looked at the Malay girls and said, "I know that you all will not admit to this but wait till my staff and I catch you red-handed."

After saying what she had to say, she turned to Mr Suzuki, "Mr Suzuki, it's all up to them whether they want to stay at the hostel or find their own accommodation. I don't want to hear the same problem being raised again and again. I cannot always entertain all sorts of trivial requests from these and the other hostel residents. My decision is final."

Mr Suzuki turned to the girls and said, "You all have to learn to tolerate each other as you all are Malaysians, being brought up in the same community." Everyone was quiet with their heads down. "I want an answer now. Are you all willing to stay under the same roof?"

Finally, after some discussion among themselves, Cik Zalina (the spokesperson) said, "Okay, we agree to remain in the same house provided the Indian girls do not burn incense in the house and help maintain the cleanliness."

The Indian girls nodded their heads in compliance. Mr Suzuki then called the meeting to an end and told the girls to forgive each other and forget about the problem. All the girls left the room with glum faces followed by Mr Suzuki and Ms Grace. As Mr Susuki went he told her, "Ms Grace, please be cool and do not get so upset over the issue."

A week later, two other human resource department staff, Ms Sara and Ms Karen, went to the hostel to do their monthly inspection. The officers had to check on the cleanliness and report back on any repairs that needed to be done for the hostel. On their way to the hostel, they were stopped by a group of residents who were sitting and chatting in the corridor.

A resident: Excuse me. Are you from MDI?

Ms Sara: Yes, we are from MDI.

A resident: I am sorry, but I have to make some complaints. Do you know that your workers are letting men into their hostel? Our flat committee held a meeting and they want to bring in the authorities to put a stop to all these activities. I told them that it would be unfair to do so without warning and reprimanding the workers first. I'm glad I got a chance to meet with you. You'd better warn your workers. There is even a couple who are often seen kissing in the corridors. Our children always witness such incidents and this is a bad influence on them. They always ask us why the couples are behaving like that.

Ms Sara: Anyway, may I know your name?

A resident: My name is Bainun. I'm the women's representative on our flat committee.

Ms Sara: Thanks for being so considerate, Cik Bainun. We are aware of this problem but we need to be informed as soon as these incidents happen. Do you think that you could call my hand phone as soon as you see these things happening again?

Cik Bainun: That should be no problem. I hope that you will take the necessary steps to prevent this from happening. Just give me your number and I will assist you in any way that I can.

When Sara and Karen returned to the office, they related what had happened to Grace and Janet. "Ms Grace, we are truly ashamed of what our employees are doing in the hostels. They are bringing men into their rooms and are often seen kissing along the corridors. A neighbour complained about it to us and we felt so ashamed. For once I wished that I had nothing to do with MDI", Karen sighed. "We will just have to catch them in the act. We will have to do more spot checks", Grace replied.

Chapter 11
YTL Textiles Sdn Bhd*

What had been a small family business has grown so that it now has 135 employees. Yet it is still run like a family with no explicit rules, no firm disciplinary measures and all decisions being made by the Chinese owner. When trained people are brought in to manage the growing enterprise, their advice is not taken seriously. Friction develops between departments. How can the company be saved from disaster?

This case is about YTL Textiles Sdn Bhd, a company formed in 1988 principally for manufacturing and distribution of textiles for the local market. At present, the company's annual turnover is RM3.5 million. During the early years, this small business had been confined to importing textiles from China. As time went by, it was able to generate significant sales from its domestic market. As a result, the business expanded gradually in the 1990s.

The owner of this small business enterprise was Mr Yap Thye Leong who arrived from China in the late 50s. He had been recruited by an agent in China to work in a tin mining company at Ipoh. Being a young and industrious lad, he worked hard for the company and gained enough experience to run a business. Somehow, Mr Yap was able to save enough money to start to venture into a small business selling textiles. He had always been interested in the textile business as he had friends in China who produced different types of textiles popular in the Chinese market.

At that time, there were few textile suppliers and retailers in Ipoh. Mr Yap felt that it was an opportune time to start a small trading business because of the demand for textiles. To capitalise on this opportunity, he asked his friends in China to send some

---

*This case was written by Lim Yoke Khian, while a graduate student in the Malaysian Graduate School of Management at Universiti Putra Malaysia.

samples and he ordered a few rolls of fabrics to test the market. Most of his customers worked in the tin mines around Ipoh. As the Chinese community grew in size, so did his textile business. During that time, Mr Yap was helped by his wife, Siew Mei, and his three sons, Ah Keong, Ah Onn and Ah Lek, Ah Keong being the eldest son. Mr Yap had raised his children to be aware of their cultural values and beliefs. He strongly believed in the teaching of Confucius and taught his children the importance of Chinese cultural values, manners and beliefs.

In the early 1970s, they had rented a small cottage in the Chinese village on the outskirts of Ipoh and began their business operation from their home. As the company's business grew, it could afford to purchase a shop to store more stocks and its first second-hand lorry for delivery and transportation of stock to their customers. Mr Yap had planned to send his son, Ah Onn, to work for his uncle in Singapore who operated a medium-sized garment factory, in order to gain some work experience and knowledge of managing a factory. Ah Lek was sent to Singapore for further technical studies.

When the small-scale organisation was initially formed, many of the old Chinese ways of doing business were followed in the day-to-day operation of the company. In this Chinese-owned business organisation, there was no organisation chart. People worked independently and were not aware of what other workers in the organisation were doing. The level of co-ordination of work was low. To use the Chinese metaphor, 'Everyone had to kick everything with one leg' which meant one person did everything from minor errands to major tasks. Yap was in total command of the company and his sons obeyed his instructions and advice. He would recruit Chinese workers he knew from the village to assist in the business.

In the late 1980s, as a result of business expansion, the company went through a major organisation restructuring exercise. In the new structure, for the first time, professionals were employed to manage the organisation, which had a total work force of 135.

Although professionals were hired to manage the organisation, the overall management style still remained very Chinese-oriented. Yap decided to employ Mr Tan, a qualified and experienced accountant, to head the Finance and Accounts Department. For the last few years working with YTL Textiles,

Mr Tan had been constantly beset with the same problems of non-compliance of standard operating procedure (SOP). Although written procedures had been set in the company, people simply refused to follow them. All the staff liked to do things that suited their individual preferences and habits. Hence, the controlling activities in the company were vague and weak. All the undisciplined workers were penalised for infringement of the rules and regulations, and were scolded by Mr Yap.

In this organisation, changing the behaviour of people, especially old ones, was much more tedious and difficult than structural or technological change. In a Chinese organisation, usually little or no attention is paid to standardising procedures. Non-standardisation of procedures does allow high flexibility and autonomy in getting tasks done; however, it turns into 'old habits', which are extremely difficult to change. In addition, in this organisation, many people saw neither need nor benefit in adopting a more standardised approach. To them, it just meant more administration and more paper work. Therefore, much time was spent tracking down the person responsible for any particular transaction.

In the production department, a Chinese employee bought some spare parts for the production floor without going through proper procedure. He was supposed to obtain a Purchase Requisition Form and forward it to his supervisor for approval before submitting it to the Purchasing Department. Instead of following the procedure, he directed the supplier to bill the company for the purchased parts. As the supplier knew Mr Yap well, he allowed that Chinese employee to buy on credit. Subsequently, the employee resigned from the company without mentioning the purchase. His position was taken over by Mr Lee.

Several weeks later, when the bill of payment arrived, Mr Lee was shocked and would not verify the bill. As the proper procedure had not been followed, the Finance and Accounts Department refused to settle the bill. A great deal of time and effort were spent tracking down the person who actually made the purchase. However, the culprit was finally identified.

On many occasions, Mr Tan of the Accounts Department had spoken to the Head of the Production Department about enforcing procedures, but the situation did not seem to improve much. When spoken reminders failed, Mr Tan followed up with internal memos. Whatever he did, though, the company did not favour taking disciplinary action except for serious misconduct or mistrust.

The situation was constantly aggravated by office politics. People started to use office politics as an excuse for their own mistakes and failures. As relationship management is the core of a Chinese management, all decisions were centralised and in the control of the Chinese leader. The people in the company would constantly adapt their actions and behaviour to please the boss. Such office politics were highly destructive.

The question was this: Who was supposed to be responsible for ensuring the compliance of procedure? Should it be the Finance and Accounts or Production departments or should the responsibility be with Mr Yap himself? If you were Mr Tan, what action would you take, without disturbing the harmonious environment of the organisation, in order to ensure compliance of procedure at all times?

Chapter 12
Why Me?*

Some of the Malaysian staff of a fast food restaurant in Singapore think their Chinese manager is biased against them. She, in turn, thinks only the Chinese staff really pull their weight. Already the smooth running of the restaurant has been disrupted and sales have been affected. They may drop further if the restaurant does not quickly stabilise. Can the manager manage better?

Introduction

FFC (Fresh Fried Chicken) is one of the largest fast food restaurants in Singapore. Their main objective is to give their best service to the customer in order to maximise the customer satisfaction. The growth of the company's profitability is dependent upon the country's economic recovery and aggregate consumer spending. The selective capital controls imposed by the government seem to be bringing a level of cost stability and allowing better planning and implementation of programs. Recent consumption statistics and other indicators point to signs of economics recovery and growing consumer confidence. The growth in the FFC company's profits largely depends on the country's economy.

FFC Sg.Chua

FFC Sg. Chua is one of the Singaporean branches. In October 1999, sales of the month for FFC Sg. Chua decreased, compared

---

* This case was written by Anismasyiza Bt. Abdullah, while a graduate student in the Malaysian graduate School of Management at Universiti Putra Malaysia.

with those in September 1999. The productivity of the employees also decreased, and there was an increase in the absenteeism of full-time employees. Therefore, the management decided to recruit additional part timers to make up the shortage of the employees, especially during peak hours. At the moment, FFC Sg, Chua is handled by 1 manager, 2 assistant managers, 4 Bangladeshis, and 12 part time workers.

Ms Chua

Ms Chua is the manager of FFC Sg. Chua, assisted by two assistant managers, Mr Adi and Ms Munirah. Previously Ms Chua worked as an assistant manager in the FFC training institute. For the past 3 years, her performance was very good. Therefore, the management decided to promote her to the position of manager to replace Mr Seng. When Ms Chua joined FFC Sg. Chua, there were only 3 Chinese workers (part time), 4 Bangladeshi, and all the rest were Indonesian or Malay. She found that it was hard to communicate with her workers, especially with the Bangladeshis who were from different races.

Aboi

Aboi is one of the Bangladeshi workers in FFC. He has been working with FFC for the past 2 years. His record and performance with the previous manager were very good. But the situation changed when Ms Chua came in.

Situation at FFC

One day, two Malay students went to see Ms Chua.

Liza: *Assamualaikum.* My name is Liza, and this is my friend Nina. We are looking for a part-time job, as advertised in the newspaper.

Izan: *Waalaikumsalam.* Please wait here, I'll inform the manager. (*Izan went to the manager's office, to see Ms Chua.*)

At Ms Chua Office.

Izan: Ms Chua, there are two students out there who want to see you regarding the part-time job.

Without looking to Izan's face,

Ms Chua: Indonesian, Malay or Chinese?

Izan: Malay , I think.

Ms Chua: Well, tell them that I'm pretty busy right now, and also tell them that at the moment, I would prefer to have Chinese to work here.

Izan: But . . . (*still not satisfied with Ms. Chua's explanation*).

Ms Chua: Do not question me too much. That is my decision.

Izan: Okay.

(Izan walked to the place where she met the two Malay students. She feels really unsatisfied with Ms. Chua's decision).

Izan: Liza, I am very sorry for you, because the post is already full. Please come next time.

Liza: It's okay. Anyway, thank you for your help. Bye.

Izan: Bye.

(While Izan is busy doing her work)

Ms Chua: Izan, I promised to see two Chinese students today. So, please let me know, if they are here. I'm in my office.

Izan: Okay.

Izan felt really confused about the situation. She talked to her friend, Zack, about the incident. A few minutes later, two Chinese students came to the counter to talk to Izan.

Izan: Yes. Can I help you?

Li Ching:	Yes. I'm Li Ching and this my friend, Annie. We are looking for Ms Chua.

Izan:	Please wait. I'll inform the manager.

(*A few minutes later, Ms Chua turns up, followed by Izan*)

Other workers observed conversations between Ms Chua and the two Chinese students, since the situation happened in front of them. They started to realise that their new manager preferred to work with Chinese workers rather than others.

The next day, the new workers started to work. They were to undergo a training session for 3 months. Ms. Chua seemed very happy, because it was easier for her to communicate with Chinese workers than with others.

One day, in the afternoon, at the counter order, an Indonesian customer was giving her order.

Aboi:	Good afternoon. Can I have your order please?

Customer A:	Meal number 3, *pedas* (spicy).

Aboi:	This is your order. Thank you. Please come again.

(*The customer checks her order*)

Customer A:	Mr, not this one. *Saya nak pedas* (I want Spicy).

Aboi:	Sorry. (*Confused*)

Customer A:	*Tukar order saya.* (Change the order then).

The customer wanted the order changed, but Aboi could not understand what she really wanted, because he could not understand Bahasa Melayu very well. At that time, Ms Chua turned up. She managed to solve the problem. But she created another problem.

Right after the customer left the counter

Ms Chua:	Just a simple thing, but you cannot solve it. You have been working here for 2 years, but still made a mistake. I

have told you so many times, the customer is always right, he is king, So, give your best service. Do you understand me?

Aboi: Yes, Ms Chua. (*Upset*)

Aboi was really upset, because the way Ms Chua talked to him was very embarrassing, since it happened in front of his colleagues. He felt demotivated to do his work.

The next day, Ms. Chua received a call from Aboi, informing her that he was taking sick leave for two days, because he didn't feel well enough to work. Ms Chua had to call another part-time worker to replace Aboi. She asked Lee to replace Aboi, since she thought that Lee was the best person to replace Aboi as a cashier.

(*At the counter.*)

Lee: Good afternoon, Sir. Can I have your order please?

Customer B: Good afternoon. Give me meal number 3, original, plus 2-piece chicken, spicy. I'll also have a take away for another 2-piece chicken, and orange juice.

(*Lee takes the order and packs the order as requested, but he has wrongly punched the order*)

Lee: Sorry, Sir, would you mind having coke instead of orange juice, since I have wrongly punched your order?

Customer B: No. That is your fault. It was not mine. Give me my orange juice.

Lee: But . . .

(*Suddenly . . .*)

Ms Chua: What is going on?

Lee: I wrongly punched the order.

Ms Chua: Never mind. Give the customer a new one.

(*Lee punched new order for the customer*)

Lee: Here you are, Sir.

Customer B: Thank you *(paying for the purchase)*.

Lee: Thank you, Ms Chua.

Ms Chua: It's okay. That is my responsibility *(smiling at Lee)*.

Calmly Ms Chua explained his fault to Lee. The way she spoke and explained to Lee was totally different from the way she had spoken to Aboi. Once again, other workers who were observing the situation felt not very happy with the situation. The relationship between Ms. Chua and Chinese workers is different from her relationship with other workers.

The next day, without any reason, Aboi did not come to work, and nor did Izan and Zack. Ms Chua tried to get Lee and Li Ching to replace Aboi and Izan, but they had other commitments. So, she had to take over Aboi's duty in the afternoon, and Izan's duty at night shift.

For a moment, Ms Chua had to take deep breath. Why me? Why not other workers? She was trying to get her other part-time workers to fill in, but they refused to take Aboi's and Izan's duties. Ms Chua was really shocked about this incident. She had failed to get full commitment from her employees. What should she do now? Will the productivity and sales of the company continuously decrease?

Chapter 13
Hari Raya Holidays In The Year 2000*

The case is one of many which blew up in the year 2000, causing dissension in many companies. Eventually, when December was already close and bitterness had been simmering for some months, the Malaysian government decided that for that year two holidays had to be granted in December, though the total for the year remained as 10. Meanwhile great goodwill had been lost. Had you been part of the management team in the case, what would you have done?

Excel Latex Products Sdn Bhd (Excel) was established by its director, Mr Alan Tan, single-handedly twenty years back. It was known as one of those typical "China-man" businesses, which are conservative in capital investment and manpower training. Perhaps due to its careful style of management, the company evolved to be one of the Malaysian leading manufacturers in latex and nitrile gloves for industrial use. Currently, it exports more than ninety-five percent of its products to countries all over the world, including the US, Europe, Middle East, Australia, New Zealand and Asian countries.

Excel employs around five hundred employees working in three manufacturing plants in Lingui, Sg Buloh and Kelang respectively. The employees are of different races; the proportion can be briefly classified as 40% Chinese, 40% Malays, 10% Indians and the remaining 10% are expatriates from Bangladesh and Indonesia. The production operators and packers who are mostly Malays and expatriates, are the largest group within the workforce. Production operators have to work on shift rotation

---

* This case was written by Serene Ng Siew Imm, while a graduate student in the Malaysian Graduate School of Management at Universiti Putra Malaysia.

hours: 7am–3pm, 3pm–11pm and 11pm–7am. The production floor is hot, dry and has a strong smell of latex. As a result, turnover of operators is very high. Besides this, the packing department manager, Mr Alan Tan, constantly complains of shortage of workers, probably due to unattractive wages. He has an Administrative Assistant Manager, Irene, to take care of the worries with workers.

At the end of every year, one of Irene's main tasks is to work out a list of public holidays observed by the company, for the information of workers. In December, 1999, she was carrying out the same routine. Irene knew that the workers deserved ten public holidays in compliance with Malaysian Labour Law and the company had never failed to practise this policy. As she was aware, four public holidays (Labour Day, Independence Day, Yang Di Pertuan Agung's Birthday and State Governor's Birthday) are compulsory holidays that all employers must comply with. Employers have the prerogative to declare any six other days as their observed holidays. Excel's practice is to observe two days for Malay Hari Raya, two days for Chinese New Year, one day for Indian Deepavali and one day for Christmas.

When Irene was browsing through the year 2000 calendar, she realised that there were 2 Malay Hari Raya seasons, one on January 8 and 9, and the other on December 27 and 28. In order to avoid any mistake, she waited for other calendars to confirm the matter.

After having confirmed that it was absolutely true, she reported the matter to Mr Alan Tan on December 26, 1999. She wanted him to decide whether the total public holidays to be observed by workers in the year 2000 should increase to twelve days or stay at ten days as practised. The conversation went like this:

Irene: Mr Alan Tan, I have an urgent matter to discuss with you. Could you spare some time for me?

Alan Tan: What's the matter?

Irene: It seems that there are two Malay Hari Raya celebrations next year. If we were to observe both celebrations, two days holidays each, then the total number of holidays for the year 2000 would be twelve instead of ten. Two additional days of public holidays may cost the company lots of money, but on the other hand, this phenomenon only occurs once in every 30 years in the Muslim calendar, so I am sure the Malay workers would be very grateful if we could observe both the celebrations.

Alan Tan: In that case, we shall observe only one holiday for each celebration because we can't afford additional cost for those two days. It would cost about a hundred thousand ringgit. Moreover, business is getting tougher nowadays; it's not easy to make that money.

Irene: But Mr Alan Tan, I am afraid the workers may feel that the management is not considerate and may cause a lot of problems.

Alan Tan: We are not doing anything wrong. The labour laws set a minimum ten days for holidays and we are giving them. We never exploit or ignore their rights. I am sure if you explain to them in a nice way, they will understand the company's situation.

Irene: All right, I will try my best to explain to them.

After going back to her desk, Irene sat down on her chair and started wracking her brains to come up with a well-phrased holiday memo.

The next day, after the memo was put up on the notice board, not to her surprise, she received a lot of complaints from the production and packing Malay workers. But to her surprise, the non-Malays also complained. After talking to the department managers concerned, Irene realised the reason non-Malays were complaining. It seems that it was a usual practice for the non-Malays to replace the Malay workers during the Malay festive seasons who returned the favour when it came to the festive season for other groups in order to avoid production shut-down. That is the beauty of having a multi-racial country.

As usual, for next month's Hari Raya holidays, the non-Malays have been scheduled without much trouble. However, once they knew that only one holiday was to be observed, they realised that they would lose the other day's holiday pay. In other words, they would enjoy double pay only for the first eight hours and triple pay for hours exceeding eight for the declared holiday.

They complained that they had agreed to replace the Malay workers as they would be compensated with holiday pay but to their disappointment, it turns that will not happen. As they felt that they were being unfairly treated by the management, they threatened that if two days' holiday were not observed for Hari Raya, they would not turn up to work since they would not receive the anticipated pay. As this would cause production shut down, the production manager, Mr Khoo sought Mr Alan's opinion.

Khoo: Mr Alan Tan, I have a problem getting staff to work during this coming Hari Raya celebration.

Alan Tan: I thought you had scheduled the non-Malays to take over the job during those days as you have done for years.

Khoo: I did, and they agreed before the memo was put up. But after reading the memo, they felt that it is unfair as they agreed on the grounds that they would be paid holiday pay for those two days as usual.

Alan Tan: Have you explained to them the logic behind the decision, that we are deducting one day holiday this time since there is another Hari Raya at the end of the year? And that it is going to cost the company a hundred thousand ringgit for two additional holidays, which the company is not ready to bear as business is bad?

Khoo: I did, but they argued that this happens only once every 30 years in the Muslim calendar and that the management is not respecting the Malays' culture. They ask what is a hundred thousand ringgit compared to an occasion that only happens once every 30 years? Many other factories are observing both, and there are some even observing more than two days each. For instance, since the second Hari Raya falls on December 27 and 28, and December 25 is Christmas day, there are companies declaring December 26 as their holiday as well. Aren't we too calculative and inflexible by sticking to ten days holidays a year? Besides this, I heard that the Malays are very unhappy and that about 50% of them will resign immediately after Hari Raya. This is going to jeopardise our production and thus affect the delivery date we committed to our customers.

Alan Tan: It sounds serious. But we cannot surrender and be driven by them just because they protest. I cannot allow this to become the company's culture. Anyway, I don't think we are doing the wrong thing.

Khoo: What if the Malays resign? It's going to affect our production.

Alan Tan: I don't care, just get Irene to recruit additional staff for their replacement.

Khoo: But isn't it costly to lose our experienced workers who have been working here for years? And it is expensive training new workers. They will take weeks before they able to carry out work properly.

Alan Tan: Those workers are trained by you, right? As long as you are here, I am sure you are able to train the new recruits to be as good as they are. I feel no mercy for workers who lose loyalty to our company just to fight for additional holidays.

Khoo: How about those non-Malays who refuse to work on the Hari Raya days?

Alan Tan: I am going to get Irene to tell them straight that if they fail to show their commitment when we need them, meaning if they are not turning up during Hari Raya days, the management is not going to pay them a year end bonus and salary increment.

Khoo: But Mr Alan Tan, can we think of another better way? For instance, workers are given these two Hari Raya days off but they must work on one of the Sundays as replacement working day?

Alan Tan: My decision is final.

After Mr Khoo left his office, Mr Alan Tan leaned back and wondered if he had made the right decision.

Chapter 14
The Mess In The Technical Department*

This case study presents a situation where adequate understanding of cross-cultural management is important in dealing with problems and misunderstandings that arise in organisations with employees from different cultural backgrounds.

The case is about a promotion exercise in the technical department of ABC Utility Sdn. Bhd. that resulted in misunderstandings regarding the criteria for the promotion. The company was set up as a joint venture between a local company and a Japanese company with an agreement on technology transfer. The company's employees were nurtured with local and Japanese working cultures. The unsuccessful candidate accused the management of the department of being biased against the female gender. However, the management decided that, other than work performance, it also put high value on ability to work in teams and group cooperation.

The Company

ABC Utility Sdn. Bhd. was involved in providing petroleum gas to factories and households as a cheaper alternative source of energy. The company started supplying gas to factories in the federal territory and later on to all other states in Malaysia. It was a fast growing company with annual sales of more than RM100 million per year. It had approximately 500 employees and ten branch offices located all over Malaysia. Originally it was set up as

---

* This case was written by Che Ruhana Isa, while a doctoral candidate in the Malaysian Graduate School of Management at Universiti Putra Malaysia.

a joint-venture company between a local company and a Japanese company with an ownership ratio of 80%: 20% respectively. Since the industry was relatively new in Malaysia, the joint-venture agreement included clauses on transfer of technology from the Japanese within the first four years of the company's operation. To facilitate the transfer of technology, certain departments, especially the technical department, would be assisted by experienced Japanese staff in training, planning and operation during the period.

The Technical Department

A Japanese general manager, Matsuda, headed the technical department. A deputy general manager, Mohamed, who was an experienced local engineer, assisted and reported directly to him. There were four managers, two locals and two Japanese, and four local assistant managers, who reported directly to the deputy general manager. In addition, four local and four Japanese engineers, with various levels of working experience, along with other support staff were recruited to work in the department.

The staff in the department worked long hours and maintained a close relationship with each other. The general manager tried to cultivate traditional collective orientation, which was typical in Japanese firms, in the department's working environment. This included strong emphasis on loyalty and duty to the group and harmony and cooperation among group members, rather than individual functions and responsibilities. Informal communication among the staff was also encouraged.

The staff normally engaged in sporting activities after working hours during the working days and went for golf games during the weekends. The company provided sports facilities for its staff within the office building compound. Occasionally, they went out in groups for dinner and drinks after work. However, the female employees in the department rarely took part in these activities, as many of them preferred to spend more time with their family after a long working day.

Two years after the company was founded, one of the local managers left the company to set up his own business. The company decided to promote one of the assistant managers to fill up the position. Two candidates were highly recommended on the basis of their yearly performance assessments, Ali and Maria.

The Candidates

Ali had started working with the company as an assistant manager when it was first set up. Before joining the company, he had worked with a local petroleum company for six years. Ali was 35 years old and was married with two children.

On the other hand, Maria had five years' working experience with an American oil and gas company before joining ABC Utility in early 1991 as an assistant manager. Maria was 34 years old and married with one child. In terms of work performance, Maria was more efficient and had a higher ability to work independently than Ali. One year, one of the projects headed by Maria won an award from an international body for "the fastest completed project" category. Due to her excellent track record, Maria was the only female engineer who was able to reach the assistant manager's position.

Both of them obtained their engineering degrees from American universities. And both of them were equally excited at the prospect of being promoted to the manager's position but they were aware that only one candidate would be chosen.

The Decision

For the promotion exercise, the deputy general manager evaluated the candidates with assistance from all the four managers. The recommendation was then forwarded to the general manager who made the final decision. After lengthy and careful consideration, Mohamed decided to recommend Maria for the vacant post. When he forwarded his recommendation to Matsuda, he was surprised to learn that Matsuda felt that Ali would be a more suitable candidate.

The following is an excerpt of their conversation:

Mohamed: Mr Matsuda, I have here the evaluation of the two candidates for the manager's position. In my opinion, Maria is a better candidate for the post.

Matsuda: (frowning while rubbing his forehead) Let me see about this. So you are recommending Maria for the job but I thought Ali is more senior than she is.

Mohamed: Yes, I am aware of that, but in terms of work performance, Maria is more capable compared to Ali. Even though sometimes she can be a bit difficult to work with, she will always deliver the work on time.

Matsuda: That's what I thought. I am aware of Maria's capability but we also need a team player and I know that Ali is better at this. Remember last year how one of our junior engineers who was assigned to work with Maria ended up. It was a mess! Instead of teaching him, she treated him so badly that we had to reassign him to work with somebody else. I really feel that we should choose Ali for the position.

Mohamed: What happened last year between Maria and the engineer was also partly due to the man's fault. I think he just pushed her over the limit. However, if that's what you think, I will go with it.

Mohamed left his boss's office quietly. He decided to keep his disappointment to himself until a week later when Maria went to see him.

The Confrontation

Upon hearing the news that Ali would be promoted to the manager's position, Maria was shocked and angry. She decided to talk to Mohamed to get confirmation about the news.

Maria: (*looking tense and upset*) I need to talk to you about the promotion exercise. I heard that Ali would get the position. I am so shocked to hear that because I know that I am better qualified than he is. I think you also agree with me and everybody was speculating that I would get the job.

Mohamed: Maria, I know your disappointment but the management has made its decision and I don't think that we can do anything about it. The formal letter of appointment will be issued next week after the CEO endorses it. You must know that I am also disappointed but there are other things to be considered, not just work performance alone.

Maria: I don't know about that but I feel that I am being pushed aside by the general manager because of my gender, and may be by the fact that I don't go out for drinks and play golf with the guys. I know Ali does a lot of that but I prefer to spend my private time with my family. They can't expect me to do all that.

Mohamed: Let's not jump to conclusions. You don't think that is true, do you? The general manager is also concerned with what happened between you and the junior engineer last year. He thinks that your conduct was unacceptable.

Maria: (*close to tears*) I don't believe that I am hearing this from you! I thought the issue had been settled. I have already explained everything, including to Mr Matsuda, about what actually happened between the engineer and me. I just couldn't work with him because I can't stand people who don't know how to work independently and constantly need to be told what to do next!

Mohamed: I am sorry, but my hands are tied. I am sure that it is just a matter of time and you will definitely be the next person in line for promotion. You should know that I am also disappointed with the decision and I personally think that you are very valuable to our department.

Maria: Right now I am not even sure that I want to continue working here any more. I think, with my experience and credentials, I will be better appreciated somewhere else. I would appreciate it if you could keep our conversation between us confidential because I don't want people to get the wrong idea about me. Thank you for your advice and I will keep you informed of my next course of action.

After Maria left his room, Mohamed felt even more depressed. He was afraid of losing one of the best engineers in the department but at the same time he thought that the general manager's decision was also justified.

Next day, Mohamed's worst nightmare came true when he received Maria's resignation letter with one month's notice. Mohamed was in a dilemma about what to do next. He decided to keep the letter to himself for a while before taking further action. "Should I ask Matsuda to reconsider his decision and what would he think of me after that? Should I persuade Maria to stay, but how? Was I wrong not to try my best in defending Maria?" he thought. Mohamed fell back on to his chair, closing his eyes and groaning, "What a mess, what should I do?"

Chapter 15
Mr Tan's Predicament*

Trying to please some may result in management displeasing everyone. To what extent should religious requirements be accommodated in the work place? Can a company afford to give privileges to some of its staff? Can it afford not to? And when others resent what seem unfair practices, should they be considered also.

Smart Builders is a civil and structural consulting company. At present, it has a total of sixteen workers. There are six Malays, nine Chinese and an Indian. Of these eight are engineers, six drafters and two administration executives.

Smart Builders was founded by Mr Fung Kee Seng, who had over ten years of experience in the industry. After graduating from a local university with an engineering degree, Mr Fung joined a civil and structural consulting company. He stayed with that company for five years. Then he took up a job at a construction company where he was the head of the building department. In 1993, Mr Fung decided to set up his own company.

Mr Fung started his business by renting a reasonable-sized office in the heart of Petaling Jaya. With only limited staff, Mr Fung was able to expand his business and finally was able to purchase a double storey shop lot. While the shop lot was being renovated, Mr Fung's problem started. One day Azman, one of the drafters, came to see Mr Fung in his office.

Azman: Excuse me, Mr Fung. Can I speak to you?

Mr Fung: Sure. Come in and have a seat.

* This case was written by Yap Siok Fui while a graduate student in the Malaysian Graduate School of Management at Universiti Putra Malaysia.

Azman: I am speaking on behalf of all the Muslims in the company. Since the company will have a bigger office which is now being renovated, we would like the company to provide a prayer room for the Muslims to pray in. It need not be very big but just adequate.

Mr Fung: (*Pause*) Well, why ask for it now? We never used to have a prayer room in this office.

Azman: We know that our current office is too small and renovations cannot be made since it is rented. But the new office is the company's own property and it is being renovated. The company can decide if it wants to provide for a prayer room or not. Besides the nearest *surau* or mosque is too far away for the staff who do not have their own transport. We would take turns. The women could have one time and we would take a later time.

Mr Fung: Well, let me think about it. I will let you know later.

Azman left Mr Fung's office feeling very uncertain. A few days later, Mr.Tan called Azman to his office.

Mr Fung: Azman, please have a seat. I have given your request much thought. I am truly sorry to say that the company is not able to satisfy your request totally.

(*Azman looks upset*)

Mr Fung: Let me explain to you the company's decision. First of all, the new office is not as big as you think. Secondly, since we will be recruiting new staff due to expansion, we need all the extra space we can find to accommodate these new staff. However, I would like to say that we do have a storeroom and the Muslims in this company can use this room when they want to pray.

Azman: Thank you, Mr Fung.

Azman left Mr Fung's office. Although Azman was not totally satisfied, he reported to his fellow colleagues Mr Fung's decision. They decided not to pursue the matter further since Mr Fung has promised that they could use the storeroom to pray.

At the end of the year, the new office was ready. Mr Fung decided to shift his operations to the new office. All staff helped in the shifting. At the new office, the Muslim staff found out that the storeroom mentioned by Mr Fung was very small. It was all stacked up with documents, supplies and so on. It was not air-conditioned and had poor ventilation. The Muslims found this not to be a conducive environment for a prayer room but they did not voice their dissatisfaction and kept to themselves.

All seemed fine and the company maintained good business. But then another issue came up. The fasting month was approaching and one day Azman again went to Mr Fung's office.

Azman: Excuse me, Mr Fung. Have you time to see me for a minute?

Mr Fung: Sure. Come right in and sit down.

Azman: I am speaking on behalf of all the Muslims in the company. The fasting month is approaching and since the Muslims are fasting and do not go out for lunch we would like to request that the lunch hour be treated as a working hour and the Muslims be allowed to leave one hour earlier or be given one hour of overtime.

Mr Fung: (*Pause*) I think this request is quite reasonable. All right. I will issue a memo to inform the other staff members.

Azman: Thank you, Mr Fung.

Azman left Mr Fung's office smiling and satisfied. During the first week of the fasting month, all was fine. The Muslims continued to work throughout lunch hour and everybody was happy. Then came the second week.

Janet: Have you noticed? The Muslims are not really working during lunch hour. Some of them are sleeping or resting.

Brian: Yes. But what can we do? Mr Fung has agreed that the Muslims in the company be given this special arrangement. Anyway, Mr Fung is always out during lunch hour and he does not know what is going on.

Janet: So, what should we do?

Brian: I think we should inform Mr Fung.

Brian discussed the matter with the other non-Muslims in the company and they decided to make an official complaint to Mr Fung.

Brian: Excuse me, Mr Fung. Can I speak to you?

Mr Fung: Sure. Come in and have a seat.

Brian: Mr Fung, I am speaking on behalf of all the non-Muslims in the company. We are not happy with the special arrangement that the company has agreed on regarding the fasting month's lunch hour. We would like to make a complaint. Some of the Muslim staff do not work during lunch hour and instead sleep or rest. We feel that this is unfair since they get to leave an hour earlier or get an extra hour of overtime. We would like you to look into this matter and come up with a reasonable solution.

Mr Fung: (*Looking troubled*) I will check it out and let you know later.

Mr Fung is in a dilemma. On one hand he has promised the Muslims this special arrangement and on the other hand the non-Muslims are complaining. He decided to investigate. A few days later, Mr Fung called a staff meeting.

Mr Fung: Good morning. First of all, I would like to make a few announcements. It has come to my attention that some of the Muslims do not really work during lunch hour in this fasting month and instead they sleep or rest. I will not reveal any names but you know who you are. This is unfair to the rest of us. Since this special arrangement is not working, I have decided to revert to the normal working hours irrespective of whether it is the fasting month or not. Let's get on with other matters in the agenda.

After the staff meeting, all the Muslim staff were very upset. Not only were they upset over Mr Fung's decision; they suspected that the non-Muslim staff had squealed on them. There was enormous tension between these two groups and some of the staff even contemplated quitting as a last resort. The morale of the staff was low. These two groups started to keep to themselves and were not working well as a team. Productivity was decreasing.

Some of the Muslim staff were saying that the company does not respect the Muslims because of these two incidents with the prayer room and the lunch hour during the fasting month. Word of their unease reached Mr Fung. He had tried to consider all his staff but his intentions had resulted in everyone being restless. What was he to do?

Chapter 16
On The Plantation*

When a city person, member of a close family and devout in his religion, is transferred to the outback where culture pattern and religious beliefs happen to be very different from his own, problems recur. Yet the outsider may be important to the organisation. This case keeps alive the issue of culture shock and raises question relating to foreign experts.

Setting The Scene

EC Sdn. Bhd. (EC) is in the business of oil palm plantation and palm oil mill processing. For cultivating of oil palms, EC has acquired an additional 8000 ha. of tropical jungle, located at Labuk in the Sugut Region which is in the interior of Sandakan, Sabah.

This plantation is presently accessible only by air and boat by the Sugut River, with a travelling time of 2 hours by speed-boat from Sandakan. Only the executives use the company's helicopter. Because of the plantation interior location, EC, through the years, has developed an almost self-contained settlement within the plantation to cater for the daily, social needs of the settlers, both bachelors and families. The settlement has:

- longhouses for the workers who are mainly Indonesian, Filipinos and local Sabahans;
- bungalows for the management staff, mainly Indians and Chinese;

---

* This case was written by Goh Yew Seng and Shaliza Tay Abdullah, while graduate students in the Malaysian Graduate School of Management at Universiti Putra Malaysia.

- a mini-market, bakery shop and staff canteen;
- medical facilities;
- recreational and entertainment facilities; and
- a school and church.

EC is the subsidiary company of Palmo Corporation Berhad (Palmo Corp.), which is based in Kuala Lumpur. The company was set up to manage the oil palm and processing mill business in Sabah. Palmo Corp. has invested in oil palm plantation mainly at Sugut Region in Sandakan. EC began its activity of acquiring its first plantation land in 1985. Clearing the jungle started in 1988 and planting of the oil palms began immediately. The first harvest was in 1992, and from then on there were bumper harvests.

Throughout the years from 1992 to 1997, the performance of EC was encouraging. Because Palmo Corp. was confident of the future demand for palm oil, it contemplated constructing a highway from the Sugut plantation to the coast and even planned to build a new port. The highway would act as a primary collection route to transport bulky oil palm fruit from other plantations to Sugut mill for processing. The new port would facilitate the transportation of the processed palm oil for export as well as to transport equipment and supplies to the mill. However, at present both Palmo Corp. and EC are more concerned with the staffing needs of the plantation and the suitability of the present management to meet future expansion plans.

EC has over 500 staff:

Category	No. of Persons
(i) Management Group	
General Manager	1
Estate Managers	3
Administrative Manager	1
Plant & Store Manager	1
Marketing Executive	1
Accountants Executives	2
Assistance Estate Managers	8
(ii) Technical Group	
Conductors or *Mandos*	40
Surveyor	1

Category	No. of Persons
Chainman	3
Nurse	3
(iii) Supporting Group	
Chief Clerk	1
Clerks	8
Typists	4
Drivers	2
Guards	4
(iv) Workers (labourers)	500

The composition of races was as follows:

Management & Technical/ Supporting Groups	Indians (90%) Chinese and Sabahans (10%)
Workers (labourers)	Indonesians (95%) and Filipinos (5%)

Refer to Attachment A for the EC Sdn. Bhd.'s organisation chart.

Performance of EC Sdn. Bhd.

The balance sheet for the year indicated a pre-tax profit of RM40 million derived from selling crude palm oil. Mr Lee Wong, Managing Director (MD) of Palmo Corp. and his brother, Mr Velu, the Director of EC Sdn. Bhd. are reminiscing over the good performance of EC Sdn. Bhd.:

Lee Wong: This has certainly been a good year. With the price of crude oil at RM2,315 per tonne, we could be heading for good times. (*Looking up and smiling at his brother*). I believe we made the right move to invest in an additional 8000 hectares of land in Sabah two years ago. When the mill is built and ready to run, our planted acreage will be matured.

Velu: Well, that's true. The timing couldn't be better.

Lee Wong: You will probably need additional staff to take care of the plantation.

Velu: I've already taken care of that. The plantation is currently run by senior professional staff who are experienced and capable of tackling the daily challenges of managing the estates.

Lee Wong: What I mean is more than day-to-day. Have we trustworthy people to manage the estate since we are based in Kuala Lumpur and our estate is in Sabah? It is important to put trusted and loyal staff there.

Velu: Well... you know-lah, our staff here are reluctant to leave their family and work in Sabah. I have been trying to recruit staff from our company to fill up vacancies at the estates in Sandakan. So far there is only one new Indian recruit, an accounts trainee, who has indicated some interest in working there. I think I can persuade him to take up the job as an accounts executive. My staff in Sugut can be trusted simply because they are all Indians and they share the same religious belief as I do. I mean we are all Christians.

Lee Wong: I hope your religion will further bless you with higher yield and manageable overheads; otherwise the Board of Directors will question our recruiting policy.

Velu: You have nothing to worry about. Everything is taken care of.

Recruitment of Mr. Nathan

Mr Nathan's background: age 25, fresh graduate, city dweller, devout Hindu, and his first job at Palmo Corp. was for 6 months as Accountant Executive.

The next morning, Mr Velu called Mr Nathan, the new recruit, to his office:

Nathan: Good morning, Mr. Velu.

Velu: Good morning. You have been with Palmo Corporation Berhad for 6 months. How do you find our company?

Nathan: OK. I have been given odd jobs now and then . . . I would prefer something more challenging.

Velu: This is the very reason why I called you in here. Our subsidiary company, EC Sdn. Bhd., is doing extremely well in an oil palm plantation in Sugut, Sabah. We have invested in additional land and are building another mill in Sugut in anticipation of the build-up acreage of matured fruits in year 2000. Currently, there is a vacancy for an accounts executive position in Sugut. I am looking for a person who is willing to take up the challenge, one who is proactive and hardworking. I have shortlisted a few other candidates who have an accounting background but I would prefer a young and dynamic professional who can accept challenges. So, what do you think?

Nathan: It sounds interesting but the place of work is rather far away. I am not used to the idea of leaving my parents behind.

Velu: Well, the benefits are attractive; you will be given 2 return tickets each year, an annual salary increase of 30% and food and lodging are provided. You can keep in touch with your family by phone at no cost to you . . . Not to worry! The accommodation is very comfortable, rest assured. In fact, I will be sharing a same bungalow with you. The rest of the important management staff are Indians, too. You will be among one big family. You will definitely fit right in and feel at home. Do you like outdoor life and badminton?

Nathan: Yes.

Velu: We have all kinds of recreational facilities, sporting events such as badminton, football, ping-pong and sepak takraw. Occasionally we could go to Sandakan for a social drink.

Nathan: How far is it from Sugut to Sandakan ?

Velu: It takes about 2 hours by boat. However, you can join me in the helicopter to Sandakan . . . not a problem. You will have a bright future in our company if you do what I tell you . . . You may even be promoted to Accounts Manager if you perform well. I do hope you will take up the job.

Nathan: (*enthusiastically*) OK. When do I begin?

A year and a half later, Nathan was reflecting on his decision, as he has worked as an accounts executive in this plantation. Nathan contemplated meeting Mr Velu the next day asking to be transferred back to Kuala Lumpur. The excitement he once had seems to have faded away and now he feels a sense of frustration despite the fact he is with a group of people of his own race.

(Reflection by Nathan)

Nathan went over the reasons he would use to support his request for the transfer. And that was what made him more miserable. Nathan certainly couldn't tell Mr Velu that he felt uncomfortable whenever Mr Krishnan, the Administrative Manager and Mr Bala, the Plant and Store Manager tried to persuade him to convert to Christianity because Mr Velu is himself a staunch Christian. Nathan observed that all the Indian and Chinese management staff and their families and friends in Sugut are Christians. Nathan wondered whether they had been "persuaded", too, to convert. He knows that he will be at a disadvantage if he does not comply with the wishes of the group in this settlement.

Nathan's thoughts traced back to Mr Chong, who had worked hard as an assistant estate manager for 10 years. He had been amply rewarded for his patience and loyalty and today is the General Manager, simply because he is a strong believer in Christ and the longest serving employee in this place. Nathan had a few unpleasant encounters with Mr Chong over work and until today that bitter feeling is still there. Nathan would avoid seeing Mr Chong, and vice versa. If there was any message to relay, it was done through the clerks. Nathan recalled an argument they had about the calculation of the workers' overtime pay.

Nathan: Mr Chong, I disagree with the way you calculate the overtime pay of the labourers. It should be calculated based on basic pay divided by 26 working days times 1.5, not based on a division of 365 days.

Chong: *(In an angry tone)* Who are you to tell me what to do? I have been doing it this way for the past 10 years and there is no problem. I follow the Employment Act!

Nathan continued thinking to himself, "I even asked him to show me which 'Act' and he couldn't explain the 'Act' he was referring to. Instead, he showed me a letter written by him to Mr Velu about the pay policy that would be followed. 'You do what I tell you to do!' he said".

In a fit of defiance, Nathan had written a letter to Palmo Corp. on this unlawful practice. The response was a directive from Palmo Corp. that Nathan's recommendation should be adhered to. Ever since then, Nathan and Mr Chong had not spoken a word to each other.

Going over the overtime *kong* card (record card for daily overtime), the record always showed 12 hours of work in a day. Nathan could not understand how a person could do productive work for so many hours every day of the week. Nathan once asked Mr Larry, a conductor, popularly called locally *mando*, in charge of weeding the estate, why he always filled the *kong* card for 12 hours.

Nathan: Do you always work the labourers so hard?

Larry: If the company pays a worker RM7 per day, how can you expect that he feeds his 4 children without any overtime? My workers are all hard working and obedient. They never give me any trouble. I should think it is only reasonable to help them. After all, they are very glad to do the work. At these times, when the labourer turnover is high and difficult to maintain, I give them something extra to retain them.

Strike by the Indonesian Workers

Nathan continued to reminisce: "I was so sure that Mr Chong is not qualified to be promoted that I begin to ask around to find out more about his background. The Indonesian caretaker, Mat Bu, told Nathan his experience":

Mat Bu: Our welfare here has improved a lot. We used to stay in a longhouse that is 12m x 20m per unit joined together to form a long common corridor. A couple or 2 males or 2 females are given a unit each in the same long house. We were given a kitchen, toilet, and living area. There was only a curtain partition between each unit. This did not suit us well at all. We feel that there was no privacy.

Nathan: Your people didn't raise this matter with Mr Chong?

Mat Bu: Many times! Every time we tell him about it, he will tell us that the Sabahan tribes have stayed in this type of conditions for years. He asked why we can't live the same way as they do?

Nathan: How did you manage to persuade him to give you a 12m x 40m unit with a partition?

Mat Bu: We stopped work a few days after the incident with an Indonesian couple! The wife woke up one morning and noticed that her husband was not in the room. She got up to look for him and found her husband in an intimate position with another married women whose husband had left for Indonesia.

A fight occurred with screams and insults between husband and wife. The wife went to see Mr Chong to seek help. She wanted him to catch her husband and put him in jail. When they proceeded to the longhouse to find them, her husband and his lover ran away. That was the last time we saw them.

We had to do something. The longhouse living is not suitable to our Islamic way of life. The incident created a lot of tension and disharmony among us. We were afraid that this could happen to us again. We wanted Mr Chong to provide us with decent accommodation. We took it up with Mr Chong. Nowadays, we have quarters for the different sexes and another quarter for families.

In fact, that was not the only time the workers went on strike. The reason for the strike was that no mosque was provided for them to conduct Friday prayers. There was a church to cater for the Christian management staff but no proper praying facility for the Muslims. The Christians are treated well. The management arranged for a priest to come every Sunday from Sandakan to Sugut plantation. But the management did not arrange such facilities for the Indonesian workers. The strike forced the management to build a surau in the settlement and also make arrangements for chartered buses to ferry the Indonesians to another nearby plantation for their Friday prayers.

The Proposed Sugut Bridge

There is the Sugut bridge that connects the Sugut Plantation to EC's future port. The bridge collapsed three times because the earthfill embankment eroded, because of the river current which moves back and forth according to the tide, leaving the bridge suspended at the ends. In a short time it collapsed. The bridge was made of steel sections which had to be procured from overseas through Mr Lim, Procurement Manager at Palmo Corp.

Mr Chong managed to get the survey data from the plantation surveyor, Mr Chandra, in November. In December, Mr Chow from Palmo Corp. was sent to Sugut to assist Mr Chandra. He was asked to take an hour's boat ride upstream to the location of the proposed bridge to conduct a river profile. Data taken from the river showed that the bridge Mr Chong has ordered is short by 10m. Mr Chow recalled that he told Mr Chong the river profile (one end to the other end) at high tide will be slightly below 70m width.

Mr Chong: How can it be 70m when the downstream end of the river is only 60m? The downstream river is always bigger then the upstream river end. Mr Chandra is a very good surveyor. He cannot be wrong!

When Mr Lim got to know about it, he went down to Sugut to find out more. The three of them, Mr Lim, Mr Chong and Mr Chow decided to travel upstream to the site to verify the dimensions.

Later, they concluded that the bridge they procured was short of the actual width of the river.

Mr Chow: He had the audacity to tell everyone that I gave him the wrong survey information. He blamed me for his mistake. If he is honest, he should admit that he agreed with Mr Chandra to take the survey near the settlement. I'm glad I will be going back to Palmo Corp. soon.

They had two options. Either they order an additional length of steel section or install bakau piles and backfill with earth-fill at both sides of the embankment. Mr Chong rejected the former option because the price for the bridge would be higher. The steel components arrived in June the following year and were immediately installed. The bridge collapsed within a month. EC had to fork out another RM3 million to rebuild after three unsuccessful attempts and ended up ordering the additional length.

Procurement of Equipment

Nathan continued considering. "I also observed that Mr Bala was sloppy in his work. He is responsible for the procurement and maintenance of repair work for plant and machinery. The *mandos* would complain to me that the plant, such as the backhoe, has high down time. Each time it is in need of repair; it would take a long time to be fixed.

When they asked Mr Bala the reason for taking so long to repair Mr Bala would say, 'Ran out of spare parts or no workers to do repairs!' There would always be excuses.

Mr Chong always sympathises with Mr Bala's conditions even though the excuses given do not seems to be reasonable in certain situations. There are times Mr Bala would not release the equipment to certain *mandos* for usage simply because he has personal grudges with them. The *mandos* would then put in a purchase requisition to buy new equipment. I expressed my concern about the increasing amount of plant being purchased in the meeting. They did not take any notice or pay any attention."

Local Authority dilemma

Nathan reminisces again: "The most admirable person in Sugut I will always remember is Mr Krishnan. He is friendly, easy going and helpful. I once assisted him to apply for workers' permits and material storage permits. Naturally, I had to go to the authority office to apply for those permits. My first encounter with the clerical staff was extremely difficult because I could not get the staff to expedite the application.

Even after frequent visits to the office, I still failed to get them to approve our application. Once, I was furious with them because after so many trips to the office they told me that my application forms were missing and EC has to resubmit the forms. I confided in Mr Krishnan. He told me not to worry because he is used to dealing with them. He promised he would accompany me on the next visit.

The next day, when we arrived at the counter, Mr Krishnan greeted the clerical staff heartily, '*Tuan, apa khabar?*' (Sir, how are you?). I noticed that Mr Krishnan bowed his head slightly lower and distanced himself when he spoke with the clerk-in-charge. He apologised for not coming here to apply for the permits himself and sending someone else instead. He introduced me to the clerk and signalled to me to look down. He also informed the clerk that I would be coming to apply for the permits whenever he was on outstation duty travel.

After that, they talked about their families, and friends they know. Each time Mr Krishnan addressed the clerk he would uses the word *'Tuan'*. Since that encounter, all applications have been cleared. Mr Krishnan advised me: 'If need be you have to act, or give them an impression that they are very important people you are dealing with.'"

Nathan continued thinking to himself. "It has been interesting working in Sugut and I have learnt a lot from the inhabitants of the settlement and the need to be sensitive and show respect for each other's beliefs and practices. But somehow, I am still not used to the work ethic here. What's more, I have to wake up at 5.30 am every morning and hear the *mandos* gather his workers for another day's work. My stomach still growls at 12pm and not 10am and I'm not sure what to do after work at 1.30pm.

I think my career opportunity here will be limited by religious belief. Even if they promote me to Accounts Manager and give me a high pay, I will not be able to enjoy the success of my labour without my parents, nor can I keep my identity as a Hindu. I think I will tell Mr Velu that I need to take care of my aging parents."

The Future of EC Sdn. Bhd.

Lee Wong: Velu, the plantation division pre-tax profit achieved in 1999 is RM25 million, a decrease of 38% over the previous year. I cannot imagine what will happen next year. At this rate we will end up in a money-losing enterprise.

Velu: Brother, the low pre-tax profit is attributed to lower crude palm oil prices which averaged approximately RM1,100 per tonne. The Government has imposed all kinds of taxes in this business because of just one good year.

Lee Wong: I think the situation seems to have turned around against us. The only way we can arrest such fall in pre-tax profit is to ensure that our overheads are under control. We have to tighten our belt. How do you find this Mr Chong? I heard he made a few blunders.

Velu: Yes, I am disappointed with his performance lately. His indecisive manner and poor interpersonal skills seems to bring us more trouble then solving problems. The last incident was the bridge. It cost us an additional RM3 million to rebuild, through his fault.

Lee Wong: It appears he is not up to the job. Please look into this. If Mr Chong cannot control the overheads, we will have to transfer him somehow. Oh, one more thing. Should we accept Nathan's request to be transferred back to Kuala Lumpur? Please look into that too.

Attachment A

EC ORGANISATION CHART

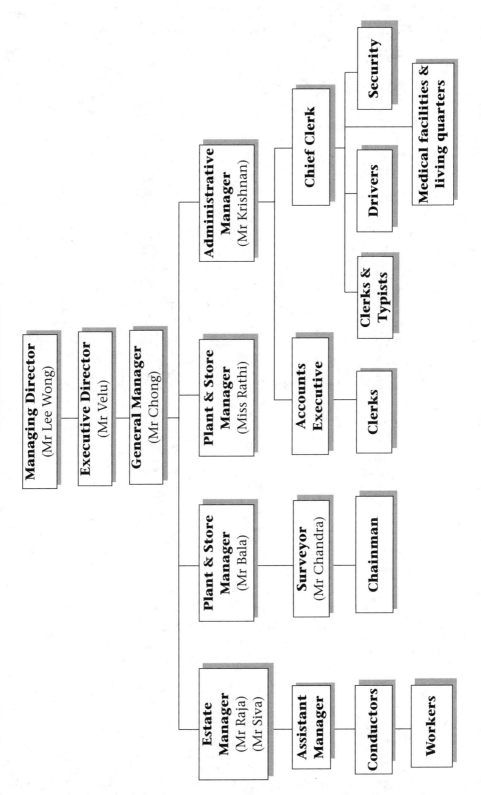

SECTION 4
CULTURE CLASH

Every organisation has the potential for differences of opinion between those in control and those who are controlled. When expatriates are brought in to technical or managerial positions, the potential for clashes increases exponentially. This section brings you some explosive situations whose causes can be traced to differences in values and habits held by people of very different cultures.

This section contains cases in which sheer lack of knowledge of other cultures creates misunderstanding that has severe repercussions on the organisations involved.

Chapter 17
The Fijian Experience-The *Tau* Relationship*

This is a case about a problem faced by Brett Taylor, an American who was an expatriate owner-manager in a resort hotel at Yanuca Island in Fiji. The Shangri-La Fijian Resort (FIJIAN) was one of the grand names of the Shangri-La International Hotel Group. The other prides of the Shangri-La International Hotel Group were the Rasa Sayang Resort in Penang and Shangri-La Hotel in Singapore. The FIJIAN was a 30-year-old resort and enjoyed a strong and widespread reputation in Australia, New Zealand and the South Pacific region as a world standard international hotel.

"We bought the hotel from the original founders; a group of three ex-Pan Am pilots. The view is as scenic as the best in the world and perfectly pollution-free. We have clear blue skies and clear blue seas. The fishes nibble at your toes and come close when you take a swim in the sea. Look at the deep sea sport fishing record; blue marlins and black marlins every year, not to mention the yellow fin tunas and bonitos", elaborated Brett Taylor, the general manager and owner of the FIJIAN.

The FIJIAN was located on Yanuca Island on the west side of Viti Levu, one of the big islands in Fiji. It was linked to Viti Levu by a 200 metre causeway. Yanuca Island, being a native reserve land, was owned by and leased from the Nadroga tribe whose main village was located on the main island of Viti Levu just

---

* This case was written by Choong Chee Yoong, while a graduate student in the Malaysian Graduate School of Management at Universiti Putra Malaysia.

outside Yanuca Island. The chief of the Nadroga tribe held the title, *Kalevu*, which means High Chief. The title was hereditary, passed down to the eldest claimant next in line, whether male or female. The present *Kalevu* was Lady Adi Mere. There was a complex and complicated web of places and relationship in the Fijian society which had developed through thousands of years by conquests and marriages in the evolution of the Fijian civilization.

The FIJIAN was a 450-room resort with about 800 local staff on its payroll. The indigenous Fijians, comprising 70% of the local staff, took positions as waitresses and waiters in the food and beverage department; as receptionists, porters, and reservation clerks in front office; as room maids in the housekeeping department; and a few as engineering maintenance staff.

The indigenous Fijians were mainly in the "front-line" or guest contact positions but the Indian ethnic staff were mainly employed in the engineering (maintenance) department and as cooks in the kitchens. The reason for the distinction was that indigenous Fijians were more apt in serving guests by their very warm and hospitable human nature. Their smiles were said to be more natural, more spontaneous and friendlier. About 80% of the indigenous staff were from the landowner Nadrogan tribe.

Many of the staff had served more than 10 years. There were staff who had been with the hotel since day one of the hotel's operations. Often the retiring staff would introduce and recommend their children and relatives for vacant positions in the hotel. It was possible to have even three generations of a family working in the hotel simultaneously, perhaps in different departments.

"Why should our children work elsewhere when there are good jobs here in our land? The hotel has treated the staff fairly and is the largest employer in this district", explained one of the long-serving staff.

Even with the personal and family ties that existed among the local staff, productivity and work were not adversely affected. A productivity survey by Shangri-La International Management found that close ties reinforced the work procedures and improved productivity.

Moala Tukana

Moala was in the first batch of three high school students selected by the FIJIAN for a 3-year hotel management course in Switzerland. His study and expenses were fully sponsored by the FIJIAN. His parents were from the Nadrogan landowner tribe.

Upon graduation from the hotel school, he returned to serve at the hotel as the Assistant Food and Beverage Manager in the Food and Beverage Department. He had shown promise for promotion with his "can-do" attitude and tireless attention to customer satisfaction. His relationship with the other staff was good. He showed proper respect for the older staff working for him and was a model worker for the younger staff. He was well regarded by his colleagues, both indigenous Fijians and Indians, as well as by his expatriate superior. It was considered by the management that he would be in line for promotion as Food and Beverage Manager at Mocambo Hotel, a 200-room sister hotel located at Nadi, Fiji's only international airport, Nadi International Airport, was at Nadi.

For a village boy who had not travelled further than the district township of Sigatoka Town (population of 5,000), the chance of studying and travelling overseas had immense appeal. It was not just the experience. He was proud of being one of the very few Fijians to have journeyed to Switzerland and also of the immense prestige and honour he gained for himself and his family. His determination to succeed was strong and unfailing. Upon his graduation, he was guaranteed a job for life with an international hotel operator. There was also the high probability of overseas posting to other five-star hotels within the hotel group. A managerial position at FIJIAN itself was an enviable position and highly regarded by the local population.

News of his return and subsequent position at the FIJIAN spread far and wide in Fiji. Moala also held the record of being the first Fijian to graduate from the internationally-renowned and reputable Larzene Hotel School of Switzerland as well as the first Fijian to hold an important executive position in a 5-star hotel of an international hotel group.

Moala became the unofficial train-the-trainer for the local indigenous staff. He undertook to train all personnel, young and old, with the knowledge and skills he had obtained while studying in Switzerland. Anyone willing to spend free and spare time was welcomed by Moala. His own lunch and free time were ultimately used to teach and train his less fortunate colleagues. Such training given by Moala was of immeasurable benefit to the FIJIAN as well.

Morale and enthusiasm among the staff were high. Cooperation and a spirit of fellowship enabled the FIJIAN to host the annual Fijian Tourism Conference with resounding success. The event was the talk of the tourism industry in Australia, New Zealand, the West Coast of America and the rest of the South Pacific for a long time. Such benefits were not achievable during the training sessions organised previously by the hotel's Human Resource Department.

"I am only doing my part for my people to bring them into the international society. We must progress from living in huts and straw mat floors, with well water and hurricane lights for the nights. My mission is to give impetus to this integration of my people with the outside world," vowed Moala during the celebration of his graduation and home coming.

Salome Suacake

Salome was hired as a trainee waitress at the Lagoon Terrace Restaurant, the 24-hour coffee house of the FIJIAN. She came from a small Bauan tribe that lived on a small island off the east coast of Vanua Levu, the other big island of the Fijian archipelago. As the fabric of the Fijian society loosened, the migration of population from their tribal lands to seek better prospects and work in lands belonging to other tribes (where their forefathers had feared to tread without raising the cries of war) was becoming a common phenomenon. Many of the younger and educated population such as Salome took the opportunity to move to the bigger towns and work in establishments such as the FIJIAN.

All local job applicants were vetted by the Human Resource Department which was headed by the human resource officer, a local indigenous Fijian. The reason for having a local to head the department was to ensure the local staff were handled correctly, according to the traditional practices and dictates of the local customs. The indigenous Fijian civilization did not have any written history, and ties among the tribes could be tenuous at times. The customs of each tribe could also differ from one to another. There were about 60 different languages within the Fijian society. Only with the arrival of the British were the languages romanised and one language, the Bauan Language, chosen by the High Council of Chiefs to be their national language.

At The Lagoon Terrace Restaurant

Salome performed well for the first two months of her employment. Negative changes in her attitude and work responsibilities began to show during her third month. Rumours started to surface of her short-changing the customers and keeping the money which customers paid for their meals and drinks. Initial reaction of the management was to ignore the rumours as there was no proof. Moreover, Moala was the supervisor of the restaurant. It was his responsibility to audit the cashiers and to make spot checks on the waiters and waitresses so that such stealing did not occur. In the past, he had been thorough and fair.

Soon after, Salome was caught red-handed taking money from customers by Brett Taylor. She was immediately suspended pending investigations. Moala was also called by the management for his explanation of the incident. He admitted that he knew Salome had been stealing. He stated that Salome needed the money to help finance the building of a church at her village. He further stated he was her *Tau*, a person committed by the ancestors to support her. As part of the company's policy, Moala was also suspended under the charge of abetting the crime.

Tau

All indigenous Fijians are Christians. The main denominations are the Methodists and Catholics. The hold of the church over the life of the Fijians is very strong. After the coup d'état by the military in 1987, the Sunday rest day was strictly enforced, though eventually employees of certain essential services and industries were given exemptions. The hotel employees were one

156   Issues and Cases in Cross-Cultural Management: An Asian Perspective

of the categories given the exemptions. The church leaders exerted immense influence over the people.

Despite such Christian influences, the indigenous Fijians are also strictly guided by their customary practices. After Moala had been suspended, one of the elders from his village sought a meeting with Brett Taylor. Apparently, Moala's ancestors owed Salome's ancestors a debt, thus resulting in an unbreakable relationship or a bond.

Salome, therefore, hailed Moala as her *Tau*. She, by virtue of such a bond, could do as she pleased in Moala's home. There was nothing Moala could possibly do to restrain or stop her, since Yanuca Island, where the FIJIAN was located, was traditional land belonging to Moala's tribe, which by extension of his family, was considered as his home. That was the reason why Moala could neither prevent Salome from stealing nor reprimand her. This relationship was uncommon and relatively unknown, even among the tribes.

The village elders appealed that Moala be reinstated without any loss in seniority and privileges. Salome simply took advantage of the bond to do as she pleased.

The Hotel Workers' Union appealed on Salome's behalf that she was unduly influenced by the church to raise funds for the church building. The money stolen was not for her own use.

The Dilemma

Brett Taylor was a manager sensitive to the local customs and practices. He had to consider the issues seriously. The local staff must not take advantage of his ignorance of such practices, and he must also be fair to the staff. He did not want to open a floodgate of staff in-subordination and abuse.

"Moala has a good record, he's definitely an asset to the resort and the people of Nadroga. He has the potential to be a leader in the future. I want him to be able to fully realise his potential. Yet the incidents of fraud cannot be condoned or played down. What options do I have?" Brett Taylor asked the human resource officer.

Chapter 18
Temper, Temper!*

Expatriate specialists, who do not understand local culture, can cause deep trouble. Sometimes small actions can take on huge significance when others interpret their meaning from a different cultural viewpoint.

FGP Sdn Bhd was undergoing a transition period because it was going to convert the system used in the company from a legacy system to an integrated system. It had employed a recognised consulting firm, Miller & Wilson, to help implement the work. FGP is a wholly owned subsidiary of a multinational firm. Other subsidiaries in other countries were converting the system as well so that all their systems could be synchronised and transparent.

The legacy system comprised a number of systems used by different departments. In particular, the system used by the administration department, was an old database system. Even though Miller & Wilson had a company in Malaysia, the consultants who were attached to FGP were mainly from Europe and America. FGP Europe attached a staff member from its Europe counterpart to help the local staff to maintain accurate data in the database before the conversion to the integrated system.

The work of maintaining correct data was tremendous. In addition to this, a large number of the staff were not very familiar with the system since they were quite new. They knew how to get things done through the system, but they did not know the way the system worked. The system itself was very old; therefore, there was no countermeasure in the system itself, which aggravated the whole problem. It also required a lot of manual work to key in all the figures.

---

*This case was written by Zailin Mahdi, while a graduate student in the Malaysian Graduate School of Management at Universiti Putra Malaysia.

The consultants had their own deadline; therefore they had to ensure that everything went according to schedule. The local staff involved with the consultants were two Malay girls, an Indian girl and a Punjabi girl. They were in a rush to complete the day-to-day work and at the same time they had to learn the old system in order to make sure that everything was done correctly. The consultants' tasks were to find information from the staff on how they did the work and to implement a process that could ensure everything ran smoothly before the cut-off date. One staff member from Europe was Anna; she was a Swede and her role was to assist the local staff in any questions they had and to help out the consultants.

One day, while the staff were having lunch, Brian, another of the consultants, also a Swede, came and slammed his fist on the table. He asked them in a normal tone to quickly finish their lunch and get back to work. The local staff were very irritated because to them he was very rude since he banged the table. His attitude implied that they were not doing their work. Malaysians value courtesy very much and if he wanted to ask them to do the work, he should not have banged the table. Brian did not mean to be rude. However, the staff took it seriously since everyone was tense. In fact, on that day they were having a late lunch because they were very busy doing the work. Everyone was working late. The ones who are married were having some problems at home since their husbands were not happy that the wives came home late and did not spend enough time with the family. Malaysians' family values are very strong and women play an important part in taking care of the family.

One evening, when everyone was busy doing their work, Brian sent out an email message saying that the staff were not keying in some of the data. Worse still, he copied the mail to the bosses. Brian was very proud of his action; he thought that he was doing his job and that, by conveying his suspicions directly to the staff, he could get the job done. He also showed that he was doing all he could to prove that he had done his job, but the staff were the ones who did not do as he told them to.

The staff were furious at his behaviour. They believed that he did not try to understand their position and that the consultants were the ones who were disturbing the others and taking their time from their work. The staff also thought that Brian had tried to make them lose face and ruin their reputations. He made them look as though they were not responsible employees.

Anna knew that the mail was sent and she partly agreed with Brian's action. The staff had befriended Anna but now they did not agree with her opinion. However, Anna agreed to the action in the interest of the company, to get things in time before the cutover date. She tried to have a session to explain the working of the old database system to the staff, but she was not even able to get the staff to agree to a date.

One morning, Anna tried to fix a date with the staff for the session. This is the conversation that took place.

Anna: Hello. I need your attention. We have to fix the date for the training session. Would it be convenient to have it today?

The staff who were facing their computers turned around to face Anna.

All: Yes, what time?

Shanti: I will be free the whole evening.

Aina: What about 3pm?

Jasmeen Kaur: Sorry girls, I have a meeting from 2pm to 4pm. We'd better fix another time. Maybe at 5 pm?

Imah: I would not be able to make it. I have not done my input yet. Can we fix another date?

She turned her back and continued doing her work on the computer.

Anna: What about tomorrow then?

Jasmeen Kaur: Oh! I have a meeting to catch, you guys decide on the time. I will be free in the afternoon, from 2pm onwards.

After saying this, Jasmeen ran out of the room

Aina: Tomorrow is impossible. I have to attend training the whole day. Can we set a later date?

Anna: Jasmeen is not around to decide on another date. We'll have to fix this later.

She sighed and shook her head. The conversation continued at lunch time.

Aina:	We still have not fixed the time for Anna yet. Everyone is busy working. Fulfilling the customers' needs is more important.
Jasmeen Kaur:	Yes, I agree with you. They asked us to do this and that and now we have to go for the training for the old system.
Imahi:	There is no point in learning the old system. It is going to be obsolete anyway in a few months. At the same time we have to learn the new system.
Shanti:	They think we are robots? We have to do our daily work and at the same time we have to learn both the old and the new system.

Another colleague, Liza, knew the process for the old system and had to settle all the errors heard in the conversation.

Liza:	Actually, you have to learn the new system so that you can prevent the mistakes before they occur. If you do this, everything will be more efficient and the figures will be accurate.
Jasmeen Kaur:	No, I do not agree with you. We do not have to learn the system since your group is helping to clear out the errors.
Liza:	They themselves are not clear on what they are doing. They are only clerks. You are the one who should prevent the mistakes from occurring.
Imah:	Yes, I agree with you but we do not have that much time. As it is, I go home late night after night in order to settle all the problems.

The next morning, Anna came to the office while everybody was busy with their day-to-day activities. She greeted everyone and the staff replied to the greetings. When she asked whether they could fix the time for the training, no one turned to face her though she was sitting on a chair nearby. She thought that she had had enough of their reaction for the past week. She had been trying to help the company but the staff seemed to be unaware of their responsibility to attend the training.

Thump! Everybody jumped from their seats and turned around. They saw a heavy file on the floor and looked at Anna who had thrown the file to catch their attention. With her action, she managed to fix the date and time. Anna looked at Liza with a smile of relief since she was able to complete her task. However, the consequence of her action was that her friendship with the staff was never the same after that. They resented her because of her action and they said she was rude and never considered their feelings.

Liza could see that there were some conflicts going on. These would create friction between them and it was only four months to go before the cutover date. Her colleagues were busy and at the same time they were pressured to maintain accurate data in the system. However, she could see the importance of the consultants' schedule and Anna's training. The understanding of the old system would help them in learning the new system and at the same time it would reduce the need to correct the errors since the work would be done correctly the first time.

Liza's colleagues, however, failed to see the importance of what she insisted on. While she understood the foreigners' position, she herself did not like the consultants. The consultants would ask the staff the same questions over and over. It seemed as though they either did not share the information among themselves or they did not understand the whole process.

In one case, when she tried to emphasise a solution, the consultants did not take note of what she said. She even tried to explain the solution to them a few times in case they did not understand it. However, they still believed their solution was right even though their solution was complicated. Only after they had experienced further difficulties, did they listen to her solutions and start asking for her advice.

She agreed with her colleague that the consultants were disturbing their work, but the consultants were the only people who could push the staff to maintain accurate data. She certainly would not be able to persuade her colleagues because they were at the same level. Furthermore if she tried to do that, her colleagues would dislike her action and would boycott her as they did Anna. Anna and the consultants would leave after they did the work, but she would still be around and would have to suffer until they managed to forget about what she did.

She expressed her concern to another colleague, but her friend was not able to suggest anything. She knew that the department was not working efficiently because of her colleagues' lack of knowledge and responsibilities towards the old system. Her conscience felt that it was her responsibility to advise her colleagues, but she would not dare risk the consequences. She was torn between responsibility and friendship. What actions should she take?

Chapter 19

Transmission Lines*

Balfour Beatty is a company that installs transmission lines. The company has staff from Italy, Pakistan, Indonesia, Thailand, Britain, Australia and Malaysia. The Malaysians consist of Chinese, Indians and Malays. Most of the Thai people are Buddhists. The works manager, Bob Harvard, is British. The chief surveyor is an Australian called Gary Bagueley. The Malays and the Thais can't converse in English. Bob and Gary can't talk in Bahasa Melayu and Thai languages.

Balfour Beatty installs transmission lines. The work involves camping in the jungle, surveying, clearing the trees to make a helipad for the helicopters to land, clearing the trees for the transmission towers, excavating earth for the tower foundations, installing tower footings, concreting, erecting towers, installing transmission lines and testing tower electrical resistance.

Religious Attitudes to Food

The Muslims do not take pork. The Muslims will eat chicken, mutton and beef only when the animals are slaughtered according to their rites. The Indians who are Hindus do not eat beef or pork. The Buddhists do not eat any meat.

Critical Incident

Balfour Beatty obtained the contract from the Malaysian Government to install transmission lines from Kenyir Dam in

---

* This case was written by Batumalay A/L Kaliannan while a graduate student in the Malaysian Graduate School of Management at Universiti Putra Malaysia.

Trengganu to Kuala Krai in the state of Kelantan. Gary appointed Batumalay to be the head of the survey team, which had Indians, Malays and Thais.

The survey team camped in the jungle and stayed in one tent. The company provided all the camping material. It also provided free food. The food was bought and sent to the campsite by Bob by helicopter. The food included pork, beef, chicken, mutton, vegetables, chillies, onions, oil and rice. Everything was packed in the same big box to facilitate easy transport by helicopter.

Everyone used the same kitchen for cooking but the different ethnic groups used different utensils. The kitchen used to be filled with smells from the groups cooking. Some of them couldn't stand the smell and silently went out of the kitchen. Gary enjoyed the smell of the various foods. He ate the food from the different ethnic groups without any hesitation. Gary liked to tell the non-eaters about the taste of the pork and beef but they said nothing in return.

The group used to camp near river sites and bathe in the river. They went fishing after work, catching fresh fish that was either fried or made into fish curry to go along with the rice. The taste was very good. Normally, all the ethnic groups shared the fish curry, but the other food was cooked and eaten by the separate groups.

After a few days of working in the jungle, the Indians, the Malays and the Thais did not want to eat the food sent by Bob. They almost completely stopped talking to Gary, and lost interest in their work. They got angry with Gary whenever he asked them to do any work. The work performance was affected badly which was serious because the company had to pay a penalty of five thousand dollars a day if there was a delay in handing over the transmission lines job.

Gary and Bob were concerned about the work performance and the working environment relationship. Was there anything they could do?

Chapter 20
Mr Braun In Trouble*

Written contracts mean different things in different cultural contexts. In this case, managers from very different cultures, with the best will in the world, find partnership difficult.

The project had been running for 14 months and the German construction company, Staud & Sohn, was satisfied with it so far. The goal was to construct a watering-dam in China on behalf of Tan & Tan, a large Chinese producer of agricultural products. Peter Staud and his son Klaus, directors of Staud & Sohn, were happy about the project as they considered it a step into the Chinese market.

The trouble began when Staud's financial department received a letter from Tan & Tan stating that they had paid their duty but had had to reduce the amount by 8.3 percent due to a sharp increase in the value of the German mark to the Chinese yuan. When Staud checked its bank statement the company found that they had even received the money one week ahead of the deadline but only the reduced amount of 40 million German marks instead of the expected 43.6 million.

The next morning the project manager responsible, Axel Braun, found a short memo on his desk that read:

> *Please meet me in my office first thing in the morning!!!*
> *Klaus Staud*

---

* This case was written by Henning Osmers & Sabri Kuskonmaz, while graduate students in the Malaysian Graduate School of Management at Universiti Putra Malaysia.

When Mr Braun entered the office, an apparently upset Mr Staud confronted him with his displeasure right away:

Mr Braun: Axel, I hope that you agree with me that the behaviour of Tan & Tan is totally dissatisfying. We cannot, and will not, accept the shortening of their payment. Please make sure that they will transfer the missing amount within three to four weeks. Tell 'em that we will otherwise stop construction work. Maybe we should also consider withdrawing you from the project and give you another project to work on. My father has indicated that he is prepared to deal with the issue himself if this should become necessary.

Mr Braun was stunned. He went over and over the position.

The Company

Staud & Sohn had been founded 19 years earlier by Peter Staud and his son. Mr Staud senior had a background as a construction engineer and had worked many years for a company building dams for water supply in Scandinavia. However, due to mismanagement, his company went bankrupt and left him with the unpleasant experience of being dismissed. As he had never thought of his employer as a good manager, he decided to open up his own company and prove to himself and others that he could do better.

His son had been educated in business engineering, providing him with both a good understanding of engineering issues as well as a comprehensive knowledge of general management. He was eager to join his father and build up a successful family business.

Staud & Sohn had specialised in the construction of dams under particularly difficult circumstances and had many experienced engineers working for it. The company concentrated on projects in Africa and Asia, but had never previously conducted business in China.

The projects were led by Staud's best-performing staff. Once an engineer became a project leader he was responsible for the entire construction work and for all communication with the base for the duration of the project.

Mr Braun

Mr Braun's bosses at Staud had every reason to be satisfied with him. During the 13 years that he had been with the company he was a reliable, committed, creative and successful colleague. Although educated as a construction engineer, he soon became a manager who organised and oversaw his own projects, the construction of dams in Asia. His projects usually achieved profit margins above company average.

His new project was the biggest he had run so far and he was the one who had got to know about it and who had managed to win the contract for his company. He had been at a conference in Hong Kong earlier and had met Tan & Tan's Mr Fu, there. They had talked about various things and kept in contact later. A few months after the congress, Mr Fu visited Mr Braun on a private visit to Germany.

During his next holidays, Mr Braun followed an invitation for a counter-visit to China. When he was in China, Mr Fu told him about his company's plan for constructing the dam. They spent evenings together discussing the details and decided to try convincing their companies to do business together.

The Project

Mr Braun had no problem convincing his bosses of the idea of entering the Chinese market. Peter Staud and his son had spoken several times about the opportunities China had to offer several times and had made the decision to take any chance to enter that market long before Mr Braun offered his project. At last this was what they had waited for.

Mr Fu's job was more difficult. His company received four offers for the project from willing partners, of which two had slightly better prices than Staud's. But in the end, Mr Fu convinced Tan & Tan's top-management that Staud was the most experienced of these companies and would be a reliable partner as he, Mr Fu, had a good relationship with Staud's project manager.

The construction work was to be finished after 18 months. But 14 months later Staud was even a little ahead with the project and as agreed upon in the contract, Tan & Tan, therefore, had to fulfil their duty and pay for the work.

Staud had calculated total costs of 38.9 million marks originally and had added its usual profit-margin of 12 percent. The plan proved to be well calculated: After 14 months, Staud had spent just a little more than forecast and the new calculation assumed a total expenditure of 39.5 million, leaving them with a margin of 10.4 percent only.

The Next Step

After leaving Mr Staud's office, Mr Braun called his friend, Mr Fu, to discuss the problem with him. He was not satisfied with the situation either but wanted to hear his friend's explanation before making any judgement and deciding on the next step.

During his call Mr Fu explained:

> I am very sorry that this situation means trouble for you, but I do not quite understand what your boss is so upset about. Neither of us could foresee an increase of the mark of 22 percent. When we agreed on our contract, our companies both talked about partnership and about looking forward to a good, long-term relationship. But does partnership not mean that we have to bear unexpected difficulties together? There is no doubt that the contract reads differently, but our view is that, insisting on the contract in such a situation, means misusing the contract in order to take an advantage on the costs of your partner. However, I will talk to my boss about this. All the same, I do not see a good chance of convincing him to pay the full amount to your company. I am sorry for your position, but hope that you will understand mine.

Mr Braun answered:

> I haven't thought about it this way and I like your argument. But my bosses view the issue the German way, which considers a contract a contract and each party is responsible to take care of potential risks itself. They say if you apply a contract according to the circumstances, and make adaptations whenever you think they are fair, what sense does it make to have a contract then, anyway?

After the call Mr Braun found that he felt even worse than before. His friend's explanation had given him a different view of the issue. Before that, he clearly thought that putting pressure on Tan & Tan to pay the outstanding amount was the right thing to do. Now he could understand the position of the Chinese. How could he please his bosses without upsetting Tan & Tan and especially without endangering his friendship to Mr Fu? What could he do?

Chapter 21
Pride And Prejudice*

*When a city person, a member of a close family and devout in his
religion, is transferred to the outback where culture pattern and religious
beliefs happen to be very different from his own, problems occur. Yet the
outsider may be important to the organisation. This case illustrates the
issue of culture shock and raises questions relating to foreign experts.*

Background

Intermedia Communications (Ghana) Ltd. is a Malaysian, Dutch
and Ghanaian joint venture company. The company is a result of
a Malaysian and Dutch global expansion to the West Africa
market. Its core business operation is a joint-venture into cellular
communication business in Accra, the capital city of Ghana.

The joint venture effort is fifty percent (50%) owned by the
Malaysian counterpart, while the remaining portion is owned
equally by the Dutch (25%) and the Ghanaian (25%) counterparts.
The company has a multicultural structure as is evident from the
different nationalities occupying the top management posts in
Ghana. The company appointed Ms Michele Lu, a Malaysian
Chinese, as the Chief Information Officer (CIO) to spearhead the
business operations in Ghana. Before her appointment as the new
CIO in Ghana, Ms Lu had been the Head of the Information
Technology (IT) department in the Kuala Lumpur office, while
Mr Philip Kroon, a Dutchman, was formerly the Business
Information System (BIS) manager stationed in Amsterdam,
Holland in charge of the Benelux operations in Europe. Mr Jabal

---

* This case was written by Wan Azhan Sahrizal Wan Hanafi & Shahrul Ariffin
Taufik, while graduate students in the Malaysian Graduate School of
Management at Universiti Putra Malaysia.

Buaben, a Ghanaian, was recruited locally. He previously had an experience of similar capacity in a telecommunication company in Accra. All three play key roles in the organisation:

- **Ms Michele Lu (Malaysian Chinese)** – Chief Information Officer (CIO), 35 years old, single, Malaysian-oriented culture.
- **Mr Philip Kroon (Dutch)** – Business Information System (BIS) Manager, 42 years old, divorcee, European oriented culture, flirtatious, easy going, egalitarian style of management and result-oriented.
- **Mr Jabal Buaben (Ghanaian)** – Technical & Operations Manager, 38 years old, married, devout Muslim from the Shiate sect (this sect is prominent in Iran), very frank, out-spoken and self-disciplined. Adopts an autocratic style of management, employee-oriented, and is extremely confrontational.

The incident

Ms Michele Lu, the Chief Information Officer (CIO) of Intermedia Communications (Ghana) Ltd. had assigned both Mr Jabal Buaben, the Technical & Operations Manager and Mr Philip Kroon, the Business Information System (BIS) Manager to lead a project on the installation of the new software system in the company's business set up in Accra, the capital city of Ghana. The problem started when Mr Kroon, a heavy drinker, could not accomplish the tasks on time and often came late to work. Mr Buaben, as a Muslim, could not stand the situation. He scolded Mr Kroon.

To make matters worse, Mr Kroon retaliated by bringing liquor to the office and consuming it during the breaks. The new software system was supposed to be ready for the trial run by 30 April, but due to the internal problems between Mr Buaben and his colleague, Mr Kroon, the project was three weeks overdue. Mr Buaben advised Mr Kroon on the urgency of the project but there was no response from him. Mr Buaben, who has been very patient with Mr Kroon's attitude towards the project, decided to see Ms Lu since he could not tolerate the situation any longer. The following conversation ensued inside Ms Lu's room:

Jabal Buaben:	Ms Lu, I would like to complain about Mr Kroon. He has been coming late to work recently. On top of that, he seemed to work individually instead of working together with me. There is certain information that he should disclose to me, but he has kept it to himself. Instead of giving full commitment towards the project, he tends to delegate the major task to his staff. Despite full delegation to his staff, I still could not proceed with certain tasks without Mr Kroon's approval. This is simply because he normally delays going through the reports and files.
Michele Lu:	What has he been up to?
Jabal Buaben:	He has not been doing his job constantly. Instead, he takes his job lightly. He usually comes around 10a.m., is always on the phone and goes away before 5p.m. I am not being prejudiced but I think people in the West are irresponsible and undisciplined.
Michele Lu:	Is he? But from my observation, he has been doing quite well in his job.
Jabal Buaben:	I don't think so, because all this while, I have been the one who has been doing all the job with some help from my staff.
Michele Lu:	All right then, I will investigate the matter thoroughly.

Mr Buaben left the room feeling satisfied with the hope that Ms Lu would look into the problem.

Inside the Meeting Room

It was Tuesday morning and the company was about to have its weekly divisional meeting. All the staff were present, including Ms Lu and Mr Buaben, except for Mr Kroon. The meeting was supposed to start at 9.15 a.m. Mr Buaben glanced at his watch which was showing 9.35 a.m. He then suggested to Ms Lu that she proceed with the meeting as there was no point in waiting for Mr Kroon. A minute later, Mr Kroon entered the meeting room, as usual very late.

Philip Kroon: Good morning everyone. I am sorry for being late, Michele, ooops, I mean Ms Lu, Mr Buaben.

Michele Lu: It is all right. Let us proceed with the meeting. Mr Kroon, what is the progress of your project? The trial run is three weeks behind schedule. Don't tell me that you have not been doing anything. I want your progress report on my table by tomorrow morning and no excuses!

Philip Kroon: Oh yes. I am still looking into it. Several issues need to be clarified.

Michele Lu: But I learned from Mr Buaben that he could not proceed without your approval on certain issues.

Philip Kroon: He should not wait for my approval in the first place. I have given full authority to my subordinates for them to make decisions on my behalf. This is how I work. This is how I developed the enterpreneurship skill among my staff.

Jabal Buaben: You as the manager are supposed to make the decisions and not your subordinates. If your subordinates make the wrong decisions, what is going to happen? We need to control and monitor the project through decision-making mechanism.

Michele Lu: This is an internal issue. Both of you need to resolve this management problem between yourselves. I am only concerned that the project can start on time. Another thing before I forget - a few departments have been complaining about the delay of the implementation of the trial run. Please pay serious attention to the matter.

The meeting ended at noon. As soon as the meeting was over, Mr Kroon rushed to see Ms Lu in her room. The following conversation ensued:

Inside Ms Loo's Room

Philip Kroon: (*in a flirting voice*) Hi honey! What was that all about in the meeting room just now? I thought you were too serious with me.

Michele Lu: I think I have to be professional here. Work is work. I do not mix our personal relationship in my work. I have to be fair to the others, too.

Philip Kroon: (*Still in a flirting mood*) Ok, forget about it. I think you are tired. Do you know that all work and no play is no fun, honey. Why don't we have a drink at my place tonight?

Michele Lu: I'm sorry, Philip. No, I can't. I have to finish up my review paper by this week for my presentation to the Management.

The next day Ms Lu went to see Mr Buaben to discuss some matters pertaining to the project.

Inside Mr Buaben's Room

Michele Lu: Mr Buaben, I need to discuss with you your proposal on the hardware appliances.

Jabal Buaben: Before that, Ms Lu, I have got something to tell you. I cannot stand it any more. Mr Kroon's erratic behaviour is getting worse. And I think you are not serious enough.

Michele Lu: Well, I have to be fair with him, too.

Jabal Buaben: I think that is your weakness. Leaders are expected to lead and direct their staff but you don't seem to comprehend my predicament. It seems that you are not a good leader. You see, in my country, a woman seldom becomes a leader. In fact in Holy Quran, it is mentioned that only man can become a leader and not a woman. I do not know why they have sent you here.

Michele Lu: Are you undermining me? Are you saying that I am not qualified? For your information, in Malaysia it is normal to have woman bosses. In fact there are also a few women who hold important ministerial posts in the Malaysian government.

Jabal Buaben: Frankly, before this, I have never had a lady boss. If you feel I'm undermining you, that is too bad.

Michele was speechless for a few seconds. She didn't expect that Mr Buaben would utter such words to her. Being a Malaysian, who is normally quite reserved and avoids confrontation, she continued the conversation:

Michele Lu: Excuse me, Mr Buaben, what are you saying?

Jabal Buaben: I guess it is too bad for you to work in Ghana.

Michele Lu: Not at all. By the way, do not think that since Mr Kroon is white, you may be prejudiced against him.

Jabal Buaben: I am not saying that I hate white people but I think about the way they have behaved since colonial days. Their mindsets have not really changed; they are still the same.

Michele Lu: Well, that is the past. My main concern now is the present time. I don't want to hear any more excuses; just work with Mr Kroon and finish up the project.

Michelle left the room feeling angry. She was annoyed by the sarcastic remarks made by Mr Buaben. She said to herself, " These Ghanaians are very rude, outspoken and insensitive towards other people's culture."

Inside the discussion room

On Friday morning, the unexpected thing happened. Mr Buaben was in the discussion room with Mr Kroon to discuss on the project.

Jabal Buaben: Mr Kroon, we have a deadline to meet. You'd better buck up or we won't meet the deadline.

Philip Kroon: What is that supposed to mean?

Jabal Buaben: (*in a stern voice*) You have not been co-operating with me in this project. You and your stinking liquor smell, coming late to work and going off early. With that kind of attitude, we will never be able to finish the project!

Philip Kroon: (*in an angry voice*) Who the hell do you think you are? You are not my boss and even Michele does not say those things to me.

Jabal Buaben: (*in an angry voice also*) Look here, since you are white, do not think that you can be arrogant and do anything you like without being sensitive to other people's feelings.

Philip Kroon: (*even more angry*) Hey, Buaben, don't try to act as if you are so smart. If it were not because for us, the so-called "white people", investing and bringing new technology to your country, I guess you would still be living in the jungle!

After that, both of them were caught up in a very heated argument and they started to fight each other.

What Happened Next?

Both of them were hospitalised. Mr Buaben suffered a few bruises on his forearms and broke his left arm while Mr Kroon had a swollen right eye and a broken right leg. Three weeks after the dreadful incident, Mr Buaben tendered his resignation. Was there anything Michelle – or any of the three of them – could have done to prevent the storm?

Chapter 22
Expat Blues*

Expat Blues is a true case study of a Malaysian executive in a foreign-transfer assignment to a South African multicultural organisation. The characters' names in the case are fictitious.

The purpose of this case study is to explore cross-cultural management issues in a foreign transfer. Many executives are simply thrown into a different culture to sink or swim in dealing with a new country and work environment. Smart transfers are the ones that have been masterminded and cultural clashes taken into account, even when the people concerned are transferred between English-speaking countries.

Benny Wong, a Malaysian-born senior executive, has been with Rj-Ap advertising agency in Kuala Lumpur, Malaysia since the agency began its operations 10 years ago. Rj-Ap is an Australian advertising agency based in Sydney and has operations in Asia Pacific and South Africa.

Benny Wong has worked very hard during these years and has been recognised with promotions for his effort and dedication. His last promotion was to the position of senior executive.

Rj-Ap's senior management in Sydney has been looking at whether the time was ripe to expand and establish their affiliated agency in Johannesburg, South Africa. After much consideration, they have decided to embark on a three-year plan to establish themselves as the leader in the advertising arena in South Africa and subsequently into other parts of Africa.

For the last six months, Benny Wong has been working closely with Sydney on all development aspects in view of global economy. He injects new ideas, plans them accordingly and

* This case was written by Leow Aik Peng & Ranjit Singh while students in the Malaysian graduate school of management.

implements them with the support of senior management and his subordinates. He is well known for coming up with creative plans, implementing them and making them work efficiently and effectively.

The top management has nominated Benny Wong for the South African job because of his reputable working history and rational management systems with the agency. He is a team player and believes in teamwork. He has also seen and learnt the way the agency grew.

Mr Charles Munro: Benny, I am not sure if you have already heard that we are trying to establish our affiliated agency in Johannesburg, South Africa.

Mr Benny Wong: Yes, I heard from Raja Usmani, our General Manager.

Mr Charles Munro: We think that you are the right person to execute the task because of your fine record and the fact that you have been with us since the beginning.

Mr Benny Wong: Thanks, I really appreciate it.

Mr Charles Munro: You will take up a new position as a management system expert. We have to look at the globalisation process based on efficiency and strength. Therefore, you will have to initiate the change process. You will work with the General Manager there, Bernard Kok, and your contract will be on expatriate terms.

Mr Benny Wong: I am not sure. I have never worked outside Malaysia and this is a foreign transfer dealing with a new country and work environment. We are an advertising agency, so at work our communication level is high.

Mr Charles Munro: Not to worry, like Malaysians they are also English-speaking and English is the language of business in South Africa. They are also a multicultural society. Anyway, I do understand your feelings.

| Mr Benny Wong: | I need some time to think over your offer. I just feel strange about that country. Anyway, thanks for giving me the offer. |

Benny Wong was in a turmoil and took 2 weeks to make his decision. He needed to talk to friends, working colleagues and to people who had worked in foreign countries. Almost everyone encouraged him to take up this foreign challenge and assured him that a Malaysian can easily adapt to a foreign country.

Benny Wong gave deep thought to the matter and told himself that South Africa is an English speaking and multicultural country, which could not be very different from Malaysia. The cultures would surely be similar. This opportunity would also enhance his career and help him financially.

So Benny Wong accepted the offer and off he went to Johannesburg. Upon arrival, he immediately checked into a hotel late that evening. On the first day at work he walked into the office, down a very long corridor where all the doors were closed. They showed him his room where he would work. He sat down in the room and was amazed that nobody introduced him or herself to him. The following day, his new General Manager, Mr Bernard Kok, formally took him around and introduced him to everybody.

Benny Wong was fast to notice the differences he faced in his work. There were two quite separate markets – the blacks and whites – with different shopping habits and extremes of wealth and poverty.

Benny Wong had to move house three times and was still not happy with his present living place. He began to realise that there are certain areas in Johannesburg where he could not live.

Benny Wong needed to speak to somebody and decided to make a phone call to Charles Munro in Sydney.

| Mr Benny Wong: | Hello, Charles. Life here is not exactly what I expected and finding a place to live is really difficult. Just in a month I have moved three times and I will be moving again for the fourth time. |

| Mr Charles Munro: | What is the problem? I don't understand. |

| Mr Benny Wong: | Each move was a total disaster. I'm just learning that I can't live in certain areas in Johannesburg. |

> The city and its conditions are very different from those in Malaysia. I am still struggling with my job and have yet to make headway.

Mr Charles Munro:	What about your work?
Mr Benny Wong:	I am still trying to settle down and getting to know office staff.
Mr Charles Munro:	You should quickly stop feeling like an alien.

Benny understood what Charles Munro was trying to tell him but the thought of looking again for some other place to live was already getting to him. Over the weekend Benny Wong could not find a place to settle down.

On Monday Benny Wong went to see his new General Manager, Bernard Kok.

Mr Benny Wong:	I can't find a suitable place to live. Can you help me?
Mr Bernard Kok:	No problem. I will take you to the suburbs and I am sure you will be able to find some place suitable to live in.

With Bernard Kok's help, Benny Wong did find a place and now he wanted to move forward in his work.

In no time though, Benny Wong was having hiccups in his job because he found that most of his colleagues had a different mindset from his, and that their thinking differed from one group to another. Most of the time non-whites had to assimilate with the culture of the whites to succeed. He could not move forward with his job simply because of the extreme diversity. There was no sense of belonging and the atmosphere was very formal with no free flow of information. The hierarchical structure was very marked and people did not seem to trust one another..

Benny Wong needed to inject a whole new spirit. Before change could be developed, a vision of assimilation would need to be accepted. Only then could the agency work in the way he planned. He wanted to tackle the attitudes, behaviour and values in the workplace.

Mr Benny Wong:	We need to change our management approach. I think that is the main problem and obstacle faced by the agency.
Mr Bernard Kok:	You must understand the history. We had our first all-race elections only in 1994, when apartheid was abolished. Since then we have been facing the challenge of managing the cultural diversity.
Mr Benny Wong:	Yes, I understand because I also come from an English-speaking and multicultural country. We should have similarities.
Mr Bernard Kok:	Listen, in South Africa, we know how to handle our problems our way. So far, my approach has been the best way.
Mr Benny Wong:	It appears to me that the organisation doesn't share the same vision and is confused in culture and ethnicity.
Mr Bernard Kok:	I do not know about your country but let me highlight to you what happens in South Africa. Over the years, separate ethnic development has led to a cultural patchwork rather than a melting pot. In our population of over forty millions, more than 75% are blacks, about 12% are whites, 9% coloured and 3% Indians. The diversity goes further; blacks are divided into 9 major ethnic groups with distinct communities, cultural practices and languages.

Benny Wong began to understand that Bernard Kok shared a vision of cultural diversity dominated by an ethnocentric approach, in which his way predominated. From that viewpoint, each group tends to attach positive traits to the in-group and negative traits to the out-groups. He also observed that the agency practised a more top-to-down information system and decisions are not really discussed.

Benny Wong was trying very hard to find creative solutions for integrating development and growth in the affiliated agency but no approach he made gave him more room to move. Benny

Wong knew that not only was corporate identity missing, but that creating one was difficult because of mental barriers.

The South African culture started to swallow Benny Wong very slowly, and the problems and obstacles he faced with the South African agency made him totally unable to function and carry out his job. The agency was led by the South African whites' dominant management style of individualism, hierarchy and authoritarianism. The white chief and the staff indirectly made Benny Wong believe that the changes he wanted to make were impossible in this South African country. He could not get their individual behaviour right because both whites and blacks have different styles of communication. Looking at time representations, he also observed that people in South Africa do not live in the same temporal world.

Benny Wong started to drown in the rainbow nation. He was emotionally upset because he had to function in the organisation and yet to bring about positive change.

The Expat Blues' tune eventually got to Benny Wong and after seven months in the South African assignment, he felt despair. The foreign transfer was a total failure and a disaster incurring high cost. Benny Wong had been simply thrown into a different culture to sink and he became history. The cultural diversity in the rainbow nation was not what he anticipated and he just could not deal with the new country and work environment. He underestimated what the cultural clashes and apparent similarities in the English speaking country meant. What should he do now? And also, what should Bernard Kok and Charles Munro do?

Chapter 23
Insya Allah*

A Malaysian Islamic asset management company is negotiating with a wealthy investor from Saudi Arabia to supply seed money for a fund whose main objective is to penetrate the Islamic international financial market. Although both parties are Islamic, other cultural factors seem likely to interfere with the transaction.

Dr Aisha paused. How was she to explain this to the Board of Directors? Their mission had not gone as she had expected. As the Chief Investment Officer of Capital Partners Sdn Bhd, it had fallen on her to explain to the Board why they had failed to secure the US$25 million investment from Shaykh Farhan ben Mahfouz for the Bushra Fund. She pondered on the events thus far.

Flashback

Capital Partners Sdn Bhd (CPSB), based in Kuala Lumpur, is an asset management company licensed under the Malaysian Securities Act. Its core activity is management of funds, including pension funds, corporate funds, family trusts and investments for high net worth individuals. CPSB invests these funds in accordance with Islamic or Shari'ah principles. When investments made are in equities, CPSB selects only stocks or shares approved by either of two bodies: the Shari'ah Committee of the Securities Commission of Malaysia for Malaysian equities and the Shari'ah Supervisory Board of the Dow Jones Islamic Market Index for international equities.

---

* This case was written by Mohd Badri Rozali & Norhayati Yusof, while graduate students in the Malaysian Graduate School of Management at Universiti Putra Malaysia.

Earlier in the year, the company had drawn up plans to set up a Malaysian Islamic fund called the Bushra Fund in Labuan. Their main objective was to promote Malaysian Shari'ah-based equities and penetrate the Islamic financial market abroad, in particular the Middle East. This was also in line with the Malaysian Government's efforts to promote Labuan as an Islamic Offshore Financial Centre.

The initial capital investment to set up the fund cost CPSB close to RM1million, excluding expenses associated with promoting and marketing the fund prior to the official launching scheduled for the end of April. To ensure the success of the fund, CPSB had targeted several potential investors, all institutional and individual investors from the Middle East countries, hoping they would provide half of the targeted seed fund amounting to US$50 million. Failure to convince these investors would certainly jeopardise the attractiveness of the fund within the Islamic investing circles and would render the fund less marketable.

Among the individuals CPSB had identified as potential investors, was a 72-year-old Saudi Arabian billionaire, Shaykh Farhan ben Mahfouz. His net worth, estimated at US$2billion, comprised an empire of trading companies and numerous investments in Saudi Arabia and abroad. Investments from him alone would enable CPSB to achieve their targeted fund base before the fund's launching. In person, the Shaykh was reputed to be a staunchly conservative and traditional man, his religious and cultural beliefs holding sway over his decisions. His nephew, Abdullah ben Mahfouz, who was an acquaintance of CPSB's Chief Executive Officer, Syed Alwi Al-Attas, had referred CPSB to him and had helped CPSB to arrange a meeting with Shaykh Farhan in Saudi Arabia.

The team from CPSB comprised Dr Aisha Johari, along with Syed Alwi Al-Attas and CPSB's Chief Operations Officer, Encik Ali Mahmud. Their trip to Saudi Arabia to meet Shaykh Farhan took place in early April, a month before the official launching of the fund.

Before the meeting, they were confident of securing the investment from Shaykh Farhan. They thought that he would be easily persuaded to part with his money. After all, his nephew recommended them and they were fellow Muslims – not to mention that they were also promoting Islamic-based investment products certified by the Shari'ah Committee of the Securities Commission of Malaysia. The amount they were asking was US$25 million, a drop in the ocean for Shaykh Farhan. How hard could it be to convince the Shaykh, given these factors? With this conviction, Dr. Aisha, Syed Alwi and Ali Mahmud flew off to Saudi Arabia to meet the Shaykh.

Preliminary Encounter

Shortly after the team from CPSB checked into their rooms at the Sheraton hotel in Jeddah, Syed Alwi received a call from Abdullah ben Mahfouz. After introductions and enquiries about their journey, Abdullah finally explained the objective of his calling. They were to have a short introductory meeting with Shaykh Farhan in the afternoon.

That afternoon, accompanied by Abdullah, the three of them went to meet Shaykh Farhan at his office. It was an awkward experience for Dr Aisha, the only woman in the entourage. Men, all garbed in their *"Thoub"*, staffed the office, even at the reception. There were no women around at all.

She preceded the men into Shaykh Farhan's office and greeted everyone, *"Assalamualaikum!"* *"Waalaikumussalam! Ahlan!"*

Shaykh Farhan bowed slightly. "How are you?" he asked.

Dr Aisha replied, *"Alhamdulillah,* thank you!" and extended her hand to Shaykh Farhan in greeting, much as she was used to doing with other potential business partners. Shaykh Farhan paused for a moment before reluctantly accepting her handshake. Only then did Syed Alwi and Ali Mahmud make themselves known to Shaykh Farhan.

"Tafaddal! Please have a seat," Shaykh Farhan gestured. They all sat down together.

"How was your flight?' he asked them.

They replied and soon found themselves engaged in small talk about their flight and about how they found Saudi Arabia, instead of getting straight into the preliminaries of the business at hand. Shaykh Farhan also seemed adept at juggling the meeting with other matters, signing documents and answering telephone calls in between, not seeming to devote much of his attention to them.

Their talk went on for an hour. Then, Shaykh Farhan stood up and said, "You will be my guests for dinner at my home tonight!"

Syed Alwi replied, "*Shukran*. We would be honoured to accept your invitation'.

Shaykh Farhan nodded, "*Insya Allah*, we will talk about business later". Dr Aisha, disappointed that they had not at least introduced their product and plans, made her way out with the men.

Dinner

That night after nightfall prayer, the three – Dr Aisha, Syed Alwi and Ali Mahmud – made their way to Shaykh Farhan's house. They were ushered in through the front door to be greeted by Shaykh Farhan. He introduced them to a few people gathered there, including some women whom he introduced as his wife and daughters, and the wives of his advisers.

"Come, let us proceed to the *Dewaniah!*" he said and led the way. Dr Aisha made her way with her colleagues. They followed Shaykh Farhan to a hall, apparently the "*Dewaniah*". There was a low table set in the middle of the hall surrounded by cushions laid on the floor and against the walls. Shaykh Farhan showed them to the head of the table. As Dr Aisha seated herself beside her colleagues, she looked around the table. She was surprised to find that the women had not joined them into the "*Dewaniah*", but she wisely kept silent.

Meanwhile Syed Alwi had started a conversation with Shaykh Farhan and Abdullah, regaling them with tales of the time when Syed Alwi and Abdullah were studying at Columbia University in New York together. Shaykh Farhan, listening to their conversation, added, "I, myself, went to Al-Azhar University in Egypt and completed my doctorate in Islamic Studies there. I am proud to say my two sons have followed my footsteps and graduated with doctorates as well. They are now working with me in our family businesses".

Dr Aisha interjected, "Oh! That is quite an achievement. What about your daughters?" Shaykh Farhan replied, "My two daughters, like their brothers, are also graduates of Harvard and Yale". Dr Aisha, seeming impervious to the Shaykh's discomfort, continued, "Then we are alumnae! I graduated from Harvard in 1985 and worked in Boston for about 5 years before coming back to Malaysia. What year did your daughters graduate and what do they do now?" Shaykh Farhan gave her an odd look before replying that his daughters did not work.

He then turned and joined the other men in their conversation. Throughout the meal there was no mention of business at all. "Maybe after dinner we can talk about business," Dr Aisha thought to herself. However, after the meal, the men relaxed against the cushions, smoking cigars and drinking Arabian coffee, the last of which she refused when served to her. "I guess it will have to wait until tomorrow!" she comforted herself.

Presentation

The next day, they arrived at Shaykh Farhan's office early in the morning. They were looking forward to this. Getting the Shaykh to invest could open a plethora of opportunities for them. They waited for Shaykh Farhan in the conference room. When he finally arrived, he came with a team of five other men whom he introduced as his senior executives and advisers. "Let's get down to business," he gestured to Syed Alwi. On this cue, Syed Alwi briefly introduced himself, Dr Aisha and Ali Mahmud as representatives of CPSB. He went on to give a brief profile of CPSB, then turned to Dr Aisha and asked her to begin the presentation. Dr Aisha began without haste.

"Good morning gentlemen. We are here to convince you to invest in the Bushra Fund," she started. Shaykh Farhan and his men looked in surprise at her. Dr Aisha delved right into the subject matter and talked continuously for 15 minutes. "Any questions?" she asked, looking around the table. Since no one responded, she assumed neither Shaykh Farhan nor his men had any questions to ask.

So she continued with her speech, occasionally referring to Syed Alwi or Ali Mahmud for clarification. When she came to the end of her speech, she looked around. Shaykh Farhan was nodding his head, and she took it to mean that he approved of their proposal. She asked again, "Any questions?"

Shaykh Farhan turned to his advisers and asked them for their comments. They engaged in a discussion of the merits of the proposal. Just as Dr Aisha thought she had managed to convince Shaykh Farhan, one of his advisers asked a question.

Adviser:	Dr Aisha, are the stocks you invest in approved by the Shari'ah Supervisory Board of the Dow Jones Islamic Market Index?
Dr Aisha:	Actually, none of the Malaysian equities are. However, they are recognised by the Shari'ah Committee of the Securities Commission of Malaysia.
Shaykh Farhan:	Who then sits on this committee?
Dr Aisha:	The committee members are all Islamic scholars. They are local and are among the most reputable scholars in Malaysia.

Shaykh Farhan nodded and asked again, "What are the expected returns on this investment?" By this time, Dr Aisha was losing patience. "At this point we cannot say exactly how much is the expected return, can we? If I could predict that, then you wouldn't need a fund manager." Shaykh Farhan kept silent, nodding his head. He thanked them for their presentation. Syed Alwi then stood up and exchanged gifts with Shaykh Farhan. Syed Alwi, being American influenced, immediately opened the gift. Shaykh Farhan looked on in silence. When Syed Alwi later pressed for a commitment, all Shaykh Farhan would reply was, "*Insya Allah*, we will do business together".

Dr Aisha wondered, "Now is that a yes or no?"

Chapter 24
Resignations*

Communication difficulties between expatriate managers and local departmental heads can be extremely serious when promotion for expert staff is the issue. When the result is a series of resignations of key staff, something must be done.

Trouble!

The Electronic Data Processing (EDP) manager, Mr Chin, opened a familiar envelope. The one page document is the standard resignation letter. "Dear Mr Chin, . . . regret to inform . . . resign with effect from . . .". Why another person? The letter was from the assistant manager, who had 4 years of service with the company and a total of 10 years in the industry. This letter would be the fourth in the last 6 months.

The EDP manager immediately went to report to the manager of the whole department. The latter, a Japanese man, 34 years old, had arrived to start his service in the company only 9 months before. *"Maitta-nah! Muzukashii desu ne!** he exclaimed.

Company background

HoseeCan Component Precision (HCP) is the pioneer in the Shah Alam Industrial Estate with 20 years experience in the business.

---

* This case was written by Tan Kok Chin, while a graduate student in the Malaysian Graduate School of Management at Universiti Putra Malaysia.
* Translation: Oh boy, this really beats me! It's just too difficult.

The shareholders consist of the HoseeCan Group of companies holding 70% equity and a local company owning the remaining 30%. The HCP company produces components for the finished product: the computer monitor, videocassette recorder and air-conditioner controller board. The components are the deflection yoke, fly-back transformer, printed wired board and the tuner. The turnover in sales amounts to about RM30 million per month and the quantity, about 1.3 million pieces in total. The workforce consists of around 1,100 locals and 12 Japanese expatriates. The land size of the factory is about 64,000-sq. m. and the building area is 26,000-sq. m.

Problem identification

The section is Electronic Data Processing (EDP), a rather old name in the industry. The EDP section is under the Finance Department. The Finance Department is located on the ground floor, front office. The EDP section is on the first floor, just beyond the factory floor.

EDP section is responsible for the computerisation activities of HCP. This section proposes the budgeting of hardware, software and application system. Recommending new technology and conducting feasibility studies are also its functions. It maintains the network and ensures that system failures are kept to a minimum.

The company has a structured remuneration scheme. The scheme has entry levels requirements and some consideration for higher salaries if the employees have relevant experience. Salary increments are based on performance, seniority and the allocated quota assigned to the section. Some rare and special exceptions do occur.

The number of staff in EDP is currently 10 persons out of a full force of 12. There has not been an increase in the number of staff for the last 3 years. In the previous 6 months there were 4 resignations. The section comprises one manager, two assistant managers, five executives and four assistant officers.

The section implemented a large-scale company-wide computerisation project within the company in 1998 and started the live run from January 1999. During 1999, the section monitored the project and solved problems that were brought to

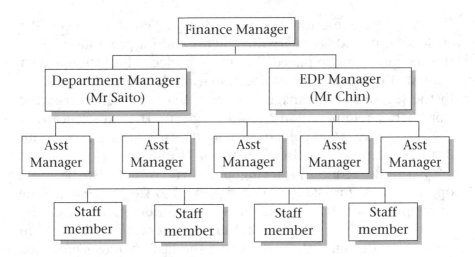

their attention. The end users had many complaints about the software being unfriendly. Conversely, the EDP people had many complaints about the end users not following instructions given to them.

The department manager rarely comes to the EDP section and the EDP manager does not report regularly to the department manager. The department manager takes care of the Finance section with the help of another manager.

The EDP manager, a family man with three children, has been with the company for 9.5 years and had only one promotion. He is pursuing his MBA, financing it himself, and is in his last semester. The company does not provide financial support nor give any study leave. The manager is expected to take care of all matters, yet his request for additional allocation of staff for the section has been rejected several times.

The proposal for faster promotion for outstanding staff in EDP has also been turned down. The management stated that if the structured remuneration scheme is not followed, other sections would be dissatisfied. The EDP section is treated like any other section, but the skills of EDP members are difficult to replace. Employees are expected to work long term, with On-the-Job-Training (OJT).

Within the company, when an employee resigns from the current employment to seek other job employment, he or she is considered disloyal. This loyalty question does not arise in Japan, where the culture is for lifetime employment, although this is changing now.

About eight months before, in June 1999, it had been the evaluation period for salary increments and for promotion. Since the section had completed the major project, the EDP manager requested consideration of additional merit awards for the staff in the section. The manager proposed that in order to keep the staff, better remuneration should be given. The experience that the staff have would enable them to earn a salary of about RM 1,500–2,000 more elsewhere in the IT industry.

With the economy picking up, there would also be more opportunities for skilled workers in the IT profession. The development of the Multimedia Super Corridor (MSC), close by posed a threat by offering better remuneration packages. In order to understand the staff better, the EDP manager proposed that the department manager attend fortnightly meetings with them. The department manager should learn first hand what the staff were asking for.

The department manager agreed and did attend some meetings but gradually his attendance was noted to be declining. Finally, he stopped attending and so the fortnightly meetings were no longer held.

In August, the first resignation from one of the two assistant managers was received. She had 8 years of service with the company but was leaving to join a consulting firm. The number of staff then was 11 persons. She had led three staff in the application area. With this loss, the members of the section would have to depend on each other until a replacement was found.

Less than 2 months later, another resignation was received. This was from one of the network specialists. He had three and a half years of service with the company. With this loss, only one person remained to handle the technical aspect of the network set-up. Then he also joined a consulting firm.

The recruitment exercise began but finding suitable candidates proved very taxing and without results in terms of time spent. There were many fresh candidates, but all needed basic training. Sifting the applications and interviewing the candidates were long, tiring processes. The candidates with experience, especially from the consulting firms, were asking about the same as the manager's salary.

In December, one experienced person was recruited. This was sheer luck; the new staff member joined up to avoid having to travel to her head office in Johor Bahru for assignments. By this time, the management had agreed to extend the head count by another three persons.

Critical Incident

Just before the year ended, the least expected person to resign tendered her resignation. This most hardworking employee, being the first to be at the office and the last to leave on most days, stated that she wanted to gain more experience. She was graded highly even though this was her first job. She managed the most difficult module, that is the production planning application. She left to become a consultant, a position that commanded double her current salary.

During the exit interview in the presence of Human Resource Manager, Mr Chin talked to the resigning staff member. "I cannot understand why you need to leave the company", he said. "We have many interesting projects being lined up for implementation. There's going to be development in the e-commerce area . . ."

The staff member, Miss Rani, explained, "This is my first job, I need to have more exposure. I have this opportunity to work with the consulting company. "If I don't leave, I will not get the exposure."

Mr Chin tried again: "Exactly what I said, we have many projects to be implemented, there will be lots of exposure . . ."

Eventually a technical person was employed and the head count stabilised with the transfer of a manager to strengthen the section. The transferred manager had been with the company for 16 years, but in the Sales Department. She was new to the IT industry. But just as these two appointments were made, Mr Chin received the fourth letter.

RESIGNATION NOTIFICATION

> **A** I wish to cease employment with the company and hereby
> tender my resignation giving _____ days/weeks notice
> according to my existing terms and conditions of employment.

My last day of service with the company is planned to be on
_____. I do hereby agree to have an interview with my
superiors and Personnel Section.

> I will return all items belonging to the company.
>
> _____   _____
>   SIGNATURE   DATE

> **B. Full Name:** _____ **E/No.:** _____
>
> **Date Joined:** _____ **Section :** _____
>
> **Job Title:** _____
>
> **Effective Date of Resign :** _____(Service year: _____)
>
> **Address (After resignation):** _____
>
> _____

EXIT Interview by Dept/Section	Personnel Section	
REASONS/CAUSE OF RESIGNATION:	Check list	Outstanding Settlement
☐ Personal/ Unavoidable	☐ Shoes	_____ _____
☐ Job Satisfaction	☐ Uniform	Business Trip _____
☐ Supervisor's Conflict	☐ Co. Handbook	SRT Notice _____
☐ Salary	☐ ID Card	PKNS Rental _____
☐ Others	☐ Others _____ _____ _____	(Include electric/water bill) Others _____

COMMENTS		Note:
_____	_____	The last salary
_____	_____	will be released
_____	_____	upon full
_____	_____	settlement of
		the above

What is Mr Chin to do? Is the resignation trend likely to continue? Is it his concern or the Finance Manager's? And how do the Japanese view the resignations? What needs to be done at once and for the long term? How can communication channels be improved so that senior management understand the resignation problem?

Chapter 25
Va bene:
A Japanese spy in Italy*

Relying on supplies from another country can be fraught with trouble. In this case, the warm, demonstrative and friendly Italians are seen as hostile by a young Singaporean instructed to keep an eye on what is happening in another country and culture. Resentment and suspicion on both sides seem to grow, but perhaps there is no way round having a representative on the spot when the supplies are indispensable.

Background

Jeff was working for a Japanese Contractor, OZUMI, on a large hotel project contracted to GEAMI, a large supplier from Italy.

Due to delay in materials delivery by GEAMI, it seemed unlikely that the project would be completed in time. This would result in financial loss by OZUMI as well as damage the company's reputation. There was extensive use of marble for the project. Without marble, it would be impossible to complete the hotel. The marble supply and delivery had been a constant problem.

OZUMI decided to send Jeff to GEAMI's production facility in Italy to monitor production and to send information back to Singapore on the actual situation.

* This case was written by Raymond Chung while a student in the Malaysian Graduate School of Management at Universiti Putra Malaysia..

THE PLAYERS:

Jeff   Singaporean Chinese in his late 20s; Australian-trained engineer who had just joined OZUMI after having lived in Australia for the previous 11 years. For all intent and purposes considered as a Japanese by the Italians.

Hano   Jeff's boss; Japanese in his late 30s; Project Manager of OZUMI

Paolo   Italian in his early 30s; US-trained architect; Managing Director of GEAMI

May, 2000; Tuscany, Italy

Jeff, after four weeks of close association with the workers and management at GEAMI is seething with anger because he feels out of his depth, unable to do anything to help his company. He is mentally going over and over his situation as he sees it.

> The Italians are a bunch of hypocrites, every single one of them! Why, only this morning, just about every one of them greeted me with *Bon Giorno** Most of them followed that with the standard *va bene*.

Jeff continued thinking to himself:

> These guys have the cheek and temerity to still ask if things are fine, when all the time they know too well that nothing is proceeding according to schedule. Procurement of raw materials is late. So are production, packing, shipping, everything! And yet, nobody's making much effort to rectify the situation. I really feel like screaming *"NO! No va bene!"* back at them so far but have stopped myself. After all, what would it achieve? They would have just smiled and said *Va bene!* Or perhaps they are mocking me?

> In addition, I reckon they're lazy workers. They're slow and do not follow the required schedules. They work only from 8 am to

---

* *Bon Giorno* is literally 'Good Morning'); *Va bene* is loosely translated as 'How's it going?' It can be used as an expression that all is well with oneself. It can also be used to enquire about someone else's well being

5 pm, Mondays to Fridays. Overtime? You've got to be kidding! And as for the long siesta at lunchtime, when it seems the whole country shuts down for a 2-hour snooze! Goodness, don't they know that this is the year 2000? Don't they know that we must finish our project on time?

It had all started one morning a month ago, at OZUMI's Project Office in Singapore.

April 2000, OZUMI Project Office, Singapore . . .

Jeff: Good Morning, Hano-san. How are you today?

Hano: Horrible!

Jeff: Why? Is there a problem?

Hano: There's a very big problem. As you know, we can't finish this project if GEAMI's materials do not arrive on schedule. And they're already running behind the agreed contractual deadlines. Worse still, I cannot get sufficient information from GEAMI.

Jeff: So?

Hano: I'm going to Italy tomorrow evening. I want to find out the true situation at the factory. If we don't know what is going on, we can't plan our site schedule. Our project will end up as a disaster. The Italians are so blasted slow. They are also dishonest and do not respect agreements. They are supposed to send us a detailed report every week, but all we get is a one-page summary which says that everything is on schedule! Yet their schedule changes every day.

Jeff: And?

Hano: I want you to accompany me. You must go and stay in Italy and keep us informed of what really is going on over there. Can you get ready please?

Jeff's first week at GEAMI went very well. The Italians were very gracious and generous hosts. He was shown round the office and production facilities. Paolo promised Hano that they would do everything in their capacity to ensure that OZUMI's project would be completed on time. GEAMI would henceforth adhere to the required schedule, as well as send regular, updated and detailed progress reports. In addition, Jeff was most welcome at GEAMI, and was free to check on all production records.

Having shown Jeff the ropes and secured an understanding from the Italians, Hano left for Singapore, and Jeff settled down to the real work. Almost immediately, the problems started.

Each request for documents and records met with a promise of quick action. However, Jeff had to wait days before he received the documents, if they ever came. More often than not, by then, due to the fast moving situation, the documents would already be outdated.

The Italians also treated him with suspicion and kept things from him. He did not greet them when he came in, and glowered at them when they tried to greet them in a friendly way. To them, he was as good as a Japanese spy. No amount of explanation could convince them that he was really Singaporean, on an assignment to help his project, that he owed no loyalty to Japan. They were reluctant to talk to him, other than exchanges of pleasantries. Even these seemed to Jeff to be rather contrived and forced. There were occasions when he was denied access to certain areas but there would always be an excuse. "Hazardous chemicals are being used, the area is off-limits" was a favourite explanation.

Language was a problem too, but again, Jeff detected that this was being used as an excuse for non-co-operation. After all, most of the technical matters did not require much verbal communication. Often, a simple yes, no, OK and dates of shipment would have sufficed. As for Jeff's explanation that OZUMI was building a landmark project within 3 years, the Italians retorted that Rome was not built in a day. Things take time and by their reasoning, delays were more than acceptable.

Jeff's problems were not just confined to Italy. He had to make daily reports back to Hano in Singapore. Due to the 7-hour time difference between Italy and Singapore, this meant that often he had to work according to the dictates of two time zones. Worse still, he often did not have the information required and demanded by Hano simply because GEAMI didn't give it to him.

He tried to gain Hano's understanding of the problems he was facing; the lack of co-operation from GEAMI, the lack of progress of production; in short, total indifference to OZUMI's requirements, in spite of their earlier promises. However, try as he might, he sensed a certain reluctance on the part of Hano to believe him. This was understandable, seeing that Paolo had promised Hano full co-operation while Hano was in Italy.

Paranoia set in. What if, thought Jeff, Hano really believed the Italians more than he believed Jeff? Perhaps Hano suspected that Jeff was just taking advantage of the situation, having a holiday in Italy rather than doing his job? Maybe this was the story that Paolo was giving to Hano.

Well, I suppose I'll just try my best and do all I can, thought Jeff, as he proceeded to yet another of those fruitless production meetings with Paolo.

May, 2000; at Paolo's office, GEAMI

As usual, the meeting with Paolo had been difficult. Despite being a month behind schedule, Paolo still maintained that they could meet the deadlines. Jeff had wanted the latest detailed shipping and production information, but as usual, information was not forthcoming. Jeff had expected this. However, what happened next was unexpected, and greatly confused him.

Paolo: I talk to your boss, Hano, at least once a week. He understands the situation. He knows what is happening here, and he's happy with it. There's no problem. What are you doing here? Why are you still here?

"Indeed. What am I doing here? Okay," thought Jeff, "I know what to do. I will call Hano tomorrow morning and tell him that I will go back immediately. After all, since he has the situation under control, there is no longer any need for me to be still here."

The next morning, Jeff arrived at work at GEAMI to be greeted by the usual *Bon Giornos* and *va benes*. He ignored everybody and went straight to the little room that he was using as an office. He rang the Singapore Office and spoke to Hano . . .

Jeff: Since I'm no longer needed here, I'll make arrangements to go back to Singapore this Friday. In any case, I was supposed to be here for only four weeks, and this is already my fifth week here.

Hano: What are you talking about? Are they giving you problems again?

Confusion reigned in Jeff's mind. Them giving me problems! Or perhaps you Japanese are the ones giving me problems, if Paolo is to be believed? If you already have the situation under control, why do you still want me to be here? Is it because once again, you Japanese do not trust anybody but want 2 pairs of eyes to be looking at any one thing? Who should I trust, the Japanese or the Italians? Of course, the Japanese pay me and I work for them. I have a duty and obligation to them. On the other hand, I owe no allegiance to the Italians. But then again, am I not but a pawn caught in between two fighting giants? What shall I do?

Jeff: Everyone is giving me problems.

Hano: I don't understand. Can you please explain to me what has been happening?

Jeff: But surely, you know everything that is happening here? Paolo told me you speak to him regularly. Since that's the case, there is no longer any need for me to be here.

Hano: You should know better than to believe Paolo. The last time I spoke with him was a few weeks ago. I can never get him and he never returns my calls. Jeff, if the company did not need you to be there, I would have asked you to return. So obviously, your presence at GEAMI is still very important for us. It is the only way we can know what really is happening. GEAMI never gives us a full or true picture. I'm sorry, but you cannot come back yet. As a matter of fact, I want you to stay at least another month. We cannot trust the Italians.

But for Jeff it was not a matter of trust. The Italians worked in their own way and he had discovered that he could not change that. What did his employers want of him? "One more month of this dreadful business!" thought Jeff. "I'll be very surprised if I survive this madness, never mind the project. Perhaps I should have stayed in Australia. What on earth can I do here?"

Chapter 26
The Cost Of Cultural Values*

This case involves a telecommunications company, a joint venture between the Malawi government and a Danish company. In Europe, funerals are a family's concern. In parts of Africa, it is a time-honoured custom for the employers to pays such costs as transporting a body, especially when the worksite is far from the worker's home. Written contracts cover such issues but workers seldom see or understand those contracts. An impasse develops when the company decides it cannot afford to transport dead members of workers' families, and the families cannot do it either. How can the situation be resolved?

The telecommunication industry in emerging markets has been transformed from a collection of mostly state-owned national companies to one with many privately owned multinational corporations.

Blantyre Telecomm is a state-owned company employing 3000 people in April 2000. This number excludes those engaged on Telecomm 2 Project. It is a major provider of telecommunication services in Malawi. The Malawi government intends to privatise the company through a joint venture with one of the Danish Multinational Telecomm firms. In readiness for the privatisation, which is aimed at enhancing the efficiency and effectiveness of the company, the governments of Malawi and Denmark engaged the services of Andersen Management International. The latter is an international consulting firm with experts in telecommunication networking.

The governments of Malawi and Denmark agreed to undertake the multimillion USD project on a counterpart-funding basis with

* This case was written by Laston Mahere, while a graduate student in the Malaysian Graduate School of Management at Universiti Putra Malaysia..

Denmark agreeing to provide the technical expertise and necessary equipment such as underground cables, and movable plants. Malawi agreed to provide manpower at various levels, and maintain the movable plants. The project was intended to expand the new network and rehabilitate the old one.

In December 1997, Mr Mart Bjerke was sent to Malawi by Andersen Management to work hand in hand with his Malawian counterparts to get the ambitious project started. Mr Bjerke is a Finnish national and so western in culture. The project team comprised nine Malawians (7 technical experts, 1 finance executive,1 human resource executive) and the consultant, Mr Bjerke. The Director of Networks in the Blantyre Telecomm headed the project and Mr Bjerke was appointed deputy.

Meetings

Meetings during this stage were conducted with project team members and heads of departments. The meetings were cordial with the usual refreshments of coffee or tea and biscuits.

Such meetings tended to be longer than equivalent western meetings but a better consensus of opinion was formed. Decision by consensus stems from the Malawian intent to ensure harmony and lack of conflict between all parties.

Implementation

The project took off in July 1998. It was labour intensive, and therefore 500 unskilled men were hired on a temporary basis. By virtue of their terms of employment, the men were not entitled to any of the fringe benefits (medical insurance, pension scheme, transport upon death of family member) applicable to permanent staff. Those supervising the 500 were permanent staff of the company seconded to the project. The actual project was, therefore, composed of two categories of employees: permanent and casual. This was the potential source of problem for the human resource executive and in turn, a puzzle to Mr Bjerke, and the consultant. Why?

In Malawi, it is a general practice that when a member of staff loses a member of the immediate family, the organisation provides transport to the home of the deceased. This is contained in the company's conditions of service or catechism. To the extent that funerals are sensitive, provision of transport is automatic and not negotiable. The human resources division is responsible for this function and knows who is eligible for what. The trend is gradually changing as organisations find it increasingly prohibitive in terms of costs.

For this project, only the supervisors qualified for the transport benefit by virtue of their positions in the company. Despite their contractual agreement they had voluntarily signed, the temporary workers expected the same treatment as their supervisors when it came to funerals. One could understand their lack of understanding of the contract. Most of them had gone up to primary school level only. Their minimal wage of US$3.00 per day was a cause for sympathy. Many were recruited at the request of their relations working for the company.

These, among other factors, prompted the human resource executive to informally relax Article 3 of their terms of contract. The article forbids provision of benefit of any kind. Consequently, transport was provided upon loss of a wife or child. Gradually, this became a norm among the 500 in the workforce. Those not married decided to abuse the facility by registering mothers as wives and siblings as children. The demand for transport to ferry mourners and corpses sharply rose to pathological levels as deaths occurred twice or thrice a week. Work could not be completed according to schedule as the utility vehicles, say 2 in a day, were sent out for funerals some as far as 400km from the workstation.

The human resources division decided to arrest the situation. Meanwhile Mr Bjerke has information that work was not progressing according to schedule. He went red with anger and quickly summoned the human resource executive to his office.

Mr Cyril: Good morning, Sir.

Mr Bjerke: Please sit down. Will you explain why men cannot go to work?

Mr Cyril: Certainly. Two of them have lost a wife and sister respectively. Two vehicles have been withdrawn to convey the deceased to their respective homes.

Mr Bjerke: Incredible! Where on earth does that happen? Is this the practice?

Mr Cyril: Yes indeed.

Mr Bjerke: Yes indeed. What do you mean? What has that to do with the organisation, let alone the project? Isn't that a responsibility of the concerned employee? Do you realise I can withdraw all the vehicles?

Mr Cyril: We have assisted others in a similar situation before and therefore a precedent was set.

Mr Bjerke: That's not my baby. I am here to ensure that work proceeds as planned. Please put a stop to this practice instantly.

Mr Cyril sought an audience with the Regional Telecom Manager, Mr Payesa, who is also the Project Manager.

Mr Cyril: I have come to brief you on the transport situation regarding the temporary employees and as directed by Mr Mart.

Mr Ekari: What is wrong with transport and what about the directive?

Mr Cyril: Since the transport benefit was extended to the temporary employees, particularly in times of death of the immediate members of their family, the demand has steadily risen. Three times a week, utility vehicles are withdrawn from the field, in order to service funerals. This has adversely affected productivity and Mr Bjerke is cross. Only this morning, he called me to his office and scolded me. He has further instructed my officers never to provide transport during funerals.

Mr Ekari: Who drew up the contract for the 500 and who approved it?

Mr Cyril: HRM Division drew it up and the project management team approved it.

Mr Ekari: Who gave authority to have the terms of contract relaxed?

Mr Cyril: I relaxed the terms because of the men's meagre pay to afford transport costs in the extended family system, and because of their little appreciation of the contract.

Mr Ekari: That sounds reasonable but crude. Was it not proper for you to consult fellow members before relaxing whatever rule? Is it because you are the architect of the contract document, and therefore you think other members should be rubber-stamping your ill-organised ideas? What do you want me to do now?

Mr Cyril: My apology, Sir. I came to consult you as to how the situation can be brought under control.

Mr Ekari: Mr Cyril, it is premature for me to accept your apology because I am not the committee. You will have to apologise to the committee. Secondly, as a human resource specialist, you should have known the problems your decision would create. Remember, this is Africa and not Europe.

Mr Cyril: Sorry, Sir, I never thought about it.

Mr Ekari: Please do as Mr Bjerke has instructed and call for an extra-ordinary meeting of the project team, to be held on 16 June in the conference room.

Mr Cyril quickly went back to his office and sent notices of the meeting to all project members. The notice was as follows:

REGIONAL TELECOMM HEADQUARTERS
P.O. BOX 1253, BLANTYRE

TO: All Project Team Members
FROM: Regional Telecomm Manager & Project Manager

NOTICE OF THE EXTRA-ORDINARY MEETING

Please take note that there will be an extra-ordinary meeting on Friday 16 June in the Conference Room at Telecomm Headquarters at 10:00 am.

The agenda will be distributed in the meeting. Kindly avail yourself of this important meeting.

Yours faithfully,
L.Cyril
For: **Convener/Project Manager.**

Mr Ekari, the Regional Telecomm Manager/Project manager chaired the meeting. He welcomed all members present and called the meeting to order at 10:10am.

CHAIRMAN: The purpose of this meeting is to discuss the transport situation in times of death of family members of the temporary workers engaged on Telecomm 2 Project. You will recall that the terms of employment for the 500, approved by this august gathering, excluded them from the list of beneficiaries of fringe benefits provided by the company.

However, and at the convenience of the human resource executive, the transport benefit was informally extended to the men. This has created a problem that our HRM Division is struggling to correct. There is nothing wrong in assisting somebody in times of sorrow provided the interests of other stakeholders are considered. The case before us disregarded other players, which is why we are here to resolve this impasse once and for all. But before members are invited to comment on the issue, I would like to request the architect of the said terms of conditions, Mr Cyril, to brief members on what has happened.

MR CYRIL: Mr Chairman and fellow members. Indeed I relaxed item 3 of the terms of conditions of the 500 men. I proceeded to extend transport benefit to the men in times of death of the immediate members of their families. Their meagre pay that certainly makes it impossible for them to afford transport costs to their respective homes motivated me. Consideration was also given to the African tradition that highly respects the dead, and to the extended family system that places responsibility on an individual. I abjectly apologise for having not consulted the authorities and the rest of the respectable members. Please accept my apology.

Some members expressed their disappointment and annoyance over the manner in which the HRM executive had conducted himself. Others threatened to pull out of the team. While members supported the idea of being humane, they accused the HRM executive of treating them as a rubberstamp to his views. They further blamed him for disrupting the fieldwork.

Mr Bjerke, the consultant, questioned the use of utility vehicles for funerals. He said that this is not the practice in the western world. "The question of extended families does not arise", Mr Bjerke continued. "People must respect the terms of contract irrespective of the level of education." He argued that ignorance of the law is no excuse. With regard to low pay, Mr Bjerke said that it was voluntary and the men were at liberty to take the job or leave it. The reasons advanced by the HRM executive were, in Mr Bjerke's strongest opinion, flawed and anti-business. He therefore, with the support of two members, called for the withdrawal of the facility.

At this point, the Chairman rose to a point of order.

MR CHAIRMAN: I strongly share your concerns about the disruptions in operations. However, I would like to draw your attention to the fact that it is a tradition in Africa to give a dignified burial to the dead. Our society is characterised by the extended family ties and places enormous responsibilities on those who are financially capable to help those who are weak. It is, therefore, not surprising to see officers taking leave to bury the dead. In saying so, I am not condoning abuse of transport, and we shall not sit on the fence to watch the situation deteriorating.

After a protracted debate on the issue, members resolved that the HRM executive should allocate transport only on recommendation from the respective supervisors. The facility should be limited to members of the immediate family declared by the employee. Any member of the team who violates the set norm will have to bear the transport charges computed at the commercial rate. The committee requested the HRM executive to prepare the memo quickly, informing the 500 men of the decision.

There being no other business, the chairman dismissed the meeting. He thanked members for their contributions and active participation.

Here is the memo that was sent out.

MEMORANDUM

REGIONAL TELECOMM HEADQUARTERS
P.O. BOX 1253, BLANTYRE

FROM: Human Resource Executive
TO: Supervisors, Telecomm 2 Project
CC: DIRECTOR, NETWORK & HEAD TELECOMM 2 PROJECT
         REGIONAL TELECOMM MANAGER & PROJECT
         MANAGER TELECOM.2 CONSULTANT, ANDERSEN
         MANAGEMENT & DEPUTY HEAD, TELEC.2

SUBJECT: TRANSPORT DURING FUNERALS

At its extra-ordinary meeting held on Friday, 16 June 1999, Telecomm 2 Project Management Team directed that transport for funerals would be limited only to members of the nucleus family. We cannot afford to go beyond this as doing so overstretches our most limited resources.

It is the responsibility of every supervisor under Telecomm 2 Project, to recommend transport assistance for only those genuine cases. Otherwise all efforts to curb abuses will be fruitless.

Supervisors are requested to bring the contents of this memo to the notice of their respective groups. The groups should also be notified that continued abuse of the facility would leave management with no option but to completely withdraw it.

We hope that you will cooperate for the good of the welfare of all and for the success of the project.

The authorities reading us in copy are requested to note.

L.Cyril
HUMAN RESOURCE EXECUTIVE

Meanwhile, one of the men lost his brother. He proceeded to HRM Division for transport. He was ushered into Mr Cyril's office by the human resource officer.

HRM Officer:	Excuse me sir; I have Mr Olhaviwa who has lost a brother. He is looking for transport.
Mr Cyril:	I am sorry, Mr Olhaviwa, for what has happened. The company cannot help you. You would better find your own means. Your group abused the facility.
Mr Olhaviwa:	Sobs strongly. I have never taken advantage of this facility and this is the first time I have ever asked for help. Please be considerate.
Mr Cyril:	I cannot help. Perhaps you should go and see your supervisor.

Mr Olhaviwa went to the supervisor, Mr Chipiliro, and entered the office while wiping out tears.

Mr Olhaviwa:	I have lost a brother and I need transport to take him home. The HRM executive says he cannot help and has instead directed me to you.
Mr Chipiliro:	*Phones Mr Cyril*: Why can't your officers assist the man?
Mr Cyril:	Because it is a brother.
Mr Chipiliro:	The brother stays with him and he is part of the immediate family.
Mr Cyril:	I feel sorry for him. Remember the resolution at the extraordinary meeting.
Mr Chipiliro:	Have you already done the memo?
Mr Cyril:	Why?
Mr Chipiliro:	Because if that has not been done yet, then you could invoke the informal rule set by your division in which case the man qualifies.
Mr Cyril:	You have missed the point of the resolution. The latter came into force straight after the meeting and the memo is only to formalise it. This is reflected in the minutes and the absence of the memo does not in anyway invalidate it. Please try to come up with something acceptable.

Chapter 27
Love Letters*

Here, to end this section, is a brief case on food. "Love letters" is the name given to small rolled sponge cakes in Malaysia.

It is Christmas time again. After Christmas comes Hari Raya – this year. After Hari Raya comes New Year and after New Year, comes Chinese New Year. In our company we celebrate them all. This year, like any other year, we have been making *kuih kabit* or small rolled sponge cakes called love letters, and I will be taking a large plate piled high with them for the office to share. They are a delicacy made of flour, sugar and coconut milk. This year, as I piled the plate high, it reminded me of an incident which occurred a few years back. We were in the process of making love letters, watched closely by a colleague from work who was staying the night for our New Year party, since her own home was so far away.

Mary: So you're taking those into work again?

Eugene: Yes. They all seem to go whenever I do.

Mary: You know, last time, straight after you put them out, Fauziah said to me *"Bagi satu"* (Give me one) and then Mimi followed her saying, *"Saya pun nak"* (I want one too.) How come?

Eugene: So? What's wrong? They're put there to eat.

Mary: But they're both Malays, Muslims to be exact. My Malay neighbours never eat anything that other races cook. And those two actually asked for the little morsels!

---

* This case was written by Eugene Tee, while a graduate student in the Malaysian Graduate School of Management at Universiti Putra Malaysia.

May Lim: (*who had been listening at the side*) I wonder if they ate it. There was one time when I took some food over to a Malay neighbour who was sick. She accepted it, but then I heard from one of my children that she poured it down the drain. And it had taken me hours to prepare.

Eugene: My colleagues never do that. But we are very conscious of what we bring in. We normally give cookies, cakes or other flour-based food. Nothing that really needs cooking with a wok or big frying pan.

Mary: You might think they never throw your stuff out. But I've done some checking. According to this Malay friend of mine, their lives run very much according to Islamic teaching. Malays will not touch anything that is not *halal* - they can't. Some Malays are worried that any food given to them is not *halal*. Just to be polite they will accept it, but then throw it away later. *Halal* and *non halal* are very complex and important matters.

Susela: (*who has joined the group*) Not my idea of being polite, throwing out someone's hours of effort.

Mary: Other than that, I have also heard that Malays will not eat food that has been cooked by using utensils which have been used to cook *non halal* food. It's not that they don't like it. It's just that it's forbidden.

Eugene: To my understanding, *halal* means food, or to be exact, meat from animals like chicken, beef and goat that have been slaughtered in a particular way. Pork is definitely a No-no. Pork, like dog meat, is considered as *najis*, or manure and dirty.

May Lim: Anyway, after that incident, I never gave any more home-cooked food to my neighbour. What about you? Will you still go to all the trouble of taking love letters to work, now you know that they may be part of tomorrow's garbage?

SECTION 5
The Power Of The Spirit

In any culture people can become caught up in a religious fervour which outsiders find difficult to understand, a fervour that can develop into hysteria when the circumstances are out of the individual's control. In Asian cultures, spiritual intensity tends to be more widespread than in the more empirical west, where scientific proof is almost a form of cold religion. This section shows the power of the spirit in very different work settings, resulting in situations hard to understand and even harder to bring under control.

Chapter 28
The Pride Of
Mr Richard White*

Belief in supernatural power, whether irrational or not, can affect workers' performance. Blue Bell Construction of Singapore has appointed an expatriate as Project Director. He comes up against religious conviction which, to him, seems empty superstition. What should he do?

Blue Bell Construction Sdn Bhd, is a subsidiary of Blue Bell Pte Ltd of Singapore, a firm that invested in Malaysia to undertake activities like construction of townships, factories, bridges, dams and roads. The company had been incorporated some years earlier to take the opportunity of the booming construction industry in Malaysia.

The projects that have been completed by the company include the new Kuala Lumpur-Shah Alam Highway, Pentas Dam and Tanjung Beruntung Township, Phase I and Phase II. The projects in progress are Tanjung Beruntung Township Phase III, Sime USP Housing Project Phase 136A and 136B and Hotel Kennesion in Kuala Lumpur, Malaysia.

Recently, Blue Bell Construction Sdn Bhd has been awarded the main contract to build a steel factory in Banting, Klang. The capacity of the steel factory will be 4 million tonnes per annum. The land, which will be occupied by the factory lot, is 158 acres. Since the company has several projects in hand, it is running short of staff. The regional manager of Blue Bell Construction Sdn Bhd, Mr Chew Eng Kee, requested the Head Quarters in Singapore, Blue Bell Pte Ltd, to send some expatriates with

*This case was sritten by Lee Chow Hooi, while a graduate student in the Malaysian Graduate School of Management at Universiti Putra Malaysia.

experience in the steel mill industry to oversee development as Project Directors.

Blue Bell Pte Ltd has considered the request of Chew Eng Kee and decided to send Mr Richard White to Malaysia. Richard White is a graduate engineer from the University of Newcastle, United Kingdom, who has specialised in Industrial Engineering. He has had eight years' working experience as an industrial engineer in a steel mill in England. After his divorce, he had decided to go away from his country to find a new life. He has chosen Singapore as his destination and has joined Blue Bell Pte Ltd as Project Director in the South East Asia region.

On this occasion, Mr Bobson, South East Asia Regional Director of Blue Bell Pte Ltd Singapore, called Richard White to his office.

Bobson: Richard, you have been with this company for almost one year and I'm very pleased with your performance. Now, our construction company in Malaysia needs somebody like you to head a project to construct a steel industry. Would you like to take up this until the project is completed?

Richard: (*After thinking for a few minutes*)
Okay, Bob. I'll take up this challenge. In fact, I'd really like to experience the life style of Malaysia. This is a good chance for me. Thank you, Bob.

Richard White arrived in Malaysia some weeks later. He met Chew Eng Kee and was introduced to the project team. The team members consisted of a site supervisor, two assistant supervisors, and a site clerk. The team was overseeing 150 workers at the construction site. The construction activity for the steel mill project was at a preliminary stage. Land clearing and site preparation were underway.

One day, Rosli rushed into the site office where Richard White was working.

Rosli: Mr Richard, we have a problem here; workers are stopping work now!

Richard: (*in astonishment*) Rosli, what! What is the problem?

Rosli: Mr Richard, there is a huge tree with about two metres in diameter at the site. Our workers dare not do anything to the tree because they believe that there is some 'superpower' living inside the tree. Last year, the workers encountered a similar tree. When they tried to remove it with a bulldozer they saw, tragically, two workers killed by the fallen tree. Also, three workers were injured on the legs and three of the workers were sick for two weeks without the doctor knowing the reason. This time, they dare not proceed until the company does something to send away the 'superpower' from the tree.

Richard: (*Amazed, but trying to keep control of himself*) Rosli, what is your suggestion?

Rosli: (*In a serious manner*) Mr Richard, I think we should engage a 'bomoh' to arrange for some praying ceremony in order to ask the 'superpower' to give way for us to continue our job.

Richard White is in a dilemma now. On the one hand, he would like to complete the land clearing work on schedule; on the other the workers are not willing to do so until a '*bomoh*' is engaged to send away the 'superpower' in the tree. Being an engineer who does not believe in superstition, can Richard White overcome his pride and succumb to belief in the 'superpower' as the construction workers believe he must? What should he do now?

Chapter 29
Disappointment*

Do religious requirements supersede all other responsibilities? When religious commitments conflict with work rules, what can be done? In this case, the work is on a 24-hour drilling rig, and requirements are tough. Many of the staff are Muslims.

Marine Exploration (M) Bhd is a company involved in the exploration and production of oil and natural gas in one of the Malaysian states. It has a diversified workforce but most of its employees at the administrative and operational levels are Muslims. The top management and supervisory positions are mostly held by expatriates who are employed on a contractual basis.

Mr Bruggemann, the supervisor, had taken up his new post just two months before. He had 80 technical staff to oversee one of the drilling rigs. The drilling rig was a 24-hour round the clock operation with crew changes every 12 hours. Mr Bruggemann had attended an induction course on cultural and religious values of the local people, the DOs and the DON'Ts, but he wasn't quite prepared for the situation at the drilling rig. For the past months he had observed the Muslim workers shutting down the operations and taking time off to pray five times a day. This was in addition to the short ten to fifteen minutes' tea breaks.

The nature of the work requires that after any work stoppage the work area must be secured and made safe before anyone can leave. In such a situation, shutting down the operations five times a day leads to an inefficient and slow operation. The non-productive time was high.

Mr Bruggemann wondered how to deal with this problem which was disrupting the operation. His job would be on the line

---

* This case was written by Linda Hii, while a graduate student in the Malaysian Graduate School of Management at Universiti Putra Malaysia.

if he didn't achieve the target production level and it would reflect badly on him as a supervisor. He decided to talk to one of the Muslim foremen.

Bruggemann: Malik, could we have a talk?

Malik: Yes, Sir. What is it about?

Bruggemann: I am concerned about our slow operation. The workers are taking too much time off for their prayers.

Malik: But, Sir, we have to pray.

Bruggemann: I understand that. But at the rate we are working, our operation is too slow. Too much time is taken to secure the area to ensure safety compliance and that's five times a day, not counting the tea breaks. Remember, we have targets to meet.

Malik: I understand your concern, Sir, but you have to respect our religion too. We have been allowed to do this in past years. I don't see why we have to change that.

Bruggemann: Malik, I am sure we can work something out. Why don't you talk to your men about this first?

Malik went off to find his crew and told them to meet him at the meeting room as soon as their shift was over.

Shortly after 12:00 noon, the workers thronged into the meeting room wondering what the meeting was about. Malik called the meeting to order and informed them what the supervisor had just talked to him about.

Affendi, who had been with the company for five years, stood up and protested, "Our past supervisors never had any problem with this arrangement so why do we have to change it now? This is our religion and Mr Bruggemann should understand."

A murmur of voices was heard and heads were seen nodding in agreement. "The management is only concerned about profits and not the welfare of the employees. Targets, productivity, deadlines are all they talk about," another grumbled. "Yes, that's right!" a chorus of voices was heard.

Malik asked them whether they had any suggestions as he had

to report back to Mr Bruggemann about the progress of this meeting. The crew kept quiet but it was obvious from their facial expressions they were not happy at all. Seeing that he was not going to get any answers at least for now, Malik told them to think about it and they would meet again after two days. He went off to tell Mr Bruggemann that he would come back with some suggestions in two days.

Razip and Mohammed, two members of the crew, left the meeting room and walked towards the pantry to have their lunch. The two friends had been saving hard to go together with their spouses to perform the *Haj*. They had accumulated 27 days of their annual leave from the past years so that they could spend more time in the Holy Land. Both of them were looking forward to the pilgrimage and were excited about it.

Mohammed: Razip, have you sent in your application for leave for the *Haj*? I have collected the form already and thought I'd sent it together with yours. We have to get our supervisor to endorse it so we better get all this done early. I don't want to be disappointed.

Razip: I have filled out the form already. I was going to ask you the same thing also. Let's go together when our work on this rig is done in two weeks' time. Now let's have lunch. I am famished. We can discuss further while we eat.

The two went into the pantry to have their lunch.

Two weeks later, the two friends met up to go to the Human Resource Department to send in their forms. They walked into Ms Sheila's office and greeted the Human Resource executive.

Mohammed: Good morning, Ms Sheila, here are our application forms to apply for leave to perform the *Haj*.

Mohammed greeted her as he handed her their forms. He noticed some completed leave forms on her table.

Mohammed: Are they also going for the *Haj*?

Sheila: Yes.

Ms Sheila took a quick glance at their forms and noted the number of days they had applied for leave.

Sheila:	(*waving them to the chairs*) Please take a seat. I can see that both of you have applied for 25 days of leave. Do you two know the company's policy about carrying over leave from the past years?
Razip and Mohammed:	(*answered almost simultaneously*) Is there a problem? We have been saving hard for our annual leave over the past years so that we can spend more time in the Holy Land.

They both were beginning to look worried. They had saved hard on money and leave and didn't want any disappointment.

Sheila:	I know that. I sympathize with you. But the company's rule is that no one is allowed to carry over annual leave for more than 15 days. You should have checked with our department first before making any booking arrangements.
Razip and Mohammed:	But Ms Sheila, we have been looking forward to perform the *Haj* with our spouses. We have made our travel arrangements and everything is confirmed. Is there anything you can do? Can't you just overlook this for once, please?
Sheila:	I am sorry. Rules are rules. Like I said just now, you should have checked with us first about the number of days of annual leave you can carry over. Those (*pointing to pile of forms at the corner of her table*) are in the same predicament as yours. You can still apply for leave to perform the *Haj* but the maximum is only 15 days (*She tried to pacify them*).

Razip and Mohammed tried to reason with her, explaining the preparations they had made and how disappointed their spouses would be but to no avail. They left her room angrily. "Why is the management so insensitive to our needs and welfare?" A couple of weeks back, they had been told to make adjustments between the praying times and working time at the oil rig and now they were being told their application for more than 15 days' leave would not be approved. How are they going to explain this to their spouses?

What about the tickets and accommodation arrangements they had already made? The disappointment was just too much.

The two decided to file a letter of complaint to the Human Resource Department. They would get their Muslim colleagues at the oil rig and various departments to add their signatures. Later in the week, they heard that several letters of complaints had been sent in concerning the leave problem.

A few days later at the Human Resource Department ...

The Human Resource Manager, Mr Ben, was in conference with his subordinates about the complaints they had received from the Muslim staff. He had also received a call from Mr Bruggemann earlier in the week seeking his advice about what alternatives could be worked out to overcome the low productivity level.

Mr Ben was going through the letters again and was wondering how he could resolve the two problems. They were isolated cases, yet linked in some ways. The Muslim staff were definitely very upset and unhappy. They made up a large proportion of the staff. One particular letter took his immediate attention. The in-house union had sent in a letter offering negotiations. His boss was expecting solutions.

What were the underlying causes of all the trouble? And how should the company act now? Mr Ben knew he and the other senior staff would have to think about those matters. Meanwhile, turning back to the staff, Mr Ben asked, "Does anyone have any ideas ... suggestions?"

Chapter 30
The Gods Must Be Angry*

Able Freight Sdn Bhd brought in a Welshman to help diversify its business. Every company has the potential for differences of opinion between those who control and those who are controlled. When expatriates take managerial or technical posts, the potential for clashes increases exponentially.

Able Freight Sdn Bhd, a home-grown international freight forwarding company, was incorporated in January 1989 primarily to serve its customers as a one-stop cargo consolidation and transhipment centre at Port Klang. In the first year of operations, the company recorded a sales turnover of RM2 million and profit before tax of RM500,000. The financial performance was even more impressive in the second year; it saw the company's revenue doubled to RM4 million and profit before tax exceeding RM1 million. This was attributed to the prevailing buoyant economy and hard work put in by the employees of the company.

"We see ourselves as a leader in the freight forwarding market and have set our vision to overcome every hurdle with enthusiasm through team work", said John Yeoh, the Managing Director to himself after reading the financial report. John then decided it was time the company diversified into warehousing and logistics business to ride on the crest of growth experienced at Port Klang, Malaysia's premier port.

One morning, John summoned his forwarding manager, Tan Ah Beng, and the marketing executive, Gopal Krishnan, to his office for an emergency meeting on a special warehouse project.

---

* This case was written by Wing Pun Yoke, while a graduate student in the Malaysian Graduate School of Management at Universiti Putra Malaysia.

John: We have signed a lease contract with the Port Authority for 50,000 square feet of "go-down" space at the old port. The lease-rental contract starts from 15 August and our first shipment of maize in bulk from the United States will arrive at Port Klang on 22 August. Can we do it?

Ah Beng: It is an exciting project, Boss, but the old port is a difficult place to work. Some of the facilities have not been used for years and some have been abandoned.

Gopal: I fear our performance may not be up to the mark since we lack experience in warehouse operations.

John: Both of you certainly look worried. Sorry, I didn't tell you earlier that I have engaged Richard Brown, my good friend from the United States, to be our project technical adviser for a year. Brown will be an asset to Able Freight.

John informed the meeting that his assessment on financial projection for the company in the third year of operations was RM7 million in terms of sales turnover and RM2 million profits before tax, including revenue from the new warehouse business.

Richard Brown

John had known Richard Brown for 15 years. They first met and did their Masters of Science in Transport Planning at the University of Wales in the United Kingdom. Brown had vast working experience in warehousing and logistic operations. He had been a port superintendent in Port Tacoma for 5 years. After his postgraduate studies he did consultancy works on supply chain management for a number of warehousing, logistic and trucking firms. He also did some market research work on global demands for maize and consumption patterns on behalf of the US Grain Council. Brown was a results-orientated sort of individual and attained personal satisfaction when set goals were achieved.

Two months later, Brown arrived in Malaysia. Ah Beng and Gopal Krishnan picked him up at the Kuala Lumpur International Airport. This was his maiden trip to Malaysia and the Far East. The company accommodated him in an apartment in the Ampang neighbourhood as this was a choice residential area among expatriates working in the Klang valley. The idea was to enable him to have some cultural interaction with other westerners since he was so far away from his family and home.

Ah Beng, aged 45, had been educated in Hin Hua School, Klang. He had joined the forwarding sector as a junior clerk at the age of 19 and rose to his position through sheer hard work and perseverance. He believed in the teaching of Taoism, ancestral worship and was quite a superstitious sort of person. He was brought up in Pandamaran New Village, married and had five children.

Gopal Krishnan, 35 years of age, came from a religious background. He was a devoted Hindu and a very pious person. He was also the chairman of the temple committee in Jalan Langat, Klang. He lived with his parents at Taman Andalas and was married with two children. Gopal joined a tally clerk company after leaving school. He obtained his Diploma in Marketing Studies by attending evening classes and since then had taken marketing as a career.

Planning Ahead

As a strategic planner, Brown knew he had a mammoth task ahead. He had about two weeks to plan and organise the warehouse operations, to recruit forklift drivers and general workers and to clear up the mess left behind by the previous tenant so that the leased go-down area could be ready to receive the first shipment of goods. Besides, the procedural and regulatory requirements at Port Klang gave him a lot to catch up with. He drew up a Gantt chart for his team members to maintain their work schedules.

Once this was done, Mr Brown called in Ah Beng and Gopal.

Brown: Congratulations to you two gentlemen. You have been hand picked to become members of a special project team. We have a big task ahead. The success or failure of the new business depends squarely on each and every one of us. I am confident we can do it together.

Ah Beng's immediate task as forwarding-cum-warehouse manager was to ensure that the rented premise was fit to store the maize in bulk. He did a good job as far as warehouse cleanliness was concerned and reported back to Brown that the possibility of contamination to the cargo was slim. The go-down was also fumigated to clear it of rodents, cockroaches and insects. But Brown told Ah Beng and Gopal he wanted more done still.

Brown: You have done a good job in sprucing up the warehouse but I see you have not removed the three Chinese altars and one Hindu shrine located within our rented premises. They are certainly obstructing operations.

Problems

Ah Beng and Gopal both tried in vain to locate the owners of the altars and shrine. They even went to seek the assistance and advice of temple priests, mediums and village elders on how best to handle the situation in order not to offend the deities. According to local beliefs, altars and shrines were put up at the work place to bless the staff and to protect them from sustaining injuries arising from industrial accidents. Offerings to deities were made by worshippers in exchange for the blessings and prosperity of the company's business and for protecting the port workers.

Just two days before the arrival of the first shipment of cargo, Ah Beng told Gopal, "I cannot solve this problem, Gopal! You see this is the month of the Hungry Ghost and the 'spirits' are all over the place." Gopal who was even more pious than Ah Beng replied with an equally worried look: "According to the Hindu Calendar, September would be an auspicious month to resite the Hindu shrine but not now."

Statistics released by the Port Authority showed the month of August usually recorded the highest number of accidents and death rates compared with other months. During the *Por Thor or Hungry Ghost* ceremony held at this time of the year in the port area, strong financial and moral support came from people working within the port paternity. When Ah Beng and Gopal could not find a solution to the problem, they had no choice but to relate their difficulties in removing those worship-structures to Brown. They were startled when Brown replied abruptly,

"Don't worry gentlemen, I will use the forklift to remove them since there are no claimants." By nature, Brown would react instinctively by making a personal decision for a solution when confronted with a problem. Without hesitation he made the arrangements for the removal of the structures.

Two weeks later, "Bintang Maju", the maize carrier, arrived on schedule at Port Klang. She was berthed alongside berth number three at the old port at 0700 hours. Under the time-charter contract between Able Freight and the ship-owner, Bintang Line Pte Ltd of Hong Kong, the ship port-stay must not exceed five days.

Based on Brown's estimation, a cargo discharge rate of 100 tonnes per hour must be achieved in order to complete the unloading operations of 12,000 tonnes within five days. There was a penalty clause in the time-charter contract stipulating Able Freight to pay the shipping company US$10,000 per day as demurrage charges should the ship overstay in port. Conversely, Able Freight could earn despatch money from Bintang Line Pte Ltd should the ship stay less than five days as the result of better than expected productivity rates achieved.

Brown, Ah Beng and Gopal took turns working round the clock to monitor the operations when the ship was in port. Despite their combined efforts, the ship could only complete work in six and a half days. Able Freight had to fork out US$15,000 as demurrage charges to the shipping company for the delays.

Other problems also cropped up. Feedmills Sdn Bhd, the importer of the cargo was not at all happy with the services provided by Able Freight. Poor delivery of the maize from the Able Freight warehouse caused their factory to shut down production for 24 hours.

John Yeoh, the Managing Director of Able Freight, also received an ultimatum from Feedmills Sdn Bhd complaining of unsatisfactory services and threatening to terminate the handling contract. Besides that, two general workers sustained serious body injuries when a pallet load of bagged maize fell on them in the warehouse. They had to be warded at the Klang General Hospital for medical treatment.

The company ran into problems with the labour office when the authorities found out the injured employees were, in fact, illegal immigrants working without permits. They had not been issued with safety helmets, shoes and apparel when working for Able Freight. The port area was regarded as an accident and fire prone area by the Port Authority.

In the operation review meeting, Brown briefed John that the delays were attributed to inclement weather, staff falling sick and high incidence of breakdowns to the mechanical handling equipment such as prime-movers, forklifts and the bagging machines. There were also reports of frequent power failure which affected the overall operations. Ah Beng added, "All of us worked very hard, yet we have delays and lost money. There could be other factors too."

"The gods must be angry", Gopal whispered back quietly to Ah Beng.

Chapter 31
Widetech Malaysia*

This incident is about a man who has made a vow for the sake of his family. He is valuable to the company because of his particular expertise but is likely to leave since staying will mean he will fail to fulfil his vow. A solution is not as easy as might appear.

It was Monday, early in the New Year. Mr Lim Kim Soon, General Manager of Widetech Malaysia was in Jakarta to attend an important meeting to finalise the opening of a new office there. He received an urgent call on his mobile phone from his senior marketing officer, Mr Raju, at about 5.00p.m.

Raju: Mr Lim, I know I should wait till you come back but I'd just like to let you know that I'm handing in my resignation tomorrow morning.

Mr Lim: Your resignation? Why? What's wrong?

Raju: I don't think that I will be able to continue working here any more.

Mr Lim: (*sensing that something major was wrong*) Let's talk about it, O.K.? I'll be back soon.

While he was on his flight back to Kuala Lumpur two days later, many thoughts crossed his mind. "Is he unhappy about his salary? Or has he got a better offer?" He called his personal assistant, Mary with questions.

---

* This case was written by Mohanan Nair, while a graduate student in the Malaysian Graduate School of Management at Universiti Putra Malaysia.

Mr Lim: What's going on in the office?

Mary: Mr Ravi said he is unhappy and would like to meet you soon. He had a quarrel with Mr Robert, the Sales Manager.

Mr Lim: There'd better not be anything else!

Mr Ravi is the most senior marketing officer in the company. He holds a Master's degree in Business Adminstration from Hull University. He is a workaholic, who seldom takes leave. However, he was given two weeks' annual leave in the previous November, and has applied for another one weeks' leave from 29 January to 3 February, this year. He submitted his leave form on 2 January, explaining to Mr Robert that the leave is very important to him for he had to undertake some religious duties.

Mr Robert is a business graduate from Hong Kong University. He has been in the marketing line for about fifteen years and in charge of WIDETECH's subsidiary, WSPL, at Shantou, China, for the past ten years. Previously he was employed by a multinational company in Hong Kong. Two years ago he was transferred to Kuala Lumpur office, but does not socialise much with his staff, preferring to travel very often to Hong Kong to visit his family. He has planned to take two weeks' leave coinciding with the Chinese Lunar festival in February, that is from 1 Feb to 15 Feb to be with his family. He wanted Ravi to be around while he was on leave.

Mr Lim arrived from Jakarta on 24 January and went straight to his office. He immediately summoned all the heads of departments, including the one from the sales department, for an urgent meeting. He briefed them on his visit to Jakarta and the need to find a suitable candidate to be in charge of the office there. Many names were mentioned including Ravi's. Mr Lim stressed the need to foster close rapport with company staff. When the meeting ended he requested Mr Robert to stay back for a discussion.

Mr Lim: What is the problem with Ravi?

Mr Robert: Ravi has applied for a week's leave during the first week of February which is around the Chinese Lunar Holidays. I cannot approve his leave because many Chinese staff will be on leave. Actually I want him to be around. He was given two weeks' annual leave last November.

Mr Lim: Did you find out the actual reason for his leave application?

Mr Robert: I think he wants to take opportunity of the Chinese New Year holidays.

Mr Lim: I want you to find out the real reason behind his leave application. If he has got some valid reason, I think you will have to reconsider your decision.

Mr Robert: I will meet Ravi this afternoon.

Miss Poon, Mr Robert's secretary, informed Ravi that he, Mr Robert, wanted to see him at 3.00 p.m. that afternoon.

Mr Robert: Hello Ravi! How are you? Actually I have reconsidered your leave application. I do not mind if you take leave at the end of February for most of the Chinese staff will be back to work after their long Chinese New Year Holidays. If this is not possible could you shorten your leave?

At no time did Mr Robert ask Ravi for his reasons for applying leave. He was not sympathetic about the whole issue. Ravi was firm in his decision. If leave was not granted for the first week in February, he was willing to tender his resignation immediately. Mr Lim, sensing problems, called Ravi to his office at 5.00 p.m. to discuss his leave issue.

Ravi was, as usual, always serious with his work. For the past three weeks he had been seen sporting a beard, less cheerful, and not frequenting the company's canteen. He had declined social functions and had become a strict vegetarian.

Since Mr Lim has been travelling overseas frequently to see the company's subsidiaries, he has not seen Ravi during January. However, he knows Ravi quite well because Ravi worked with him during his early days in the company.

WIDETECH

WIDETECH was incorporated in Malaysia on 25 January 1984 under the Companies Act, 1965 as a private limited company under the name of WIDETECH (Malaysia) Sdn Bhd and commenced operation on 1 April. The company was subsequently converted to a public limited company on 30 May 1985 as WIDETECH (Malaysia) Berhad. WIDETECH is principally engaged in the manufacture and sale of correction fluid.

There are a small number of major companies involved in the production of correction fluid. In Malaysia, the correction fluid manufacturing industry is relatively new. Its products are for both domestic and export markets.

Widetech correction fluid is a unique product which has created a niche market for itself, since no other product on the market can offer the features of this correction fluid which is widely used in offices and schools. Since the correction fluid is not a luxury product in current office and school environments, it is unlikely that its usage would be reduced during any recession. It has the advantage of steady sales, being a relatively low-cost item. The company benefits from greater market diversity by producing an almost "universal" product that can be used world-wide. WIDETECH could venture into other countries when necessary.

WIDETECH GROUP's continued success will depend to an extent on the continued demand for its principal product, correction fluid. While correction fluid will remain the Group's principal product, WIDETECH's corporate strategy is also to expand the services and products provided by its subsidiaries, EE, WMS and EPA, to external parties.

Products

Being a fully integrated correction fluid manufacturer, WIDETECH has achieved success in producing a full range of products for the correction fluid market such as solvent-based correction fluid, water-based correction fluid, correction fluid thinner, correction tape, metal tip correction pen and colour correction fluid. The solvent and water-based correction fluid are produced in the conventional bottle and brush packaging as well as in the more refined pen packaging. WIDETECH also sells its correction fluid to its customers in drums as well as in bottles. In addition to the above, WIDETECH produces fingertip moistener and correction fluid thinner as complementary products.

The correction fluid produced by WIDETECH dries fast to a paper-like surface that provides good covering for easy amendments by pencil, ink or typewriter. The soft bottle design for the pen type correction fluid ensures easy application by the consumers, while the tip cleaning cap prevents the pen tip from clotting and blockage by dried correction fluid. Correction tape allows re-writing over the tape immediately without any need to wait for drying time as in the conventional correction fluid. The correction tape uses a thin chemical film to cover the areas that require corrections.

Competitive Situation

WIDETECH's competitive edge includes the full integration in term of its design, packaging and manufacturing of correction fluid. The company's production process is highly mechanised and automated; it uses robotic arms, electronic sensors and pneumatic automation with American and German machinery.

WIDETECH also enjoys excellent synergy with the subsidiary companies, EPA, WMS, and EE. EPA designs and installs robotic arms, automated tooling systems and automated material loading systems for WIDETECH and assists the company in automating its production process.

In addition, EPA is also responsible for giving advice on the acquisition of machinery, modifications to the machinery as well as adding electronic, pneumatic, micro-processing and sensing components to the machinery in the WIDETECH Group. WMS provides micro-precision springs to WIDETECH for its plastic and metal tip pen function, enabling the correction fluid to flow to the tip. EE provides the Group with moulds that meet its specific requirements, This support enables the Group to reduce its dependence on external parties.

The company's other competitive edge includes its ability to offer a complete array of products, ranging from brush and bottle correction fluid, thinner, plastic tip correction pen, metal tip correction pen, correction tape, colour correction fluid and water-based and de-aromatised hydrocarbon-based (oil-based) correction fluid. Both the de-aromatised hydrocarbon and the water-based correction fluid are environmentally friendly products but the aromatised hydrocarbon-based correction fluid requires a shorter drying time than other products. The breakthrough in developing the de-aromatised correction fluid by WIDETECH is the result of five to six years of research, which serves as a testimony to the company's commitment in the international market place.

Distribution

Over the past 10 years, WIDETECH has established a long term and strong business relationship with some international stationary distributors such as UHU GmbH of Germany which distributes WIDETECH's correction fluid under the brand name of "UHU" and Marbig Rexel Pte Ltd of Australia which distributes WIDETECH's correction fluid under the brand name "Marbig". Its distribution channels have successfully spread over more than ten countries. WIDETECH's relationship with its customers can be seen from the growth in the sales figures, as well as the growth in the number of customers over the years. This shows WIDETECH's ability to produce quality and marketable products which suit the needs of a wide market.

Robert

Robert is from Hong Kong and he has little knowledge about local culture. He did not want to be too personal in dealing with Ravi's leave application. Being British, with Hong Kong as his home base, he is a loner in Malaysia. He places his leaves and his visits to Hong Kong as priority. He does not understand why Ravi has to take leave to perform a religious function. He could take leave for a day or two. "Why a week?" he commented. Furthermore, the function would be held at Batu Caves, Kuala Lumpur. Besides, Ravi had taken two weeks' leave in November, 2000.

Ravi

Ravi has a personal problem. His only child, a son, was born with a congenital heart disease, which required open heart surgery. His wife, a teacher, has had plaster on her right leg after meeting an accident just before last Christmas.

Ravi is always a cheerful person and has never discussed his personal problems in his office. His two weeks' leave last November was to take care of his little son who underwent open heart surgery at Institute Jantung Negara, Kuala Lumpur. He made a vow that he would carry the *kavadi* on Thaipusam day i.e., on the 2 February, the following year, at Batu Caves if his son's operation was successful. He was more convinced to carry out this solemn undertaking in view of his son's gradual improvement after the surgery. He has to carry out the vow he has made, whatever the circumstances he is in. He has been preparing for the function since the beginning of the year. He has been a vegetarian and has been fasting. During the month of January, Ravi did not attend any social functions. However, he carried out his office duties as usual. Robert's failure to understand Ravi's religious commitment was the main cause of the problem. The company cannot afford to lose a worker like Ravi.

Thaipusam

What is the significance of *Thaipusam*? *Thaipusam* is a special day for Hindus. Pilgrims throng Batu Caves to mount the 272 steps to pay homage to Lord Subramaniam. The highlight of the festival is the carrying of *kavadis* or wooden structure adorned with flowers, peacock, feathers and fruits. Devotees with skewers, spikes or other sharp instruments pierced through their tongues, cheeks and bodies scale the steps in fulfilment of their vows.

Mortification of the flesh is part of the act of repentence and the kavadi is the symbolic burden one carries. Before the ordeal begins, devotees prepare by fasting and praying. On the morning of the festival, devotees bathe in the nearby river and rub ash all over their bodies. To the chant of religious songs, the devotees in saffron fall into trance as the *kavadis* are fixed to their bodies. They then begin their arduous ascent of 272 steps.

Many of the devotees carry *kavadis* to fulfil their vows. Some of them carry *kavadis* for three consecutive years. They come from all over Malaysia. Some come from Singapore, Thailand and Indonesia. Every devotee has a specific reason for performing his pilgrimage. Robert had simply failed to understand the significance of Ravi's religious commitment. What should he do now? And what can the company do?

Chapter 32
Thaipusam Tragedy*

The previous Thaipusam case is a reminder of another true incident that occurred in the nineteen seventies. This case was written by a senior army officer, about a soldier who had made a vow and was confronted with circumstances in which he could not keep the vow. Was the outcome inevitable?

In 1975, 25 members of the security forces were killed during an operation. Because Communist activities were very active, all securities stationed at Sibu were deployed along the Rajang River to fight the insurgents. Reinforcements were sent to the area to help the existing troops.

The government put all its effort into curbing the situation. The public lived in fear. More areas along the Rajang River were declared under curfew. One of the army battalions stationed at Oya Camp, about 10 KM from Sibu, was 23rd Para Regiment which had been in and out of the fighting. The government put all its effort into curbing the situation. The public lived in fear. More areas along the Rajang River were declared under curfew. One of the army battalions stationed at Oya Camp, about 10 km from Sibu.

RASCOM HQ

On 20 November, 1975, Brigadier-General Alang Abu, a Sarawak Malay, was military commander at Rajang Security Area Command (RASCOM) Headquarters in Sibu. He called for a

---

* This case was written by Basrun B. Husain, while a graduate student in the Malaysian Graduate School of Management at Universiti Putra Malaysia.

meeting at RASCOM headquarters to deliver his new orders. Representatives from various units under his command came for the meeting. Besides the military commanders, there were police and civilian authorities. During the meeting he said:

> Gentlemen, communist activities in our area of command are very active. There are reports that their movements have been spotted at various locations, and that they are gaining sympathy from the natives. Higher command has allocated two more battalions for these operations. We expect them to arrive here in a few days.
>
> All commanders will be given new tasks for these operations. I want you to reorganise your troops and deploy them according to plan. My intelligence officer will distribute to you the new deployment plan for these operations. For your information, from now until further notice all leave will be frozen except compassionate leave.

After the meeting all the commanders were busy drawing new maps and getting more details about the deployment. Most of them rushed back to their units to pass down the news to their men.

23rd Para Battalion

Lieutenant-Colonel (Lt. Col.) Soo Ah Chai, commanding officer of 23rd Para Battalion, arrived at his unit late in the afternoon. After he settled down in his office, he called his adjutant and asked him to tell the other staff officers to be available at the Operations Room in two hours' time.

When all his staff officers had assembled, Lt Col. Soo Ah Chai arrived at the unit Operations Room. He first briefed his officers on the situation in RASCOM area, and then deliberated on the plan of operations.

> Well, gentlemen, we are going to face tough challenges ahead of us. This situation might last a few months before we can see the results. Besides carrying out the plan of operations, we have to provide two-man standby troops from our battalion. They will be deployed as soon as we know the location of the enemy. The whole troop will be very mobile.

Captain Sarlan, of Jawanese origin from Johor, was the officer in charge of the standby troops. His assistant was Sergeant Malang, an Iban from Sarawak. The troop comprised 20 men from all the companies (coys) in the battalion, A Coy, B Coy, C Coy and D Coy.

Back in his room at the Officers' Mess, Captain Sarlan looked through the list of names of the standby troops. Some of those he had selected were seniors, some juniors. Tomorrow he would start his training with them.

Private Kupusamy

Private Kupusamy had been with the battalion for four years. He was a very dedicated soldier. He was married, blessed with a two-year old son. That January 1975, his son had fallen ill and since then, the boy had been in and out of the hospital. Besides sending his son into hospital, Private Kupusamy also made an effort to cure the boy through traditional medicine. Nobody seemed to know the reasons for his son's sickness.

On 12 December 1975, after spending a sleepless night due to his son's sickness, he got up early in the morning. He sat down and prayed. He made a vow that if his son was cured from the sickness, he would carry the *kavadi* and would celebrate the coming *Thaipusam* at Batu Caves.

The Situation In 197

In March 1976, operations were still going on. The security forces were deployed according to the operation plan; the standby troop of 23rd Para had been deployed no less then five times since the operations started. However, the communists were fighting aggressively. The security forces had had no success so far and so a new plan to curb the situation was formulated.

For more than three months, personnel in RASCOM were not allowed to go on leave. Most of them celebrated their festival celebrations in their camp or in operation areas. During Christmas and Chinese New Year, no one went on leave, including the Commanding Officer of 23rd Para. Sergeant Malang, being a Christian himself, celebrated his Christmas in the camp.

Private Kupusamy conducted his daily life as normal. His son's health was improving. In photographs, the boy looked so cheerful. "At last my prayers have been answered", said Kupusamy.

The Tragedy

5 March 1976, the standby troops under Captain Sarlan were training as usual. After the training, Private Kupusamy came to Sergeant Malang's office.

Private Kupusamy: Good morning Sergeant, can I see you for a while?

Sergeant Malang: Well, good morning, come in. Yes, anything I can do for you?

Private Kupusamy: I have a personal problem and I would like to apply for 15 days' leave. I plan to go back to Kuala Lumpur to celebrate Thaipusam, which falls on the 25 March. I would like to apply for leave starting from the 15th to 30th March. Here is my leave pass.

Sergeant Malang: Well, I'll forward the pass to the officer, but as you know no one is allowed to go on leave unless it's compassionate leave.

Private Kupusamy: Please Sergeant, I need the leave very badly, I have something on.

Sergeant Malang: Well, I'll look into it, but I am not sure of the approval.

Sergeant Malang sent his leave pass to Captain Sarlan though an officer, but the latter did not allow the leave pass to reach his commanding officer. He insisted that nobody go on leave except for compassionate leave. He insisted that nobody go on leave except for compassionate leave. To him any religious celebrations could be celebrated in the camp. So far, nobody had been allowed to go, including the commanding officer.

Five days had passed since he submitted his leave pass to Sergeant Malang. Private Kupusamy inquired about the situation from his superiors. The answer he received was that it was not approved, and he felt distressed about that.

On the night of 24 March 1976, Kupusamy had a sleepless night, worrying that he would not be able to fulfil his vow. He did not want to see his son back to the condition that he had been in a few months before.

Next morning after the normal training, he went to the barracks to draw his personal rifle and some ammunition. He rushed to the end of the field and fired a few shots. Sergeant Malang, realising that it was his man, tried to cool him down. As he approached Private Kupusamy, the rifle was pointed at him. Private Kupusamy pressed the trigger. Sergeant Malang was shot and died on the spot.

In the afternoon, after the situation calmed a little, the CO visited Private Kupusamy at the Guard Room, asking him why he had shot Sergeant Malang. Private Kupusamy said, "I'm afraid of my vow."

Chapter 33
The Month Of The Hungry Ghost: Custodial Services Of CSQ Bank*

A previously successful company is plagued with selfish petty behaviour, constant bad weather, unprecedented staff sickness and a high incidence of machinery breakdowns and power failures. In the month of the hungry ghost, an expatriate manager might not recognise the cause.

Company Background

CSQ Bank was among one of the top custodian banks in Kuala Lumpur. The Custodian Services department served both foreign and local investors, in particular institutional investors. There were 24 staff in this department: fifteen clerks, one office boy, three junior officers, 2 assistant managers, an assistant Vice President and a Vice President.

The assistant Vice President, Ms Wong, was a Chinese lady in her mid-forties. She was promoted on seniority. Every officer in the department knew that she was quite difficult to deal with. She liked to mingle with the clerks and to start telling them about all the loopholes that the officers (except her) had taken advantage of. They knew that her intention was nothing more than to find

---

* This case was written by Zarazila Mohd Ripin while a student in the Malaysian Graduate School of Management. It has been considerably altered.

fault with others and show the Vice President that the officers did not perform their duties as they should.

As a result of her improper office conduct, some clerks did not show respect to their respective officers. However, none of the officers had the courage to inform the Vice President what was going on in the department.

Most of the officers believed that she was behaving like that because the other officers had tertiary qualifications and it would be a matter of time before her position was taken by any one of them. To complicate matters, she felt that the officers did not respect her, by-passing her on many occasions and only taking commands from the Vice President.

Susan Chua was an assistant manager in the Corporate Actions department. She was in her late twenties and apart from her office work, she also studied part-time in the MBA programme at a local university. Susan had received her high school diploma from an American High School and college education from Brown University, USA. She had spent fifteen years in the United States of America. She spoke with an American accent and her character was more like that of an American rather than a Malaysian-Chinese. She reported to work on Monday, 27 July 2001 after being away for one week of study leave.

One morning, the moment she stepped into the department, she could sense that the office environment was tense and her heartbeat became very fast. She had a funny feeling and knew that something must have gone wrong while she was away on her study leave. From her experiences, when she took leave for more than two days, problems always surfaced or cropped up in her supervision area, Corporate Actions. However, those problems were merely teething problems which could be solved or settled easily.

As usual, her first day was busy with clearing off all the outstanding work which had piled up on her table but she sensed trouble. Nobody informed her that anything had gone wrong during her absence. She preferred open two-way communication and directness and so tried to get some clues from her colleagues and clerks. However, much to her disappointment, she could find out nothing. She dared not ask the assistant Vice President because that lady could be temperamental and was very likely to have Monday blues.

Critical Incident

At 4.30 p.m., Susan was summoned into Ms Wong's cubicle. Susan knew that this could be her D-day on which she could anticipate being fired by Ms Wong for reasons unknown to her. She did not have any ammunition with which to defend herself as she did not know what the problem was. In short, she was not prepared at all and she felt very awkward and strange.

The following conversation went on between the two:

Ms Wong: I am sure you will know by now why I am calling you in?

Susan: Gosh! To be honest to you, I have no idea at all. You know, I have had a strange feeling all morning. I had butterflies in my stomach the moment I walked into the department.

Ms Wong: All right! During your absence, many clients' issues surfaced which put our business operations at risk. Clients have threatened to pull out from us. Did you know that?

Susan: Please come straight to the point. Don't make me shoot in the dark trying to know the reason for your dissatisfaction.

Ms Wong: Here's an example. On 21 July this year, our valued client, AGF Asia Limited, Singapore, rang up our Vice President complaining that we failed to send them circulars on the Extra-Ordinary General Meeting (EGM) of MBA Company. You knew that they are the substantial shareholders of MBA! The Financial Controller, Mr James Muthiah, claimed that his company received the notification from other sources and not from us as their custodian bank. This is a really embarrassing situation as we have allowed the client to express dissatisfaction with our service.

Susan: The EGM's circular reached our office on Saturday, 19 July at noon. I instructed my staff to prepare the advice and fax to the client by Monday morning, 21 July. I explained the importance of giving prompt notification as the client is highly sensitive and requires a world-class service from us as the custodian bank.

Ms Wong: Whatever explanations given were too late. The damage is done. You can argue until the cows come home but our reputation has been tarnished. I have got enough scolding from the Vice President and I think it is fair that you should also share in that! After all, it is your area and you are responsible for your staff's work. I was just relieving during your absence. Another issue is the complaint received from Credit Agricole Indosuez, Paris. Why did you wait until the second reminder came before answering their swift query? Do you know that our Vice President was really mad about this matter? We checked with your staff and found that you drafted the reply but why didn't you monitor the outgoing reply? You have delegated to your staff but you have failed to monitor their work!

Susan: Ms Wong, don't expect a sparrow to fly like an eagle! For the swift reply, I reminded the staff several times before proceeding on study leave. If a staff member promised me to do something by Monday morning, but failed to honour her promises, what else do you expect me to do? I was not around during that day and I am sure if I were around, this thing would not have happened in the first place.

Ms Wong: I have another issue to bring to your attention. The filing system in your staff area was in a terrible mess. It took me half an hour to find a dividend voucher. You can't allow this to happen. What have your staff been doing all this while? You can't expect me to find a needle in a haystack! I had to get assistance from other sections to help re-arrange the files in your section. I even found some tax vouchers lying on Kumar's table. Well, he told me that he did not know what to do with them. Come on, Susan, what is happening to you?

Susan: For the filing part, we have tried our best. You already knew that my dividend clerk is on five-month, no-pay leave. Of course, her area was in a mess as she has been on medical leave for every alternate day. And besides, the other clerks were busy with processing rights and bonus issues and sales of shares. As for the tax vouchers, I explained to Kumar that I would be looking into the matter when I came back from my study leave. Why wasn't he telling the truth? Why is he getting me into trouble? O.K., never mind, I will check with him after this for clarification.

By now, Susan was already tense, as she knew that someone had been trying to stab her in the back during her absence.

Ms Wong: I have also received a complaint from the Branch Operations Manager that your staff have been utilising the "Quick Cheques Deposit Box" to deposit our dividend cheques at the Banking Hall. Do you know that the box is meant for external customers only and not for our usage? Why didn't your staff follow the procedures which I laid down?

Susan: I have never instructed my staff to use that box and I didn't even know that the box existed. Let me double check with my staff on this matter to ascertain who instructed them to use the box.

Ms Wong: No need! I don't want to know.

Susan: Ms Wong, if I don't ask them, then how am I going to clear my name since I seem to be blamed for this whole business?

Ms Wong: I repeat, it is not necessary.

When Susan heard this statement, she started raising her voice unintentionally because of her emotional dissatisfaction.

Susan: Ms Wong, I think someone is just jealous of my achievements. I have not been given a fair chance to defend myself. After all, the Vice President will know by now, based on your report on me that I was not performing well. It is more a personal attack than trying to give justice by looking at the problems objectively. You have on purpose tried to prove my weaknesses to him! Instead of trying to improve the work processes, you are just blaming me for nothing!

Ms Wong: You have gone overboard by accusing me. It is my job to report any irregularities happening in this department!

Susan: (angrily) There you are! Very smart at finding a scapegoat. When you did something wrong, you cautioned us not to highlight the matters to the Vice President. You are just playing a double standard. Have you heard of a level playing field?

Ms Wong: I am warning you, Susan! If you accuse me like this again, I
am going to slap your face!

When the heated discussions took place, without Susan's
knowledge, the Vice President was at the corner of the room
listening to the conversation. When Susan saw him, she suddenly
realised that her reputation was at stake, as she would have been
seen as being insubordinate towards her superior.

Susan was smart enough to protect herself. She immediately
wrote an official complaint letters to the Officers' Union and The
Human Resource Manager telling them that Ms Wong, her
superior, had threatened her. She quoted exactly what Ms Wong
had said to her.

During her entire seven years working, she had never
encountered this kind of heated argument. She had been a very
energetic, responsible and highly resourceful officer. Because of
her capabilities and good managerial skills, she became the Vice
President's "blue-eyed" girl. On top of this, it was based on the
Vice President's recommendations that she was hired into the
department.

Susan had a sleepless night thinking about what had
happened during the day. She tried to analyse the situation and
could not find any solution. All this while, she was cool, polite
and rational in her reasons and discussions.

The following day, Susan confronted her staff on the issues
brought up by Ms Wong. The staff could not give any
explanation. To them, the best answer was to say that they did
not know anything because saying that meant they would not get
themselves into any trouble.

At 3 p.m. one week later, the departmental officers' meeting
was held. Throughout the meeting, the Vice President sounded
very serious about operational efficiency, customers' complaints
and outstanding items for officers who proceeded on vacation
leave for more than three days.

Susan knew that the meeting was focused entirely on her even
though the Vice President did not mention any specific names.
The worst part was when he mentioned that officers were to be
more tactful in tackling their respective staff problems and must
not allow their emotions to overcome the rationale or logical
explanations. According to him, he lost respect towards officers
who allowed their emotions to control their minds.

Once the meeting adjourned, he instructed both Ms Wong and Susan to come into his room for another serious matter. He had personally requested Susan to withdraw her complaint letter against Ms Wong as he felt that, as a departmental head, he was in a position to settle the disputes amicably without any interference from the Union officials and the Human Resource Manager. Furthermore, if the complaint letter was not withdrawn, then Ms Wong's personal record would be affected.

At the same time, Ms Wong apologised to Susan and explained that she had no intention to threaten her at all. What happened during their heated discussion was entirely out of her control as she believed that a supernatural power had taken possession of her. She claimed that her normal behaviour was not like that at all.

As well, she mentioned to Susan that as a Chinese, she should be aware that the "Month of Hungry Ghost" was around the corner. Ms Wong believed that these ghosts, coming from the restless spirits, would have roamed the earth and caused trouble for her. She claimed that she was the victim of these hungry ghosts.

However, Susan refused to withdraw her complaint letter outright. She did not categorise herself as a Chinese because she was a Christian and had been indoctrinated with American culture and beliefs since she was a teenager. She strongly believed in justice. For her, believing in superstitions like the existence of a "Hungry Ghost" was ridiculous. The two-day unpleasant episode had made Susan feel very disturbed.

Chapter 34
Insensitive*

This case, like most of the others, is based on a real life situation. It revolves around a German electronics company in Malaysia. It touches on the issues of the culture, characters and races in Malaysia in general and how a foreign manager tries to fit into the cultural system. The case evolves around the main issue of a delivery order, the fasting month and the coming Hari Raya Puasa celebrations. The majority of the workers are Malays who are Muslims. They make up 46 of the total of 70 personnel. They also control the important aspect of the factory as most of them work in the production department.

The Hari Raya Puasa is an important celebration in the Muslim calendar and has a designated 2-day national holiday in Malaysia. Prior to the celebrations, all Muslims are required to fast from dawn till dusk. The breaking of fast is usually between 7.00 pm till 8.00pm depending on the areas in Malaysia as specified by the religious councils.

Prayer times are also within that period. Though the labour law mentions that employees must work provided that overtime is paid, it is very important, too, to explain tactfully to the staff concerned what misconceptions a foreigner could have of their religious attitudes and their work commitments.

On a Friday morning, 2 months before Hari Raya Puasa, Mr Peter Haessler sat at his office sharp at 8.00 am just as any other day. This was in line with his German working characteristic of precision timing.

---

* This case was written by Loo Wai Thien and Anthony Dylan when they were graduate students in The Malaysian Graduate School of Management.

He got up and looked out the window facing the factory floor below, sighing. He then made his way to the little German coffee machine on his right to make a cuppa to start off the day as always.

Company Background

Autobahn (M) Sdn. Bhd., is a German-based electronics based manufacturing company specialising in car ignition systems. Its products are exported only to Europe. The company was established in Malaysia in 1998 and is located in the Penang Free Trade Zone. The factory is semi-automated and the non-automated process requires use of specialised, skilled personnel to monitor the equipment. The total manpower is 70 male personnel (69 local and 1 expatriate).

Mr Peter Haessler is a 40-year-old German. He has had 20 years' experience in manufacturing and human resource development. His job is to oversee the profit and loss of the whole operations and to report to Autobahn International Ltd. in Hamburg, Germany.

His personal assistant, Mr Chin Peng Aik, is a 35-year-old Malaysian Chinese. He has had 15 years' experience in various manufacturing firms. He reports to Mr Haessler and oversees 2 other superintendents. One of these is En. Ahmad Yahya, a Malaysian Malay, aged 43 years. He has had 24 years' experience in various manufacturing firms. He reports to Mr Chin Peng Aik and oversees the Production Department and ensures deadlines in production are met. He is also in charge of staff welfare.

The other is Mr K. Param, a 38-year-old Malaysian Indian. He has had 10 years' experience in manufacturing firms specialising in electronics. He reports to Mr Chin Peng Aik and oversees the Quality Control and Technical Department to ensure quality control and smooth operations. He is also in charge of staff welfare.

Management Chart

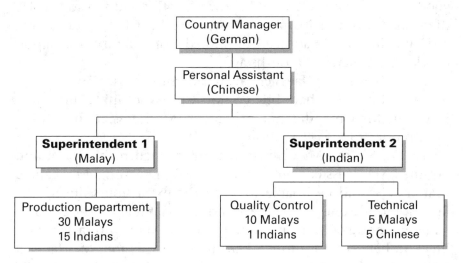

The Challenge at Work

The Hari Raya celebration is in 2 months' time and the company has a delivery order worth RM1 million, also due in 2 months' time. Most of the workers are Malay. Mr Haessler proposes they work 3 hours extra each day next month to ensure delivery in 1.5 months' time. He is totally unaware of the sensitivity of the fasting month.

Mr Haessler was new and as a foreigner arriving on shore 2 months ago, he has tried hard to get used to the way of life here. He was a strict and respected man back in Germany and he badly wanted to be liked by the locals here. Mr Haessler indeed had something exciting in his mind today. He was thinking of Hari Raya Puasa and his Malay staff under him. He also focused on the delivery order on his table which was due in 2 months' time. The order could be delivered on schedule but that would mean that he would not be able to grant any leave to his Malay staff longer than 2 days for Hari Raya Puasa. The delivery order was valued at RM1 million and considered the biggest so far.

He thought that, in order to be able to grant all Malay staff leave of at least 5 days around the celebration period, he would require them to work an extra 3 hours straight from next week for 1.5 months. This way he could get the delivery done in 1.5

months' time. He was confident that this would make him look good in their eyes as it would show empathy and sensitivity. He then sat down anticipating the arrival of Mr Chin, his personal assistant. Mr Chin had been promoted from factory head upon Mr Haessler's arrival 2 months ago.

At 11.00 am, Mr Haessler called Mr Chin asking him to come to his office. He then briefed Mr Chin, outlining his plan. However, Mr Chin did not explain to Mr Haessler the fasting month prior to the celebrations.

At 11.45 a.m., Mr Chin called En. Ahmad to his room and outlined Mr Haessler's proposal. However, En. Ahmad explained that they would be unable to work the extra hours during the fasting month due to tiredness and prayer times as the 3 hours straight work would mean from 5p.m. till 8p.m. with a 1/2 hour break in between for dinner. During the discussion, Mr Haessler was passing by Mr Chin's room and thought it would be splendid if he could explain his brilliant idea to En. Ahmad.

Mr Haessler: Good morning Encik Ahmad! How are you today?

En. Ahmad: Good morning Sir. Mr Chin has explained your proposal and (*interrupted*) . . .

Mr Haessler: Yes! I think it is brilliant! En. Ahmad, I am sure that you are aware that the Hari Raya Puasa festivities are coming. So, in view of this, I insist that you inform your staff they must work an extra 3 hours per day from next week for 1.5 months so we can meet our delivery order schedule. This is due in 2 months and with the extra effort, (smiling), I will give all Malay staff 5 days' leave for the festivities.

En. Ahmad: But Sir, we are fasting then. I do not think that we can work longer hours. We have prayers and fasting. We would be tired and unable to concentrate for the extra hours. I am afraid that we are unable to do so.

Mr Haessler: Hmmm . . . Are you saying that I am being unreasonable? (*hint of anger in tone*) I am trying to help you here and I have a schedule to keep. You must accept. I insist.(*stern tone*)

En. Ahmad: But Sir . . . we just can't. We . . . (*interrupted*)

Mr Haessler: Listen here Encik. Ahmad! I am running this factory and all success is my doing. Now, you can either accept or you and your men will not be allowed to take leave longer than 2 days for the festivities. You would also have to schedule the manpower in order to have adequate manpower for smooth operations during the period. Leaves cannot overlap among staff. What did you say your (*in a sarcastic tone*) decision was?

En. Ahmad: Sir, please understand that we must serve our religious obligations. We cannot work long hours. We would also like to let you know that we need longer holidays as all of us come from outside this area. We ask that you allow us to work at this present pace and get some other departments to help us in the extra hours. All they need to do is to learn the bit to maintain the machines for the said 3 hours. I am sure Mr Param would not mind.

Mr Haessler: Mr Chin, please call Mr Param in.

Mr Param: Good morning, Sir.

Mr Haessler: Mr Param, would you mind getting the technical and quality control men to help out in working extra hours to help En. Ahmad here?

Mr Haessler proceeds to explain the situation carefully.

Mr Param: I am sorry but no. We don't have the expertise and besides, it is not in our job specifications. I am sorry.

Mr Haessler: Very well then. You may go. En. Ahmad, I think my decision is clear. You either accept my proposal or take the alternative.

En. Ahmad: (*politely*) May I ask why you did not impose the directive on Mr Param?

Mr Haessler: (*angrily*) Are you questioning my authority? I don't care for Mr Param! I don't trust him anyway and that is why I did not impose an ultimatum on him. I trust you but you disappoint me! So? Decision?

Encik Ahmad keeps silent a while, controlling his disbelief and anger, sighs and says . . .

En. Ahmad: OK. I will let you know after we come back from prayers. I will discuss this issue with my co-workers and I will try to convince them.

Mr Haessler: (*coldly*) Let me know by 3.30 pm. Mr Chin, please ensure you get the answer from En. Ahmad then. Thank you.

Chapter 35
Flooding the Indigenous Voices*

Black magic may seem a real part of life to some, and empty superstition to others. But there is no doubt that the results of belief in black magic are real, and can stymie the attempts of an organisation to do what it sets out to do.

This is a case about Hydro Energy Inc., which is 70% Korean owned and 30% Malaysian. It was incorporated on 20 April 1980 as a dam construction company. As time went by, it acquired an enviable reputation for its hydropower projects in the Asian region. At present, its main headquarters are in Seoul, Korea, with a branch in Kuala Lumpur, Malaysia. It has about 10,000 Korean as well as Malaysian employees, not including the labourers, who are mostly employed locally. Its client base usually includes the public sector agencies and private developers. Currently, its work is confined to projects within the Asian territories.

The company recently won a new hydroproject to build a dam in Sarawak, Malaysia. The work of clearing the 69,000 hectares of land began two months ago. The project site was situated at a remote area where there were some illegal "*orang asli*" (indigenous people) settlements. The "*orang asli*" at the illegal settlements were the Penan. The Penan are one of the few remaining nomadic people of the rain forest. They live in a place of immense beauty, a diverse forest intersected by rivers and the world's most extensive network of caves and underground passages in Sarawak. Some Penan feel threatened by this massive dam project.

---

* This case was written by Fiona Lim Ai Suan & Jennifer Lee Chow Ching, while graduate students in the Malaysian Graduate School of Management at Universiti Putra Malaysia.

The proposed dam will flood the 69,000 hectares of land, displacing the Penan people and wildlife and destroying even more rain forest. The traditional nomadic Penan community survives by hunting and gathering wild animals in the jungle. Only a handful of such societies remain on earth. The nomadic hunting-gathering lifestyle represents the original human condition. It was the way our own ancestors lived for millions of years.

While most Penan now have permanent homes by the riversides, they continue to make long journeys into the forest to collect food, medicine, and other jungle products. The physical and spiritual well-being of all Penan, whether nomadic or settled, depends on the survival of the forest. Both men and women are gentle and soft spoken. Outsiders who observe them are invariably struck by the complete absence of violence among the Penan. However, the building of this massive dam near one of the settlements has angered them.

The company has hired Mr Cheah Kim Chuan as the site supervisor. He is a civil engineer and a local resident of Sarawak itself. He has been in this industry for 10 years and is very familiar with the area where the project is situated as well as with the "orang asli" people. Mr Cheah has for several years been friends with an "orang asli" called Upih Guling who is a Penan himself. He is one of the very few Penan that have decided to change their lifestyle and earn a living outside their community. Previously, Upih Guling was working with a construction company until he was retrenched. For this reason, Mr Cheah had recommended that the company employ Upih Guling as head of the local labourers and had persuaded Upih Guling to accept the job immediately.

One night after dinner at the labourers' camp, the head of the Penan settlements near the ongoing project confronted Upih Guling, the labourers and some of the Korean engineers.

(The conversation below took place in the Penan native language but has been translated into English)

The head of the	Stop destroying our precious forest or we will be forced to protect it. The forest is our livelihood. We have lived here before any of you outsiders came. We fished in the clean rivers and hunted in the jungle.

We made our sago meal and ate the fruit of the trees. Our life was not easy as yours but we lived it contentedly. Now the clearings have turned rivers to muddy streams and look, the jungle is devastated. The fish cannot survive in dirty rivers. The wild animals will not live in devastated forest. You took advantage of our trusting nature. You cheated Mother Nature. By your doings, you take away our livelihood. You threaten our very lives. You make our people discontented. Don't any of you feel some guilt? We want our ancestral land, the land we live and feed on! We can use it in a wiser way than any of you could. When you come to us, come as guests with respect. You (*referring to Upih Guling*) as a Penan should know better. Have you forgotten about your ancestors' land?

Upih Guling: Please calm down. Let's discuss this in a harmonious manner. Remember the authorities have also given all of you ample notice beforehand.

The head of the Penan settlement: We want all of you to leave us alone. Go back to where you came from. Remember we will come with our blowpipes if you do not leave and we will not be reluctant to use our black magic!

Upih Guling was worried and approached Mr Cheah with this problem on the next day. This was their conversation.

Upih Guling: Good afternoon, Cheah.

Mr Cheah: Yes. How is the work getting on and how are our labourers?

Upih Guling: Well, not good. We have a problem. Two nights ago some of the Penan men came to our labourers' camp. They were unhappy with the clearing of the rainforest. They say that we are disturbing their ancestors' land, which is sacred to their people. Some of them threatened to use physical force on our men if we do not stop our work. Some even said that they would cast black magic on our labourers.

Mr Cheah:	This is serious, Upih. They are threatening to use black magic. You and I do know that the *"orang asli"* are very serious about the casting of black magic.
Upih Guling:	Yes. I am worried too. Two of our men have fallen sick with high fever today. They were also having delusions. I am afraid the black magic has been cast.

The next day some of the labourers tendered their resignations. Some of them even left the site immediately without giving any notice. They were all afraid of their own safety and wellbeing. They were not taking any chance of being the next victim there. The numbers of labourers were dwindling. This was getting worse. The clearing of the site had to go on and the project had to be completed on time. At present, they were already a month behind their schedule.

With this problem at hand, Mr Cheah went to seek advice from Mr Park Sang Hyon. When Mr Cheah told Mr Park about the shortage of workers, Mr Park, the newly-appointed regional manager for the company, was puzzled. He has been in the company for 15 years and was previously the department manager in the Korean headquarters. When he was promoted as regional manager, he was transferred to Malaysia and had now been in Malaysia for about 3 months to overlook the ongoing project in Sarawak.

Mr Park:	Shortage of workers? Why? Everything was all right a couple of days ago.
Mr Cheah:	Well . . . errrmmm . . . They are all resigning because they are afraid of the black magic cast by the Penan people who refuse to move from our project site.
Mr Park:	Black magic? Don't be ridiculous! This is the twenty-first century. There is no such thing as black magic.
Mr Cheah:	But Mr Park, a few of our men are seriously sick. I think this black . . .
Mr Park:	Enough. I do not want to hear anything about black magic any more. Send these men to town and get them checked. I want the work to resume as usual. Tell Upih to settle the problem with the illegal settlers or else he will be fired.

Mr Cheah: What about the labourers? We are way behind the schedule.

Mr Park: Well that is what you are here for. You deal with them.
               I am sure you can solve this petty problem by yourself.
               I have other serious problems to deal with.

Five days later, the problem was still not solved. None of the workers came back to work and the Penan refused to leave their settlements. Mr Park fired Upih Guling on the ground that he was not efficient enough. Upih Guling was unhappy and felt disappointed that Mr Cheah did not stand up for him in front of Mr Park. Mr Cheah felt sorry for Upih Guling for he was the one who persuaded Upih Guling to work with the company and he also recommended the company employ Upih. He felt that Upih would not trust him any more.

When the headquarters got to know about the delay of work at the project site, some of the directors from the Korea headquarters and Kuala Lumpur branch came to meet Mr Park and Mr Cheah to discuss the problem. A day before the meeting, Mr Park sat and wondered if he had done the right thing – firing Upih and not taking this problem of black magic seriously. Was it too late for him to change the situation? If he were to admit that he had made a mistake to the directors, he would feel very embarrassed. The delay in the progress of the site work might also imply that he was not committed to his job. Thus, this in the end might damage his image as the newly promoted regional manager as well as his career progress in the future. Was there anything he could do?

Recommended Reading

Adler, Nancy J. (1991) *International Dimensions in Organizational Behavior*, 2nd edn, PWS-Kent: Boston, Mass.

Beamer Linda, Varner, Iris (2000) 2nd edn. *Intercultural Communication in the Global Workplace*. Irwin: Chicago.

Erskine, James A., Michiel R Leenders & Loiuise A Maufette-Leenders (1998) *Teaching with cases*. London, Ontario: Richard Ivey School of Business

Gudykunst, W.B. and Kim Y.Y. (1992a) *Readings on Communicating with Strangers*. 2nd edn, Addison-Wesley: Reading, Mass.

Gudykunst, W.B. and Kim Y.Y. (1992b) *Communicating with Strangers*. 2nd edn, Addison-Wesley: Reading, Mass.

Hall, Edward. (1976) *Beyond Culture*. New York: Doubleday.

Hall Edward. (1983) *The Dance of Life*. Doubleday: New York

Hofstede, Geert. (1991) *Culture and Organizations. Software of the Mind*. McGraw-Hill: New York.

Lustig, M.W. & Koester, J. (1996) *Intercultural Competence*. Harper Collins: New York.

Maufette-Leenders, Louise A., Erskine, James A. & Michiel R Leenders (1997) *Learning with cases*. London, Ontario: Richard Ivey School of Business

McLaren, Margaret C. (1998) *Interpreting Cultural Differences*: Peter Francis: Norwich, U.K.

Mead, Richard. (1990) *Cross-Cultural Management Communication*. Wiley: London.

Oberg, Kalvero.(1960) "Culture shock: Adjustments to new cultural environments. *Practical Anthropology*, 7: 177-182.

Peters, T. and Waterman, R. (1982) *In Search of Excellence: Lessons from America's Best-Run Companies*. Harper & Row: New York.

Porter, M. E. (1980) *Competitive Strategy: Techniques for Analyzing Industries and Competitors*. Free Press: New York.

Poulin, Bryan, Mills, Bob & Spiller, Dorothy. (1998) *Strategy and Management: A New Zealand Casebook*. Addison-Wesley Longman: Auckland, NZ

Samovar Larry A. and Porter Richard E. (1995) *Communication between Cultures*. Wadsworth: Belmont, CA.

Samovar Larry A. and Porter Richard E. (1994) *Intercultural Communication: A Reader*. Wadsworth: Belmont, CA.

Tayeb, Monir H. (1996) *The Management of a Multicultural Workforce*. Chichester: Wiley.

Trompenaars, Fons,(1993) *Riding the Waves of Culture: Understanding Cultural Diversity in Business*. London: The Economist Books.

Victor D. (1992) *International Business Communication*. HarperCollins.

Bibliography

Adler, Nancy J. (1986), *International Dimensions of Organizational Behavior*. Boston, Mass.: Kent Publishing Company.

Aini Suzana Haji Ariffin. (2001) *The United Kingdom of Belgium*. MBA paper submitted to the Malaysian Graduate School of Management.

Asma, Abdullah (1992), The Influence of Ethnic Values on Managerial Practices in Malaysia, *Malaysian Management Review*. Vol. 27, No. 1, p. 30.

Asma, Abdullah (1996), *Going Glocal – Cultural Dimensions in Malaysian Management*. Kuala Lumpur: Malaysian Institute of Management.

Beamer, Linda & Varner, Linda (2001) *Intercultural Communication in the Global Workplace*. Boston: McGraw-Hill Irwin.

(Note: This is the second edition of Varner and Beamer listed below. Both are included Asian libraries one might be available but not the other. A single entry would not cover them both since the authors' names are reversed in the second edition)

Berger C. R. & Calabrese R. J. (1975) "Communicating under Uncertainty" in W.B. Gudykunst and Y.Y. Kim (eds) (1992b) *Readings on Communicating with Strangers*. New York: McGraw-Hill.

Burke, W. Warner, & Goodstein Leonard D. eds. (1980) *Trends and Issues in OD: Current* Theory and Practice, San Diego, CA.: University Associates Inc.

Danandjaja, Andreas A. (1987), Managerial Values in Indonesia, *Asia Pacific Journal of Management*, Vol. 5, No. 1, September, pp. 1-7.

De Leon, Corinna T. (1987), Social Categorization in Philippine Organizations: Values Toward Collective Identity and Management through Inter-group Relations, *Asia Pacific Journal of Management*, Vol. 5, No. 1, September, pp. 28–37.

Dong Ki Kim (1981), The Korean Manager, in *Profile of an Asian Manager,* ed. P.N.Singh, Bombay: A Forum of Asian Managers Publications.

Druckerman, Pamela (7 August 2001) *Asian Wall Street Journal*. p. 1, col.1.

Elashmawi, Farid, & Harris Philip R. (1994), *Multicultural Management – New Skills for Global Success,* Kuala Lumpur: Gulf Publishing Company.

England, G.W. (1975) *The Manager and His Values: An International Perspective from the United States, Japan, Korea, India and Australia,* Cambridge, Mass.: Ballinger Publishing Company.

Gudykunst, W.B. and Kim Y.Y. (1992a) *Readings on Communicating with Strangers.*2nd edn, Addison-Wesley: Reading, Mass.

Gudykunst, W.B. and Kim Y.Y.(1992b) *Communicating with Strangers.* 2nd edn, Addison-Wesley: Reading, Mass.

Guthrie, George. M. (1968), *The Philippine Temperament, Six Perspectives on the Philippines,* Philippines: Bookmark, Inc., pp. 49–83.

Hall, Edward. (1976) *Beyond Culture.* New York: Doubleday.

Hall Edward. (1983) *The Dance of Life.* New York: Doubleday.

Hall, Edward T. & Reed, Mildred (1990). *Understanding Cultural Differences: Germans, French and Americans.* Yarmouth, ME: Intercultural Press.

Heller, F.A. & Yuki, G. (1969) "Participation, managerial decision-making, and situational variables". *Organizational Behavioral Human Performance.*Vol. 4, pp.227–241.

Hofstede, Geert. (1980) *Culture's Consequences: International Differences in Work Related Values,* Beverley Hills: Sage.

Hofstede, Geert (1984) "Cultural dimensions in planning and management", abridged version published in W.B. Gudykunst and Y.Y. Kim (eds) (1992b) *Readings on Communicating with Strangers.* New York: McGraw-Hill.

Hofstede, Geert (1991) *Culture and Organizations: Software of the Mind.* London: McGraw-Hill.

Ikeda, Daisaku (March 2000) caption to a photograph, from a lecture given at Moscow University in 1975, printed in *Sunrise,* p 12.

Ikeda, Daisaku (1996) *A New Humanism.* New York: Weatherhill.

Jones, Merrick L. (1986) "Management Development: An African Focus", *Management Education and Development,* 17, 3, pp. 202–216.

Kelley, Lane; Whatley, Arthur; Worthley, Reginald & Lie, Harry (1986) "The Role of the Ideal Organization in Comparative Management: A Cross Cultural Perspective of Japan and Korea", *Asia Pacific Journal of Management,* Vol. 3 No 2. January, pp. 59–71.

Kluckhohn, Florence & Strodtbeck, Frederick (1971) *Variations in Value Orientations.* New York: Row and Peterson.

Locker Kitty O. & Kaczmarek, Steven Kyo (2001) *Business Communication: Building Critical Skills.* Boston: McGraw-Hill Irwin.

Lynch, F., (1970) "Social Acceptance Reconsidered, in *Four Readings on Philippines Values,* Institute of Philippines Culture Paper No. 2, Frank Lunch and Alfonso de Guzman II (eds), Quezon City, Phillipines: Ateneo de Manila University Press, pp.1–64.

McLaren, Margaret C. (1998) *Interpreting Cultural Differences: The Challenge of Intercultural Communication.* Norfolk: Peter Francis Publishers.

Md. Zabid Abdul Rashid, Anantharaman, R. N. & Raveendran, Jaina (1997) "Corporate Cultures and Work Values in Dominant Ethnic organisations in Malaysia" *Journal of Transnational Management Development.* Vol. 2(4) pp.51–65.

Md Zabid A.R. and Choong, W.Y., (1994) "A Cross-Cultural Study of Managerial Values and Practices in Malaysia", *Third World Business Congress,* June, Penang: Malaysia

Peters, T. and Waterman, R. (1982) *In Search of Excellence: Lessons from America's Best-Run Companies.* New York: Harper & Row.

Porter, M. E. (1980) *Competitive Strategy: Techniques for Analyzing Industries and Competitors.* New York: Free Press.

Pottinger, Matt (July 31, 2001) "Hong Kong Railway Loses Appeal", *The Asian Wall Street Journal,* p.4, col.1.

Poulin, B. J. (1990) "A New Gestalt of Organisation: Implications for Quality Management", *Australian and New Zealand Management Educators' Conference Proceedings.*

Poulin, Bryan, Mills, Bob & Spiller, Dorothy. (1998) *Strategy and Management: A New Zealand Casebook.* Addison-Wesley Longman: Auckland, N.Z.

Ronen, Simcha, (1986) *Comparative and Multinational Management.* Singapore: John Wiley & Sons.

Runglertkrengkrai, Somkao and Suda Engkaninan, (1987), The Pattern of Managerial Behaviour in Thai Culture, Asia Pacific Journal of Management, Vol. 5, No 1, September, pp. 8–15.

Samovar Larry A. & Porter Richard E. (1991) *Intercultural Communication: a Reader.* (6th edn) Belmont CA: Wadsworth.

Samovar Larry A. & Porter Richard E. (1995) *Communication between Cultures.*(2nd edn) Belmont CA: Wadsworth.

Sarachek, B., Aziz Abdul Hamid, and Zakaria Ismail, (1984) "An Opinion Survey of Malaysian Middle Level Managers and Professionals", *Asia Pacific Journal of Management,* Vol. 2. May , pp. 181–189.

Shephard, Peter, (2001)," Expats working with Malaysians", in *Understanding the Malaysian Workforce – Guidelines for Managers* ed.Asma Abdullah and Aric H.M. Low, rev.edn. Kuala Lumpur: Malaysian Institute of Management.

Smuckarn, S., (1979) *The Conflict, Problem, and Future of Thai Society: Cultural Value*, Bangkok: National Institute of Development Administration.

Sumner, William Graham (1906) *Folkways*. Boston: Ginn.

Trompenaars, Fons (1993) *Riding the Waves of Culture,* London. The Economist Books.

Varner, Iris & Beamer, Linda (1995) *Intercultural Communication in the Global Workplace*. Chicago: Irwin.

(Note: This is the first edition of Beamer and Varner listed above. Both are included Asian libraries one might be available but not the other. A single entry would not cover them both since the authors' names are reversed in the second edition)

Victor, David (1992). *International Business Communication*. New York: Harper Collins Publishers.

Index